THE STORY OF SOUTH AFRICA

THE STORY OF SOUTH AFRICA

by

LEO MARQUARD

FABER AND FABER LIMITED
24 Russell Square
London

First published in mcmlv
by Faber and Faber Limited
24 Russell Square, London, WC1
First published in this edition mcmlxvi
Printed in Great Britain by
Latimer Trend & Co Ltd Whitstable

TO

JENNIFER AND TERENCE

CONTENTS

MAPS

PREFACE

This book does not pretend to be a full-scale history of South Africa. It is, rather, an attempt to trace the story of the different peoples that have contributed to the making of modern South Africa, to describe the main events in that story, and to re-assess some of those events.

I have made use of a large number of primary and secondary sources, too numerous to detail; but I must record my gratitude to Prof. Eric Walker, Prof. W. M. Macmillan, and Prof. C. W. de Kiewiet whose scholarly writings have made all South Africans their debtors.

I wish to thank the following: A. Wheaton and Co. Ltd. of Exeter for permission to use the maps on pp. 54, 89, 130, and 161 taken from Juta's *Historical Atlas for South African Schools*; George Philip and Son for the map on p. 194, taken from Philip's *Large Print Atlas for South African Schools*; the Van Riebeeck Society for permission to quote various extracts from their invaluable publications of original documents; the Oxford University Press for permission to use the map on p. 241 taken from my book *The Peoples and Policies of South Africa*. The map on p. 50 is based on information contained in three maps in the Official Year Book of the Union of South Africa, Number 18, and is reproduced under Government Printers Copyright Authority No. 2164 of 26th October 1954.

I am grateful to Mr. D. Marquard of Bloemfontein who read the manuscript and made valuable detailed and general suggestions.

My greatest thanks, as always, go to my wife who, like

Sir Toby Belch, hates a false conclusion, and whose criticism has been invaluable.

Stellenbosch, L. M.
February 1954

PREFACE TO SECOND EDITION

Much has happened in the nine years since this book was written and I have tried in the last chapter to bring the main threads of the story of South Africa up to date. I find it impossible to remain entirely detached when describing contemporary events in a country in which my own past, present, and future are so deeply involved; but I hope I have been at least partly successful in presenting both sides of the story.

I wish to thank the Oxford University Press for permission to use material from the third edition of my book, *The Peoples and Policies of South Africa*, published in 1962.

L.M.

Claremont
April 1963

Chapter One

EARLY INVADERS

When European explorers discovered the world outside Europe, in the latter half of the fifteenth century, the country we now call South Africa was inhabited by primitive peoples with no written language. Towards the end of the century, when Columbus was rediscovering America, Portuguese sailors rounded the southern tip of Africa and found a new trade route to the East. Until then we have no written records to help us in reconstructing the story of South Africa; and for the next century and a half we have only romantic tales told by travellers who, on their way to and from the East, had occasional contact with inhabitants living near the coast.

In the middle of the seventeenth century, men of European stock began to settle round Table Bay, and from then onwards we have written records of some of the things that happened in South Africa. These records consist of instructions to, and reports of, governors and other officials, minutes of meetings, private papers, and diaries; and as we reach the nineteenth and twentieth centuries the records swell in volume and are supplemented by books and periodicals. It is important to bear in mind that practically all the available records were written by Europeans, and the historians who interpret the records are, with minor exceptions, Europeans—members, that is, of the conquering race that took South Africa from its original inhabitants and whose descendants constitute one-fifth of the total population to-day. It is natural, therefore, that these records should be mainly concerned with matters that interested and affected Europeans, and that, as far as the rest of the population is concerned, there are large gaps in the story.

The written history of four-fifths of the population tends to be either a scientific description of such habits, customs, and institutions as are different from those of Europeans, or else an account, from the European point of view, of how tribes were overcome, of the triumph of superior technical skill over superior numbers, and of the effect of this conquest on the institutions of the conquered. What is missing from the story is the human element, social history as distinct from the mere chronicling of kings and emperors and wars. People are described as clans or tribes rather than as human beings, and we forget that tribes are made up of individual men and women.

Another way in which European-written history is likely to fall short is in the matter of impartiality. In South Africa the past intrudes into the present more than in most countries, because her main problem is still what it has always been: the relations between the different groups that live in the country. As a result of this the converse becomes true, and people living to-day, and having to cope with existing problems, are inclined to let the present influence their view of the past; and as long as those who write South Africa's history come from the white minority only, it is likely to be biased against the non-European majority or, in an effort to be fair, it may be biased in the other direction.

The gaps in South Africa's story will only be filled when Africans and Coloured people begin to write history. That day is not far off,[1] but until then we must let our imagination assist us in arriving at a more complete story. At least we must let it remind us that the complete story has not yet been told.

We are not, of course, wholly dependent on written records for our knowledge of the past. Archaeology and other sciences have reconstructed past civilizations for us,

[1] There have been a few halting attempts but they have been more in the nature of chronicles than disciplined historical writing.

and where there are still remnants of an ancient people living, like the Bushmen in South Africa, anthropologists have been able to fill in many gaps by studying what someone has aptly called 'our contemporary ancestors'. From such sources we are able to say, in general terms, what seems to have happened in South Africa before its conquest by Europe. Such a sketch cannot give the answers to many interesting questions, and we are free to indulge in the amusing pastime of speculation. This is not harmful so long as we do not try to use it to 'prove' some modern political or racial theory, such as that African society is either inferior or superior to European, or that all men are equal or, for that matter, unequal.

When Dutch settlers arrived at the Cape in 1652 their first contact was with Hottentots, but as soon as the settlement spread they found still earlier inhabitants, the Bushmen, who had lived in South Africa for at least a thousand years, and probably much longer. Skulls. and stone implements in which South Africa is rich, show that the Bushmen themselves were preceded by people of earlier cultures equivalent to the early stone-age cultures of Europe and India. We do not know whether there was a break between the earlier cultures and that of the Bushmen, or whether, as seems more likely, the Bushmen infiltrated into the earlier tribes and mixed with them as the Hottentots subsequently did with the Bushmen.

The original home of the Bushmen was somewhere in the eastern part of Central Africa from where, thousands of years ago, they migrated southwards. Bushmen skulls, stone implements, and rock paintings and engravings are found in most parts of southern Africa and as far north as Uganda and the Sudan, showing that at one time Bushmen had the whole of the present South Africa as their hunting grounds. They were nomadic hunters and gatherers of food, and their social organization was suited to that life: there were no real clans, only hunting parties which probably never exceeded a hundred people, men, women, and children; only the rudiments of tribal organization and chieftainship existed; they had no collective name for themselves though the Hottentots called them *San*, and the Dutch *Bosjesmannen*, the men of the bush.

There are still about 10,000 Bushmen living in the Kalahari Desert and in parts of South-West Africa, and though their culture has been influenced by contact with other aborigines and with Europeans, we can form a fairly good idea of their distinctive way of life. To a primitive nomadic people it is natural that the moon and the stars, the wind and the rain, thunder and lightning, and all forms of animal life should be regarded as gods to be prayed to or ancestral spirits to be propitiated. Bushmen are great tellers of tales, and their stories are mostly about animals and natural forces which they personify. Many of the stories are about animals that were once men and women of the race that preceded the Bushmen, so it is probable that these stories have been handed down through thousands of years; and we shall never know where, by whom, and in what dim age they were first told.

Living in the wastes of the Kalahari, Bushmen are seldom seen by Europeans. Those who have learnt to know them say that they are shy with strangers but cheerful and merry among themselves. They are passionately fond of miming and dancing, and the dances imitate animal life, hunting scenes, fights, and stories from their own history. They are skilful hunters and trackers, using poisoned arrows to wound larger game and then tracking them down for many miles; they hunt smaller game by stalking them to the water-holes and stunning them with an accurate blow from a knobbed stick thrown from as much as thirty yards away. Bushmen do not cultivate the soil but depend on herbs and roots. They are notoriously hospitable and improvident, eating what is available and not worrying to save food for future use.

The Bushman is slightly built but tough and his average height is about five feet; he has a yellow-brown complexion and his skin wrinkles easily; he has little hair on his head or body, a flat nose and prominent cheekbones, and, as a rule, his ears have no lobes. His practical knowledge of poisons, edible roots, and herbal medicines is considerable but is not based on anything that can be called scientific theory. Bushmen have no mathematical divisions of time, of the seasons, or of distance, and they do not show any signs, as many primitive people do, of craftsmanship.

In most parts of southern Africa rock engravings and, usually on the walls of caves, rock paintings, are to be found. This primitive art is commonly associated with Bushman culture, though some authorities regard it as pre-Bushman. Using a small, hard stone to make the engraving, these early artists ground mineral ores and mixed them with animal fat to get their colours. They chose as their subjects hunting and battle scenes, domestic life, cattle raids, and scenes from their mythology. The drawings are realistic and accurate except for their human figures which are impressionistic and in which different features are exaggerated. Their paintings are lively and vigorous and, according to many critics, shew a high degree of artistic talent.

The existence and the wide dispersal of rock paintings pose many questions to which no certain answers can be given. Are they evidence of a link with prehistoric cultures in northern Africa and southern Europe where similar rock paintings are found? Have the paintings in the caves of Lascaux and in South Africa a common origin? Why is it that a people, primitive in all other respects, should show such remarkable artistic abilities? Why did the art die out—was it some natural catastrophe that overwhelmed the people or was it a gradual change in their way of living, forced on them by outside circumstances, that turned them from such a congenial occupation? What were the individual artists like, and did they have an honoured position in society? We shall never know the answers to these questions, but to ask them is exciting, and it is because historians and scientists have asked similar questions, and tried to find the answers, that we know as much about the past as we do.

The first aboriginal inhabitants of Africa to see people from Europe were the Hottentots. To them it must have been a strange and frightening sight to see white-skinned people of peculiar dress and habits who arrived in ships, used a wonderful new animal, the horse, had wheeled transport, and fired guns instead of arrows.

The Hottentots probably came from the region of the Great Lakes in Central Africa and were the result of intermarriage between Hamitic tribes and Bushmen of that region. Their language is a Bushman language with traces of Hamitic influence, and they have many beliefs and myths in common with Bushmen. Like them, but unlike other races in Africa, they worship the moon and personify natural forces, particularly those associated with water and rain. There are, however, considerable differences between the cultures of these two primitive peoples. The Hottentots were pastoral and kept cattle and sheep; their clan and tribal development was more advanced than that of the nomadic Bushmen; and they had a fairly well-defined system of chieftainship. While the Bushmen still used stone implements, they knew how to smelt iron and copper.

By the beginning of the seventeenth century, Hottentots in scattered clans and tribes were occupying what is now the western and southern portions of the Cape Province, and were in process of driving the Bushmen out of those areas towards the north and east. This process was, as we shall see presently, assisted by the arrival of Europeans.

The next people to arrive on the South African scene were the Bantu or, as they are more generally called to-day, Africans.[1] While there are now only about 10,000 Bushmen left, and very few pure-bred Hottentots, there are eight and a half million Africans who constitute two-thirds of the

[1] The words Native and Kaffir are still used to describe the Bantu-speaking people of South Africa. The first is no longer distinctive, since Europeans are also natives of South Africa; the second was used historically, and is so used later in this book, but it has a derogatory sense to-day and its use is distasteful to many Europeans and most Africans.

population and continue to play an important part in the life of the country. They are at all stages of cultural development, from illiterate tribesmen, living much as their forefathers did, to industrial workers and professional men and women who have thrown off tribalism and adopted the ways of an individualist society.

The original home of the Bantu was probably near the highlands of East Africa. There, more than two thousand years ago, Negroes from West Africa and the Congo mixed with Hamitic tribes from North Africa and, to a much smaller extent, with Bush people. From this mixture of races there grew the people who, in hundreds of tribes all over southern Africa, are known as Bantu-speaking people. They have many languages and dialects that, like English and German, are different from one another but have a common origin. They shew a wide diversity of features, colour, and stature, depending on the proportion of Negro, Hamitic, or Bush blood that goes to make up an individual. Though they have certain basic characteristics in common, the tribes differ from one another in customs, in organization, and in institutions.

At least seven centuries B.C. Arab traders, and later Indians, settled on the east coast of Africa as far south as Sofala and bartered hatchets, lances, daggers, and glass to the inhabitants for ivory, palm oil, and slaves. It is possibly from these Arabs that the Bantu learnt to smelt iron. From the eleventh century A.D. Chinese and Malayan merchants traded regularly with the east coast though they never settled there to the same extent as the Arabs. On the coast the direct influence of Arabs on Africans was profound, and in the interior, from where the South African Bantu came, the effects were no less profound, for it was there that the full impact of the slave trade was felt.

By the time slavery was abolished, in the first half of the nineteenth century, it had been going on for at least two thousand years on the east coast. It has been estimated that during three hundred years of slave trade on the west coast of Africa, about twelve million slaves were taken to America and the West Indies. Though the volume of trade from the east coast was smaller, it must have run into many millions during the course of two thousand years, and it took Africans to Arabia, India, Malaya, and China. The effect of slave raids on the tribes of the interior was devastating. Clans and tribes were broken up, tribe was set against tribe by the foreign raiders, and tribes and remnants of tribes migrated to evade the enemy. The slave trade was possibly the greatest single factor in initiating those mass migrations which took the Bantu southwards and ever southwards, along the central highlands and down to the eastern coastal belt, until, by the beginning of the eighteenth century, African tribes were occupying the eastern portion of South Africa as far south as the present Port Elizabeth.

When Europeans first began to come into contact with them, the southern Bantu were agriculturalists and pastoralists. They had well-developed political and social institutions, much in advance of the Hottentots and based on clearly-defined clans and tribes; chiefs and elders ruled in peace and war and administered customary laws that had their roots deep in the past. Chieftainship was normally hereditary, and chiefs were treated with the respect given to those who are not only natural leaders but who are believed to embody the traditions of their people.

Social life in an African village was, and in some parts of South Africa still is, at once simpler and more complicated than in a modern village. Beehive-shaped huts were constructed of wood, clay, and grass, and the position of each hut was decided according to strict social rules. A minimum of clothing was worn, and cooking pots, baskets, sleeping mats, and other household utensils were made by hand. Generally, there was a division of labour; women and girls did the domestic work and ploughed the fields, sowed millet, hoed, and harvested the crops, while men looked after the cattle, hunted, attended tribal councils, and went to war. The education of boys and girls consisted of learning tribal laws and custom and of finding out how to do the things they would have to do when they became men and women. There was plenty of leisure for games, story-telling, dancing and ceremonial.

But life was complicated, as it seems to the twentieth century, by innumerable and rigid rules that governed all social and economic behaviour and activities. Birth, initiation, courtship, marriage, and death were surrounded and governed by ceremonial ritual based on strict taboos that were designed to propitiate natural forces and ancestral spirits. Rites had to be performed before ploughing, sowing, reaping, or hunting could be undertaken, and almost all of what are now regarded as natural occurrences were ascribed to magic or witchcraft.

African beliefs and customs, like those of any other people, have ancient roots, and it is interesting to speculate on their origins. All over Africa south of the Sahara, Bantu tribes that have had no contact with one another for more than a thousand years have many things in common besides a parent language and similar physical features. Beehive huts, tribal initiation, and rituals associated with cattle are found everywhere, with local variations, from South Africa to the Central African cradle of the Bantu, and it is probable that these things had a common origin more than two thousand years ago. How much of these is Hamitic and how much Negro? Is it possible, for example, that the division of labour between men and women owes its existence to the fact that the Hamites were pastoralists and the Negroes cultivators? And why is it that the Bantu, who were far in advance of the more primitive Bushmen in crafts, metalwork, and in social and political institutions, had practically no art? What factors made the nomadic hunting life of the stone-age people more conducive to the growth of representational art than the pastoral and agricultural life of the iron age? Here, too, there is no certain answer.

Over a period of thousands of years, then, South Africa has suffered a series of invasions. The later stone-age Bushmen conquered and mixed with early stone-age people whose implements and skulls have so far told us very little about them. Bushmen were followed by a Hottentot invasion of a similar kind, and the Hottentots were followed by the much more numerous African invaders who drove Hottentots and Bushmen, fiercely resisting, further south and settled on the plains of the high veld and on the fertile eastern coastal belt. From the middle of the seventeenth century there began another invasion, a mere trickle at first, that had more far-reaching and astonishing results on South Africa than any of the previous invasions. These new invaders, the Europeans, came from a different continent, six thousand miles away, and were equipped with physical and spiritual weapons, and with a restless energy, that enabled them in the short space of two and a half centuries to conquer and rule the whole of southern Africa.

There is no need to describe the origins and history of Europe and of Western civilization, but it may be useful to say something about the stage that civilization had reached when its representatives began to enter South Africa. By the middle of the seventeenth century the transition from provinces of the Roman Empire to modern European states was well on its way. Though the emotionally powerful doctrine of nationalism was still in its early stages, the nations in which it was engendered already existed, and national rivalries for trade and colonies had begun. The great discoveries of men such as Cabot, Columbus, da Gama, Diaz, and Drake had laid bare the New World to the astonished gaze of Europe and had opened the trade route to the East round the Cape of Good Hope. Trade followed the discoveries, and by 1650 the flags of Spain, Portugal, Holland, Britain, and France had either followed or were beginning to follow trade: in other words, conquest and colonization had begun, and Europe had set her feet on the path that was to lead her to the domination of the world.

Ideas of hereditary kingship and government by a nobility were firmly entrenched in the five colonizing nations; but in two of them, England and Holland, the theory of controlling the actions of kings and rulers by elected parliaments and by law courts was already successfully challenging the doctrine of the divine right of kings. Hampden, Pym, and Cromwell in England, and van Olden Barneveld and de Witt in Holland, are a few of the names associated with the revolutions that ultimately turned those two countries into parliamentary democracies, firmly based on individual freedom that was safeguarded by the rule of law.

The Christian religion that has been such a powerful agent in giving shape and form to European civilization had passed through a great crisis: the Protestant Reformation of Luther and Calvin. Holland and England had broken with Rome and were Protestant countries, while Spain, Portugal, and France remained Roman Catholic. The religious wars that accompanied this cleavage in the Christian Church were not over, and they were not wars of religion only. Emerging nationalism and trade rivalries became mixed up with national religions, and, in freeing themselves from control by Rome, England and Holland, frequently in alliance, overthrew the might of Spain and Portugal. Holland's long war with Spain was a war for national as well as for religious freedom, and it was also a war for commercial and colonial supremacy based on sea power.

Following on the Reformation came the question of personal religious freedom and of toleration, and this in itself became involved in questions of freedom of speech and of the press. It was during the seventeenth century that English, French, and Dutch thinkers and statesmen laid the intellectual and legal foundations on which modern democratic freedom rests; and it is those foundations which, in the twentieth century, are most bitterly attacked by those who seek to destroy democratic freedom. It was in defence of those principles that civil wars and revolutions were made, and it was with the hope of enjoying liberty that Englishmen immigrated to America and Frenchmen to South Africa.

By the middle of the seventeenth century the achievements of Europe in literature, art, music, and architecture were immense. The Bible had been translated into all the main European languages and the invention of printing had made possible the spread of learning. Milton was writing in England, and Vondel in Holland. In Holland, too, Rembrandt, Hals, Vermeer, van Dyck, and Rubens were painting their great masterpieces. The finest age of music was still to come, but already Monteverdi had written his operas. In architecture, the great cathedrals which, to-day, we alternately admire and bomb, had been built.

Galileo, Harvey, Kepler, Descartes, Newton, and Huyghens were among the seventeenth-century scientists whose restless and inquiring minds were re-examining old beliefs and superstitions and applying to them those experimental tests that are the mark of the new scientific age. By the end of the century a steam engine had been invented, the same engine which, seventy years later, James Watt repaired and perfected. The seventeenth-century scientists, whose contemporaries invaded South Africa, thus paved the way for the industrial revolution that enabled their descendants to conquer southern Africa, to develop its mineral and agricultural resources, to span it with land and air transport routes, and to plant Western civilization firmly on the soil of Africa.

There was, of course, another side to seventeenth-century Europe. Illiteracy and learning; superstition and science; great wealth and abject poverty; beautiful houses and filthy slums; a humane literature and art and inhuman punishments and cruelty; a religion of love and the burning of witches and torture of prisoners; a passionate love of freedom in Europe and the wicked slave trade in Africa—all these existed side by side.

Just as the previous invaders of South Africa had brought with them their habits and customs, their stone and metal implements, their social and economic institutions, so the European invaders took their civilization with them. Some of their customs and institutions suffered a sea change, not always into something better. Pitted against Nature and a less developed but numerically far superior people, Europeans lost some of the humaner and more gracious ways of Europe at its best and retained the harsher and less pleasing habits. Art and literature had little hope of flourishing in a society that was so small and much occupied with a struggle to survive; and the development of individual liberty in Europe became, in South Africa, either stunted through the institution of slavery or a rather undisciplined individualism. But the great traditions of Europe did not die. They could be, and were, revived in later centuries.

The European civilization that came to South Africa, with its inevitable mixture of good and bad, was much more complex and powerful than those it overcame. In religion, in political and legal institutions, in technical knowledge and skill, in weapons, and in organization, Bushmen, Hottentots, and Africans were no match for the people of Europe. How they were conquered, and with what results, will be seen in subsequent chapters.

Chapter Two

DUTCH SETTLEMENT

'December 1651

On Board The Ship *Drommedaris*

14th. About two hours after midday, the weather being unsettled, squally and rainy and the wind westerly, the said Riebeeck departed with his family from the city of Amsterdam. Previously at eleven o'clock he had taken his final leave of the Hon. Lords Directors at the Counting-house as well as at the slaughter-house of the aforesaid Chamber. On the

16th. he came on board the ship *Drommedaris*, having on the previous Monday at a full meeting of these Lords Directors in the presence of all the skippers—obtained leave to proceed on his way. He had received orders to hoist the flag of the ship *Drommedaris* and to take command of the departing ships according to an extract from a resolution of 4 December by the distinguished meeting of the aforementioned Hon. Lords Directors. This extract was taken to Riebeeck in Texel by the two commissioned Directors Roch and de Lange and handed over to him.'

These opening extracts, translated from the official journal of Jan van Riebeeck,[1] first Commander at the Cape, give the sequel to 150 years of exploration and trade and the beginning of 150 years of Dutch rule in South Africa.

During the Middle Ages world commerce centred round the Mediterranean and Adriatic seas. From India, merchants sent spices, precious stones, incense, perfumes, and carpets

[1] *Journal of Jan van Riebeeck*, Vol. 1, p. 1. Published for the Van Riebeeck Society by A. A. Balkema, 1952.

up the Persian Gulf and the Euphrates and then overland to Beirut and Antioch. Sometimes this Eastern merchandise might be taken to Trebizond on the eastern shores of the Black Sea or carried in Arab dhows, running before the monsoon to Aden and the Red Sea, and then to Egyptian ports. From Europe, merchants of Venice, Genoa, and Marseilles sent shiploads of grain, cloth, leather, wool, soap, furs and manufactured metal goods to Beirut, to Trebizond, or to Alexandria, there to be exchanged for the products of the East. From the European ports Eastern goods were distributed by overland routes to the market towns of France and Germany to be sold by pedlars or at fairs; or they went by sea to Lisbon, London, and the Netherlands where the town of Bruges was for many years the chief commercial centre.

The trade routes on which Europe depended for its traffic with the East were difficult, dangerous, and expensive; moreover, they were under Mohammedan control. There were, thus, powerful motives to seek an easier and less expensive route, and these motives were greatly strengthened when the Turks, having taken Constantinople in 1453, extended their rule along the eastern and southern shores of the Mediterranean. Even before this, Portuguese sailors had been exploring the Atlantic coast of Africa, and by 1445 Cape Verde had been reached. In 1486 Bartholomew Diaz rounded the Cape of Good Hope, and twelve years later Vasco da Gama reached Melinde on the east coast of Africa and there found an Indian pilot who guided him to Calicut. The sea route to India had been opened.

Six years earlier, in 1492, Columbus had reached America, and the effect on Europe and the world of his and da Gama's voyages was revolutionary. The weight of world commerce shifted from the Mediterranean to the Atlantic, and by the cheapening of the cost of transport the volume of trade was increased. Much of the wealth that had formerly gone to Venice and Genoa now flowed, in ever-increasing volume, to the Atlantic ports of Portugal, Spain, France, the Netherlands and England, and it was from these Atlantic countries that the conquest and colonization of the non-European world came.

For the first hundred years after the discoveries of sea routes the carrying trade was almost entirely in the hands of the Portuguese and Spaniards. Within fifty years of da Gama's voyage to India the Portuguese had captured the Indian Ocean trade from the Arabs and had established themselves on the East African seaboard, while the Spaniards had conquered Mexico and Peru and virtually destroyed their ancient civilizations. The Dutch, the French, and to a lesser extent the English were at first content to play the role of importers and distributors to the rest of Europe, leaving to Portugal and Spain the long and hazardous voyages to India and the New World. Indeed, lack of sea power made it impossible for them to compete with the powerful navies of Spain and Portugal, for successful trade, then as now, depended on naval power; and it was not until the end of the sixteenth century that England successfully challenged Spain, nor until the seventeenth that a Dutch admiral was able to tie a broom to his masthead as a sign that he had swept the seas of a rival.

By 1580 the Dutch were casting envious eyes on the enormous profits—as much as 600 per cent on a voyage—that were to be made by direct trade with India, and were planning to take part in that trade. In this they were spurred on by two political events: both Portugal and the Netherlands were subject to Philip II of Spain who believed himself to be divinely commissioned to stamp out Protestantism everywhere, but particularly in his own realm. As a move in the long fight with his Dutch subjects he closed the harbour of Lisbon to Dutch merchants in 1581, and the Dutch, who had been fighting for their right to be Protestants, now had to fight for their very existence, which depended on commerce. There was nothing left for it but to trade direct with India, and in this they were helped by the second political event: the destruction of Spanish sea power when

England defeated the Armada in 1588. This marked the end of Spanish and Portuguese monopoly and the beginning of English, French, and Dutch expansion.

Profitable as direct trade with India was, it was far too expensive for individual enterprise. The merchant adventurers therefore combined in small companies, which in turn soon amalgamated into the great chartered companies that played such a significant role in national and international affairs for more than two centuries. In England and France East India Companies were established, and in 1602 the Dutch East India Company received its charter from the States General, the government of the United Provinces.

For the business of such vast enterprise as direct trade with the East, Holland was fortunately placed and well equipped. Her great seaports of Amsterdam and Rotterdam are situated where roads and rivers of Europe meet the sea, thus making her the natural middleman between Europe and countries that could be reached by sea. Dutch merchants, bringing spices from Lisbon and corn from the Baltic ports, and exporting the products of the European hinterland, had built up the reserves of capital that were required for expansion of trade. Philip II of Spain once more assisted them unintentionally: he repudiated his debts to Italian bankers and practically ruined them, and, for religious reasons, drove Jewish merchants and bankers to seek refuge in Holland, which soon became the banking centre of western Europe. The Dutch were, moreover, an industrious and skilled people who used every square yard of land that they had won from the sea for cultivating crops and for dairy and wool farming. The capital wealth of Holland was thus securely based on a sound internal economy.

Within twenty years of the establishment of the Dutch East India Company the Dutch had ousted the Portuguese, had captured Bantam, Amboyna, and Java, and had set up a government at Batavia, in Java, for their East Indian possessions. Soon they occupied Ceylon, Banda, Malacca, Macassar, the Moluccas, and other trading stations, and by

1651 the Company had decided to establish a half-way house at the Cape, a refreshment station at which ships could put in for fresh food and repairs on their long journey to and from the East. It was as a servant of the Dutch East India Company, and it was to fulfil this mission at the Cape, that Jan van Riebeeck went on board the *Drommedaris* in December 1651.

The decision to set up a refreshment station at the Cape was not a sudden one. After one or two unfortunate experiences with Hottentots, Portuguese ships avoided the Cape and used St. Helena and Mocambique as their half-way stations; but Dutch and English ships soon got into the habit of putting in at the Cape to take on fresh water and leave letters under the so-called 'post office stones'. The prevailing winds on which sailing ships must depend made the Cape a natural port of call both on the outward and homeward journeys, and it was a toss-up which of the two Companies, English or Dutch, would be the first to decide to establish a regular station. In 1620, two English captains, FitzHerbert and Shillinge, 'annexed' Saldanha Bay in the name of King James I; but James rejected the offer. In 1648, a Dutch ship, *Haarlem*, was stranded in Table Bay and the crew was forced to spend a year there before being taken off. They lived off the land, growing their own food; and although they had had a hard time of it the commander, Janssen, on his return to Holland, advised the Company to establish a permanent station at the Cape. Thus it was that, in 1652, the Dutch did what the English might have done in 1620.

Jan van Riebeeck left the sheltered waters of Texel for the open sea on Christmas Eve of 1651. His flagship *Drommedaris* was about 200 tons, and he had under his command the much smaller *Reijger* and a yacht, *Goede Hoop*, of about 40 tons: such was the fleet in which Europe set out on a journey that was to end in the colonization of southern Africa. The commander had his wife and son with him, and two attractive nieces who subsequently were married at the Cape; and the rest of the company consisted of just over 200 men of whom 80 were to remain at the Cape. Of these, only a few had their families with them, for none of them regarded the expedition as emigration from Holland to colonize a new country, in the way that Englishmen and their families were at that time immigrating in the American colonies. The expedition was simply a job that servants of the Company had to do. When it was done they would return home.

Into these small ships had to be stored all that was required for the voyage as well as the picks, shovels, spades, wheelbarrows, timber, nails, and tools needed to build houses and construct a fort. Guns and ammunition there had to be, not only for dealing with hostile tribes and wild animals but because Holland was at war with Portugal, and because pirates were an ever-present danger, even in the Bay of Biscay, where van Riebeeck sighted a Turkish pirate on the third of January. Water and food were always a great difficulty on these voyages. Beef that went bad in spite of being heavily salted and pickled, rancid water and a lack of green vegetables resulted in diseases of which the worst was scurvy, a wasting disease that took a heavy toll.[1] One of the main reasons for establishing a settlement at the Cape was to be able to supply ships with the fresh water, meat, fruit and vegetables that would save many lives.

Jan van Riebeeck's expedition was fortunate. A voyage in the seventeenth century, over largely uncharted seas, was a perilous affair, for apart from enemy ships and pirates, there were dangers from storms and unknown rocks. Even more dreaded than these were the dangers of being becalmed in the doldrums and of dwindling food supplies that drove men to kill rats and fight over the corpses. Van Riebeeck

[1] Scurvy, which is due to lack of vitamin C, was a scourge in England that diminished at the end of the sixteenth century when the common potato was introduced from Spain. It was not until a hundred years after van Riebeeck's voyage to the Cape that James Lind published his *Treatise on the Scurvy* and showed conclusively that the only preventive and cure was a diet of fresh fruit and vegetables.

was becalmed on both sides of the Equator, but for the most part he had favourable weather and only once had the water and beer ration to be reduced; there were only two deaths, one from scurvy and one from dropsy; but he reported that when they finally landed in Table Bay many of the company were weak from lack of proper food.

The route in those days when ships were entirely dependent on trade and anti-trade winds, lay almost due south to the Canaries, then, keeping close to shore, south-west to the Cape Verde Islands. After that it was due south to the Equator, once more south-west to within fifty miles of the Brazilian coast, and only then did the ships begin to veer eastwards. For the last twenty-three days of the three-and-a-half-months' voyage van Riebeeck was sailing practically due east, and on the fifth of April the chief mate of the *Drommedaris* sighted Table Mountain and was rewarded with five Spanish *reals*, about one pound. A gun was fired from the *Drommedaris* and flags were hoisted to inform the *Reijger* and the *Goede Hoop* that land had been sighted, and, having assured himself that there were no Portuguese or pirate ships in the bay, van Riebeeck dropped anchor on the sixth of April 1652. The long journey from Holland had ended and a new and eventful chapter in the story of South Africa had begun.

The directors of the Dutch East Company had instructed van Riebeeck to lay out a vegetable garden, secure the supply of fresh water, build a small fort, remain at peace with the inhabitants and obtain cattle from them by barter. The first few months were months of great activity as van Riebeeck proceeded to carry out his instructions: shelters had to be built before the stores could be unloaded; sites were selected for a fort and for gardens; and exploring parties were sent out to find timber, collect greens for food, and try to barter cattle. There was plenty of fish, but the Hottentots were at first reluctant to part with cattle and the settlers were glad enough to kill and eat a hippopotamus which, as van Riebeeck reported, weighed as much as two oxen. It was the first fresh meat they had had for four months.

Van Riebeeck had to contend with many difficulties. Storms washed away the gardens and new ones had to be laid out; baboons and other wild animals were a constant source of danger; wheelbarrows and other equipment wore out, and the copper wire used to repair them was stolen by his men for trade with the Hottentots. Lack of sufficient food, hard work, and illness made the men discontented, and when, six months after his arrival, it was necessary to cut rations, van Riebeeck faced a mutiny. A few of the men deserted, and there was much grumbling; theft of rations and equipment increased, and at one time the commander's life was threatened. Any sign of disobedience or insubordination was treated with the cruel severity customary in those times: a hundred lashes, the chains, or the terrible keel-hauling from which few escaped alive or unmaimed.

Van Riebeeck persevered against all these odds and gradually the little settlement began to take shape. The cattle trade improved, and to supplement it the Company started its own herds of cattle and sheep. In 1657 the commander persuaded the directors to allow a few of their servants to take their discharge and become free burghers farming on their own account on land allotted them by the commander. This step was taken in the hope that it would increase production at no expense to the Company. It was not an attempt at colonization, and van Riebeeck kept strict control over the free burghers, compelling them to produce only what the Company needed, and forbidding them to sell except to the Company, or to trade direct with Hottentots. Nevertheless, whatever object van Riebeeck had in mind, these nine free burghers and their families were the first real colonists in South Africa—colonists as distinct from Company's officials; and they soon began to assert their rights as freemen by protesting against restrictions and demanding that their interests as well as those of the Company should be considered.

In the same year that free burghers were granted farms, the first slaves arrived in South Africa from Java and Madagascar, and from then onwards slaves were imported regularly from East Africa, Madagascar, and the Indies. Soon slaves were doing all the unskilled and some of the skilled work at the Cape. They were, on the whole, not ill treated, and regulations provided that they should be christianized and taught to read and write; when they had these accomplishments they might be freed. Children of slaves were the property of the owner; often they were his own children by slave women, and it was by mixture between Europeans, Hottentots, and slaves from Madagascar and the East that the present Cape Coloured People of South Africa came into being as a distinct group.

The first Hottentots the Dutch met were a band of about twenty beachcombers, *strandlopers*, as the Dutch called them, under a picturesque leader known as Herrie. He spoke a little English and Dutch, having once been taken on a visit to Batavia, and he acted as interpreter and general liaison officer between the Dutch and the Hottentot clans of the interior. Like many a man in similar circumstances Herrie used his position for his own advantage: he tried to induce greater liberality among the Dutch by telling them that the English were more generous; and while he kept in with the Dutch and persuaded other Hottentots to bring their cattle for barter, van Riebeeck strongly suspected that he was egging them on to demand better prices—that is, more copper per beast. Whenever the opportunity offered Herrie and his little band stole copper, tobacco, knives, and even the buttons off children's clothes, and on one occasion they went so far as to murder a herd boy and steal his cattle. Van Riebeeck put up with most of this, partly because he had been instructed to avoid the expense of war with the inhabitants, and partly because Herrie really was useful to him.

North and east of Cape Town lived larger nomadic Hottentot clans with their herds of cattle and sheep, and it was with them that the Dutch hoped to establish friendly trading relations. Some of the clans were accustomed to bring their herds to graze, for two or three months every year, on the lands which van Riebeeck's men were now beginning to cultivate, and the Dutch were able to buy cattle from them. But that was too small and irregular a supply to satisfy the demand for beef. Exploring parties were therefore sent to induce the Hottentots to bring more cattle to Table Bay at regular intervals; and these expeditions, undertaken so that van Riebeeck could carry out his instructions to supply passing ships with fresh meat, constitute the first exploration of the interior, and it was by these that news of fertile lands fit for occupation was brought back.

It is clear to us, looking back, that the conscientious way in which van Riebeeck tried to carry out his instructions led him into a number of contradictions. To produce his supplies of meat as economically as possible he wanted the Hottentots to drive it to market at Cape Town, and when they did so, thieving and quarrelling disturbed peaceful relations. Underpaid Company's servants saw in the presence of the Hottentots an opportunity for private trade in elephants' tusks and cattle, and this led to more quarrelling and to dissatisfaction with the Company for prohibiting private trade. When the supplies from Hottentots were insufficient, van Riebeeck began to establish his own herds and to encourage free burghers to farm; this meant that grazing lands which the Hottentots regarded as their own were occupied by Europeans. Finally, the Company wanted to limit its occupation at the Cape to what was strictly economic, but the very establishment of a class of non-official free burghers and the introduction of slaves were bound to lead to expansion of the settlement.

Van Riebeeck tried to solve some of the difficulties into which contradictory policies had led him by establishing a boundary. At one time the Company thought of digging a canal across the Cape Peninsula to cut it off from the mainland and so prevent expansion. Van Riebeeck was against this, and instead planted a bitter almond hedge as a boundary from the mouth of Salt River to the mountain, and built three blockhouses which he called *Kyckuyt* (Look-out), *Keert de Koe* (Stop the Cow), and *Houd den Bul* (Hold the Bull), names that show clearly what his policy hoped to achieve. But these measures were of no use. The very economic demands that van Riebeeck tried to serve broke all boundaries. Hottentots and Europeans wanted to trade; and nothing the Company could do would, in the long run, prevent quarrels about land. In 1658 this quarrelling ended in a regular small-scale war, and the Hottentots were compelled to accept the fact that they had lost their grazing lands near Cape Town.

We have clear proof of the important part played by land in the relations between Europeans and Hottentots. In a letter to the directors, van Riebeeck said:

'The prisoner . . . who could speak Dutch fairly well, having been asked the reason why they caused us this trouble, declared for no other reason than that they saw that we kept in possession the best lands, and grazed our cattle where they used to do so, and that everywhere with houses and plantations we endeavoured to establish ourselves so permanently as if we intended never to leave again, but take permanent possession of this Cape land (which had belonged to them during all the centuries) for our sole use; yea! to such an extent that their cattle could not come and drink at the fresh water without going over the corn lands, which we did not like them to do.'[1]

A contemporary writer, Olfert Dapper, describing this incident, and the questioning of the prisoner who was a wounded Hottentot, adds:

'He asked finally what we would have done had the same thing happened to us. Moreover, he added, they observed how we were strengthening ourselves daily with fortifications and bulwarks, which according to their way of thinking could have no other object than to bring them

[1] This, and the next two extracts, are quoted from *The Early Cape Hottentots*, Van Riebeeck Society Publications No. 14, pp. 14–16.

and all that was theirs under our authority and domination.'

And when the Hottentot clan sued for peace, van Riebeeck reported:

'They pressed this point so hard that their lands should be evacuated by us, that we were finally compelled to say, that in consequence of the war made against us, they had completely forfeited their rights, and that we were not inclined to restore them, as the country had become the property of the Company by the sword and the rights of war.'

Without realizing the full implications of what they were saying, the wounded Hottentot clansman and Commander Jan van Riebeeck were speaking for Africa and Europe. What they saw and said went to the heart of the matter and was to be repeated with monotonous variations in the centuries to come. It was the dim recognition of the tremendous fact that Europe was conquering Africa. The white man had come to stay, and the black man was losing his land.

We have a number of records written by Dutch officials and by other European travellers, describing the habits and customs of the Hottentots and reflecting the interest and scorn, the amusement and disgust with which Europeans regarded the indolent, carefree, and crafty ways of these primitive people. Van Riebeeck describes a Hottentot baby drinking from the udder of a ewe, and calls it 'charming'; he calls the parents 'dull, stupid, lazy, and stinking'. From the other side we have no evidence of what the Hottentots thought of the Europeans, except from a Hottentot prisoner interpreted by a European. We can assume, however, that there must have been arguments and debates about these white-faced invaders with their curious ways and deadly implements. The question most discussed would have been how to deal with the new situation: whether to keep away from them altogether, and forgo the delights of brandy, tobacco, and copper; whether to make a friendly approach or to try fraud; whether to fight for the land they saw being occupied by the enemy. Whatever they may have thought, the end was surrender to superior force and eventual absorption into the civilization of the European invaders.

The Dutch East India Company which ruled in South Africa until 1795 was administered on principles in which economic and political considerations constantly clashed. It was neither a purely business concern, though this side of it came first in the eyes of the directors and shareholders, nor a system of political government. In Holland supreme control of the Company's affairs vested in the Chamber of Seventeen, a federal body representing six provincial chambers. One of the seventeen directors was appointed by the government, from whom the Company received its charter and monopoly to trade in the East and to take possession of and administer such lands as it thought fit. In Batavia, the capital of the Company's possession in the East, a governor-general and council managed business affairs and ruled politically over the Company's territory. The Company had its own civil service and, in effect, its own army and navy. The status and rank of the officials are evidence of the mixed economic and political nature of the Company's activities: governor-general, governor, commander, councillor, senior merchant, junior merchant, captain, corporal, and so on. Everyone in its employ took an oath of loyalty and obedience to the Dutch East India Company.

The administration that van Riebeeck established at the Cape bore all the marks of the dual nature of the Company. Van Riebeeck, himself holding the rank of merchant, was commander. (It was not until 1691 that the Cape was considered sufficiently important to have a permanent governor.) Assisting the commander was a Council of Policy composed of the commander and senior officials which was really a ship's council transferred to land; it could become a Broad Council when officers of visiting Dutch ships attended, and if a visiting officer was senior to the commander, he took the chair. The Council of Policy was legislative, executive, and judiciary rolled into one. It issued local regulations, called *placaaten*, controlling trade and private conduct; it administered laws made by the Council in Batavia or the Chamber of Seventeen in Holland; it regulated religious matters and performed marriage services. As the settlement expanded other boards and councils were created to meet the needs of civil government; but in van Riebeeck's time the Council of Policy performed all the functions of government.

After ten years at the Cape, Jan van Riebeeck, to his great joy, was allowed to go to the East Indies on promotion; he remained there for fifteen years and died in 1677 without having returned to Holland. In the eyes of the shareholders whom he served, van Riebeeck had done a good job. At comparatively small cost he had established a half-way house which, by providing repairs for storm-tossed ships and fresh supplies for scurvy-stricken sailors, must have saved the Company much money and many lives. Van Riebeeck himself regarded all that he had done as serving this single end. The fort, the houses and barns, the gardens and fields; free burghers and slaves; cattle trade and Hottentot war; expeditions inland and along the coast—all these were undertaken, one step leading to another, in the interests of his masters and with no thought that he was doing more than that or that anything else was of the slightest importance. It is natural that a later age should place a different emphasis on events and regard the ends he sought and the means he used as important, not because they increased the dividends of the shareholders in Holland, but because they were the beginning of European settlement in southern Africa.

Chapter Three

EXPANDING FRONTIERS

Though the Cape had been established as a refreshment station it soon became clear to the Dutch, as it has been to the world ever since, that its real value lay in its strategic position astride the sea route from Europe to the East. Whoever held the Cape held a shield to defend its own trade and a sword to threaten the trade of other nations. This fact, so obvious in the two world wars of the twentieth century, was forced on the attention of the Dutch when war broke out between Holland and England in 1665, and was driven home when France attacked Holland in 1672.

It was for strategic reasons, then, that the Dutch East India Company changed its policy at the Cape and, for the next forty years, looked upon an increase of the free burgher population as desirable. It might be truer to say that it retained its old outlook on the Cape as 'an item in the East India ledger' but that it superimposed a policy designed to serve strategic needs. It did not abandon the view that its prime object was trade with the East and that it was not interested in colonization except in so far as it promoted that object; it still maintained that expenses at the Cape must be kept as low as possible, and that to that end production, trade and prices must be strictly regulated by the Company and in the interest of the Company. But it hoped to serve two ends by an increase in the burgher class: to produce more cheaply the meat, corn, vegetables, and wine that its ships needed, and to provide at little cost the manpower required to defend the Cape against attacks from without.

The new and the old policies were contradictory, almost mutually exclusive, and the long-term results of the contradictions became apparent in the eighteenth century; but the immediate result of the new policy was a fairly rapid expansion of the settlement by assisted immigration. In 1679 the directors made a happy choice in appointing Simon van der Stel as commander. He was an enthusiastic colonizer who saw the potentialities of the Cape as a colony and carried out the Company's new immigration policy so heartily that he had to be reprimanded by the directors for inducing artisans, on their way to India, to settle at the Cape. Dutch and German settlers were welcomed and Company's servants were urged to take their discharge at the Cape and become free burghers. He tried, but with little success, to bring orphan girls from Holland as wives for his young farmers.

Simon van der Stel explored the immediate hinterland of Cape Town, beyond the sandy flats that surround it, and established a new community at Stellenbosch, thirty miles from Table Bay. There, in the fruitful valley of the Eerste River, he granted farms in freehold and established South Africa's first village. More farms were granted ten miles north-east of Stellenbosch, at Drakenstein and Paarl in the Berg River valley, and by 1688 the burgher population had risen to 600. Van Riebeeck's bitter almond hedge, planted as a boundary to contain the settlement and keep out Hottentots, had ceased to be a frontier, and the refreshment station was in a fair way to becoming a colony.

In 1688 the Cape received the largest single dose of immigration that she was to have until the nineteenth century. Louis XIV of France had, in 1685, revoked the Edict of Nantes which had guaranteed religious toleration to French Protestants; and Huguenots, as they were called, fled to Switzerland, Germany, England and Holland in search of the religious freedom denied them in their own country. The Company seized the opportunity to offer refugees a free passage to the Cape, and farms, when they got there, on the same terms as the other free burghers. It will be remembered that Philip II of Spain had, by expelling Jews and Protestants, benefited the Netherlands. Centuries later, Germany impoverished herself and benefited other nations by persecuting Jews and Germans who would not conform to Hitler's racial doctrines. In the same way Louis XIV benefited South Africa by denying religious freedom to his subjects. The rebels who refuse to conform to man-made doctrines are likely to be the staunchest and most enterprising members of the community, and what the expelling country loses other countries gain.

The total number of French refugees to the Cape between 1688 and 1690 was not more than 200, but they had a far deeper influence on their new country than their co-religionists had on the countries of Europe to which they fled. At the Cape, the Huguenots constituted a significant proportion of the free burgher population; they were industrious, skilled, independent, and freedom loving; they were of a better social class and had more education than the normal run of discharged Company's servants who had become free burghers; and their firm religious beliefs, for which they had left their homes in France, strengthened moral standards at the Cape. It was a much-needed infusion of new blood at a time when those moral standards showed signs of sagging under the influence of slavery and of contact with a primitive race.

Of deliberate policy, and to the anger of the newcomers, van der Stel dispersed them as much as possible among Dutch farmers in Drakenstein and Fransch Hoek. The Company was afraid of creating a French minority which might, at a pinch, side with a French squadron attacking the Cape, and was anxious that the refugees should be assimilated as soon as possible. For this reason, too, it discouraged the use of French in church and school, and, in 1701, actually forbade it; the French naturally objected and, though the order remained, it was never strictly enforced. What could not be done by force, however, happened naturally. Intermarriage and the needs of social and official intercourse and business compelled the refugees to let their children learn Dutch, and in three generations the French language had died out at the Cape. To-day it survives only in numerous names such as Marais, de Villiers, du Plessis, and Joubert.

The process of settlement and assimilation was not easy. The refugees were poverty stricken and had, in the first years, constantly to be helped by the Company; homes and farms had to be built in untamed country where danger from wild animals and marauding Bushmen and Hottentots was ever present; and the newcomers had to adjust themselves from the civilization of Europe to the more primitive life at the Cape. Holland and France had been at war and French squadrons had threatened the Cape. No wonder then that Dutch and French, neither understanding the other's language, were suspicious of one another and tended to remain aloof. Differences of national customs and language were bound to produce friction, and friction there was in plenty. When the French, rightly thinking that their mother-tongue was being suppressed, petitioned the governor, they were called ungrateful; and a Frenchman was banished to Mauritius for publicly wishing that 'the French would come and would stay'. Relations became so strained that a Dutch farmer said he would rather give food to a dog or a Hottentot than to a Frenchman.

When two groups are quarrelling there is nothing like a common grievance to unite them, and that grievance was supplied in 1705 by Willem Adriaan van der Stel, who had succeeded his father as governor in 1699. The younger van der Stel was an able man who did much to improve stock farming and agriculture at the Cape; but he was arrogant, ambitious, greedy, and dishonest, and seized the opportunities offered by his official position to enrich himself and a few of his friends. He used the Company's materials, men, and time to establish a beautiful country estate called *Vergelegen*, still one of the show-pieces of Cape architecture. In spite of the prohibition against private farming and trading by Company's servants, he and a clique of seven or eight high officials each acquired large farms, the total extent of which was about one-third of the whole farming area at the time.

All this was bad enough, but it was not all. By 1705 the Company's policy of increasing the number of free burghers was being only too successful, and in a reasonably good year the restricted Cape market was easily saturated. When, therefore, van der Stel and his friends decided to corner that market the farmers were faced with ruin. Using his official powers over the sale and price of produce he saw to it that contracts to supply the Company went to his friends. The valuable meat contract, for example, was taken away from a farmer called Husing and given to four of van der Stel's underlings.

It was the direct threat to their livelihood rather than the dishonesty of the officials that roused the farmers, Dutch and French, to action. A petition to the directors was secretly organized and the names of the leaders—van der Heiden, Husing, Adam Tas, du Toit, des Pres—are a sign that bitter feeling between Dutch and French was passing. Adam Tas, a recent arrival from Amsterdam and an 'elegant writer', was appointed secretary to draft the petition and to collect signatures with as much secrecy as possible. Sixty-three burghers signed, a large number when we consider the risks involved in what might be regarded by the Company as conspiracy; and the petition was smuggled out to the Council at Batavia from where two copies were sent, one to the directors in Holland and one to the governor at the Cape, van der Stel himself.

Van der Stel took immediate action. He organized a counter-petition and by use of bribery, fraud, and force induced 240 to sign. He then arrested Tas and a few of the leaders and tried to force them to recant, which, under threat of torture or banishment, some of them did. Meanwhile, in Amsterdam, the directors appointed a commission of inquiry, and on its recommendation recalled van der Stel and the senior officials to Holland where, after a long trial, van der Stel and two officials were dismissed from the service of the Company. It was a victory for the burghers. But though they had won the battle for economic rights against the officials, who were once more forbidden to own or lease land or to trade privately, they were still at the mercy of the Company with its policy of strict control, and the economic difficulties of the young colony were by no means at an end.

The reaction of the directors to the quarrel between the burghers and van der Stel was to abandon the policy of assisted immigration. They felt as the British government was to feel later about the American colonies, that colonists were a nuisance and distracted the Company from its real business of trading; besides, colonists tended to demand rights that conflicted with the interests of shareholders. When van der Stel left in 1708 there were 1,700 men, women, and children belonging to the free burgher class, and the Company made no further efforts to add to their number. In 1713 a smallpox epidemic killed off 25 per cent of the population of Cape Town and wiped out several Hottentot clans, and the Directors asked the officials at Cape Town whether the resulting labour shortage should be made good by European artisans or by slaves. With one notable exception they replied that slaves would be far more economic; European labour was lazy and inefficient. Captain de Chavonnes, brother of the governor and the one man who voted for free European labour, pointed out all the disadvantages of slave labour: that it was, in fact, uneconomic, that it encouraged plantations rather than intensive cultivation, and that it induced habits of sloth and inefficiency among the owners. His prophetic words were unheeded, and the directors plumped for more slave labour.

Earlier in this chapter it was pointed out that the Company, in assisting immigration, was following contradictory policies. The commercial policy, as it was understood in Europe in the seventeenth and eighteenth centuries, demanded that the Company should have a monopoly in trade, that it should buy as cheaply, and sell as dearly, as possible, and that it should keep down expenses. To retain its monopoly and to keep the prices of its imports from the East high, the Company resorted to a practice that is not unknown in the twentieth century; it limited supplies and destroyed 'surplus' stocks of spice. To keep down expenses, low salaries and wages were paid and severe punishments were meted out to officials who indulged in private trade; but despite the punishments, officials were compelled to add to their meagre incomes by private trading, and the result was a corrupt civil service.

This policy, as applied at the Cape, demanded that food and defence, the two needs which the settlement was designed to serve, should cost as little as possible. When, for a short time, the Company imposed a new policy of assisted immigration on the old commercial policy, it was with no idea of turning the refreshment station into a colony; it was simply in the hope that the cost of food and defence at the Cape would be reduced. The Company wanted the burghers to produce just enough corn, meat, vegetables, and wine to satisfy the limited demands of the Company at a price decided on by the Company—just enough and no more. Such a policy could never work. Had the Company resolutely stuck to its original idea of using only paid servants to produce what it needed, it would have had no colonization problems and the Cape would have remained a refreshment and strategic station until, possibly in the nineteenth century, a more natural and healthy colonization could develop it. By assisting immigrants and at the same time limiting the market for which they produced, the Company was trying to have it both ways. And by abandoning this policy after forty years the Company secured for itself the worst of both worlds. The Cape became neither an efficient refreshment station nor a vigorous colony; it remained economically and culturally backward until it was rescued by the nineteenth century.

The attitude of the Company towards colonies was common in Europe until the nineteenth century. It was believed that colonies were useful only in so far as they served the needs of the mother country. This was England's belief about her American colonies. But the American colonies were peopled by real immigrants who had gone out in hundreds of thousands to found new homes for themselves where they could enjoy religious and political freedom; and when, in the middle of the eighteenth century, England began to apply to the American colonies the policies which the Dutch Company applied at the Cape, those colonies rebelled and fought a successful war of independence. The semi-colonists at the Cape were too poor, too few, too backward, and too dispersed to make any effective rebellion against the Company. The younger van der Stel had shown that it was indeed possible for the Company's servants to supply the Cape market; but by then the free burghers, too weak to make effective rebellion, were just strong enough to prevent the Company from making use of van der Stel's discovery.

Other factors besides the economic policies of the Company determined the way the Cape was going. From the narrow coastal belt the land rises steeply over the mountains and on to the vast plateau that constitutes the greater part of South Africa, and the fruitful valleys of Stellenbosch and Drakenstein, with their good winter rainfall, give place to the great stretches of rolling veld and a fickle summer rainfall. Along the southern and eastern coastal belts winds from the warm Indian Ocean bring rain which diminishes from the east, across the mountains, to the west; and the cold Atlantic current causes desert or semi-desert conditions over the western half of South Africa. Nowhere is the soil as good as even the medium soils of Europe, and poor soil combined with poor and uncertain rainfall make intensive cultivation impossible without irrigation. Most of the country is essentially sheep and cattle land.

Van Riebeeck's nine free burghers and van der Stel's immigrants could, for the most part, be accommodated on land in the more fruitful winter-rainfall area to produce

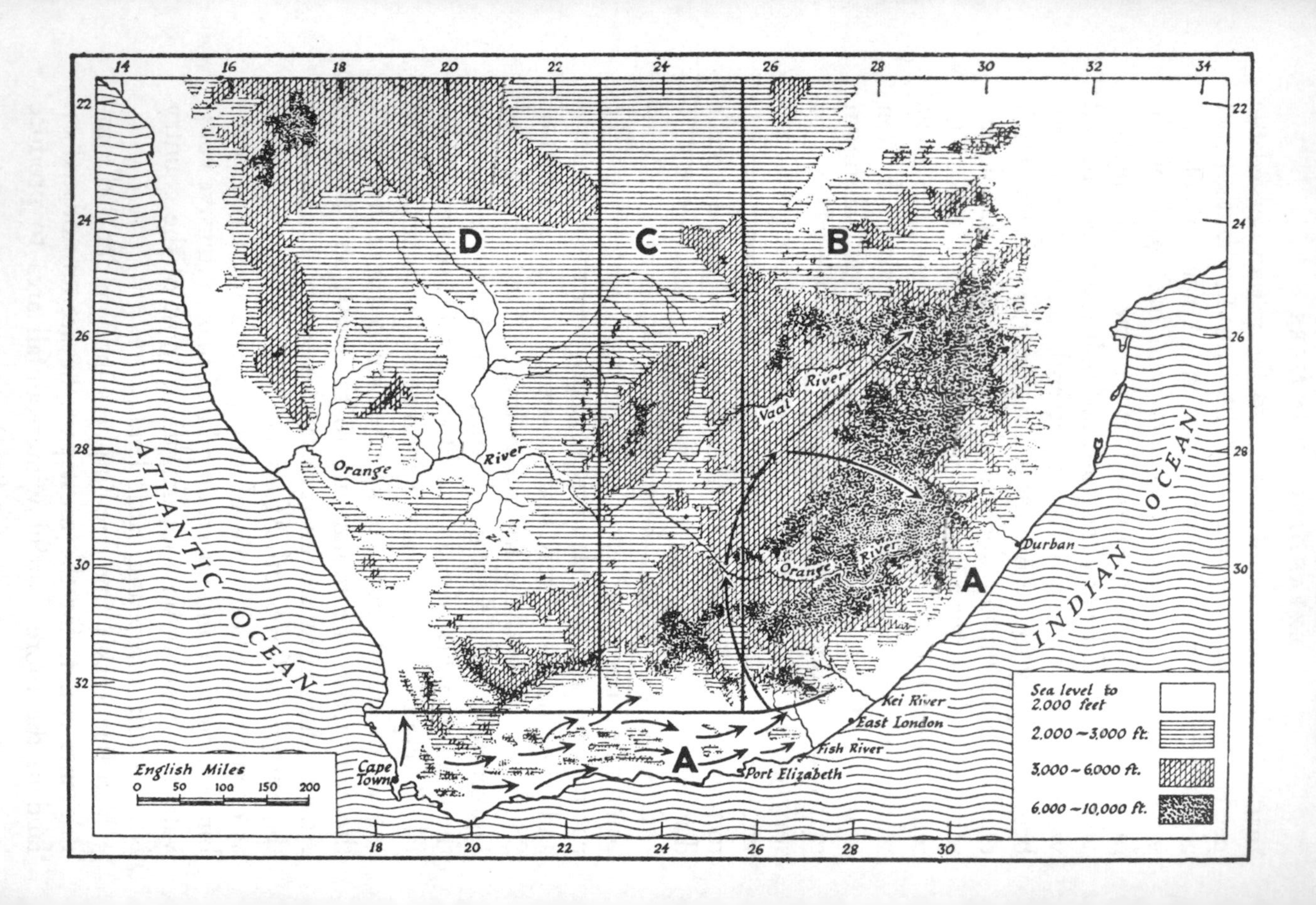
ATLANTIC OCEAN
INDIAN OCEAN
A
B
C
D
Orange River
Vaal River
Orange River
Durban
Kei River
East London
Fish River
Port Elizabeth
Cape Town
English Miles
0 50 100 150 200
Sea level to 2,000 feet
2,000 – 3,000 ft.
3,000 – 6,000 ft.
6,000 – 10,000 ft.

This map is intended to show how the physical features and the distribution of rainfall and vegetation influenced African and European migration. South Africa consists of a coastal belt and an interior plateau.

Rainfall decreases from east to west. The area marked A, the southern and eastern coastal belts, has an annual rainfall varying from 15 in. to 75 in. Evergreen forests, subtropical bush, and grasslands are found in this area. B has a rainfall, diminishing from east to west, between 40 in. and 25 in. It consists largely of grasslands and parklands. C has a rainfall, diminishing from east to west, between 30 in. and 15 in. It, too, consists of grasslands which become poorer as the rainfall diminishes. D has a rainfall, diminishing from east to west, between 15 in. and less than 5 in., and consists of shrub which eventually gives place to semi-desert and desert.

The arrows mark the path of European expansion. Almost the whole of area A north-east of the Fish River, and the eastern half of B, were occupied by African tribes, and this forced European expansion northwards, on to the central plateau. But the tendency always was to turn east, to the better-watered lands. A. B, and C were, therefore, the areas most desired by both black and white cattle farmers.

corn and wine. Even they found that the restricted Cape market and the low prices fixed by the Company gave an inadequate living, and they resorted to the more profitable keeping of cattle runs beyond the Hottentots Holland Mountains, which they frequently stocked by illegal barter with Hottentots. The Company itself had, before the beginning of the eighteenth century, given up trying to limit its own cattle runs to the Cape Peninsula and had established cattle posts beyond the mountains. For the succeeding generations of free burghers farming in Stellenbosch and Drakenstein held few prospects. One of the greatest drawbacks to the development of the Cape was that it had no staple export product, such as the West Indies had in sugar. The Company did occasionally export surplus corn, but its quality was poor and its price too high because the farmers lacked skill and the good soils of Europe and because slave labour was uneconomic. In spite of the efforts of the van der Stels and the French refugees, Cape wines were of such a poor quality that the Council of Batavia sarcastically suggested that the Cape should concentrate on vinegar; and the vinegar they did make was not of much better quality.

If farming corn and wine became an overcrowded and unattractive profession because of restrictions, there was nothing else for younger sons but to turn their backs on Cape Town and cross the mountains to keep cattle, to hunt, to fight against Bushmen, and to trek ever further away from government and civilization. East along the coastal belt until in due course they met the black cattle farmers, and north-east over the escarpment and on to the Little and Great Karroo, these trekboers[1] went. The only form of capital that was plentiful was land, and though the Company would no longer give freehold because it wanted to stop the trekking, it compromised in the worst possible way by allowing anyone to occupy a farm of about 6,000 acres on

[1] The word boer, pronounced like the German *bühr* and not *boor*, means farmer. In the nineteenth century, Boer with a capital letter came to mean the European inhabitants of the two Republics.

payment of a quitrent of £5. These farms were called loan farms and a man 'surveyed' his farm by walking from a central point for half an hour in each direction, north, south, east, and west, and thus marking his boundary. So far from stopping the trekking this system encouraged it. Farms were easily obtained by the Boers and easily left, frequently without their informing the Company's officials or paying the quitrent; and these conditions induced a restlessness which militated against permanent settlement of farms and the building of proper houses and cultivating of fields that this would have demanded.

In adopting the life of the trekboer the sons and daughters of Europe were reversing the usual process of development from nomadism to settled agriculture and industry. They moved from settled agriculture to the nomadic life of the cattleman, the life which the earlier inhabitants of Africa had led. It has been pointed out[1] that it was, economically speaking, a successful adaptation to environment. It is true that the settled and intensive agriculture of Europe was not possible in the circumstances, but these nomadic conditions left distinct marks on the society that grew up in them. The trekboer became hardy, independent, and self-reliant; but his freedom was anarchic, not the disciplined freedom of Western Europe, and his individualism was that of the frontier, not that of a democratic society. His freedom and individualism were bred in isolation, far from the settled society in which a man's rights are limited by the rights of his neighbours.

There were other disadvantages attached to the evolution of the trekboer. Wherever he held land, that land belonged to the Company; but the Company was not prepared to spend the necessary money to follow up expansion by administration, and for many years it contented itself with issuing instructions that the latest frontier should not be crossed and that the trekkers should not have dealings with Hottentots, or, later, with Africans. These instructions went

[1] See de Kiewiet, *A History of South Africa*, chap. I.

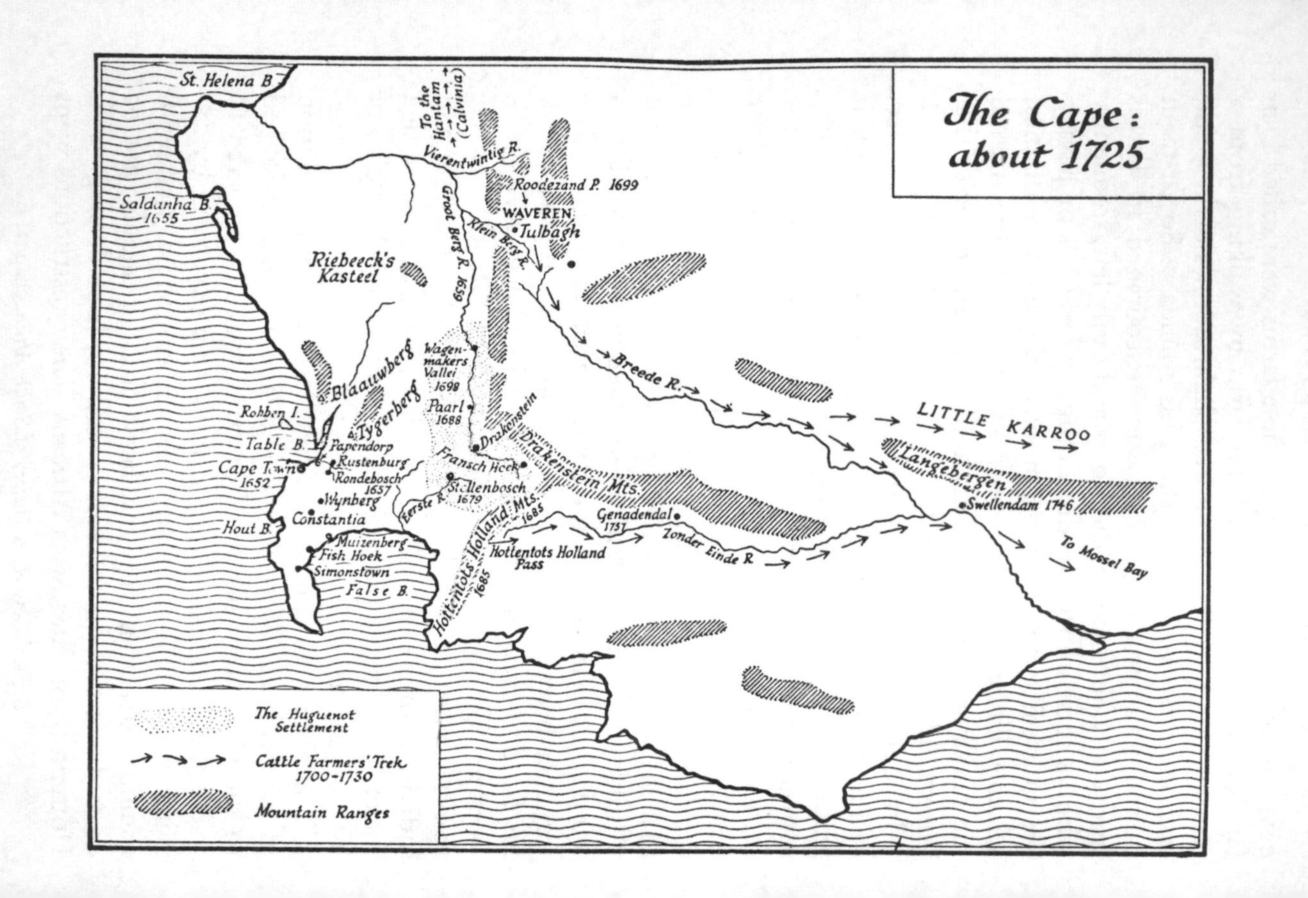
The Cape: about 1725
St. Helena B.
Saldanha B. 1655
To the Hantam (Calvinia)
Vierentwintig R.
Roodezand P. 1699
WAVEREN
Tulbagh
Klein Berg R.
Groot Berg R. 1659
Riebeeck's Kasteel
Breede R.
LITTLE KARROO
Langebergen
Swellendam 1746
To Mossel Bay
Wagenmakers Vallei 1698
Paarl 1688
Drakenstein
Drakenstein Mts.
Blaauwberg
Tygerberg
Robben I.
Table B.
Papendorp
Rustenburg
Cape Town 1652
Rondebosch 1657
Wynberg
Constantia
Fransch Hoek
Stellenbosch 1679
Eerste R.
Genadendal 1737
Zonder Einde R.
Hottentots Holland Mts. 1685
Hottentots Holland Pass
Hottentots Holland 1685
Hout B.
Muizenberg
Fish Hoek
Simonstown
False B.
The Huguenot Settlement
Cattle Farmers' Trek 1700-1730
Mountain Ranges

unheeded and the frontier continued to expand. Indeed, it was the one thing at the Cape that did expand—far too rapidly for the slowly increasing population. The trekboer developed an attitude to land which he passed on to his children: that there was plenty of land and that it was the natural right of a white man to own a farm.

Finally, the isolation of the trekboer left him outside the stream of European civilization, except for his Calvinist religion. He had no part in such culture as there was in the settled districts, and he hardly felt the winds of reform and revolution that were beginning to blow in Europe and America and even at the Cape itself. When at last the nineteenth century caught up with him he had developed many sterling qualities but he was unprepared for the new ideas that were changing the world. By the end of the eighteenth century the contradictory policies of the Company had combined with geography and climate to produce a frontiersman who differed markedly from his Dutch and French ancestors in Europe; and it was this frontier population that was, in the following century, to push the boundaries of South Africa to the Limpopo River and beyond.

Chapter Four

SOCIAL LIFE AT THE CAPE

Looking back on the eighteenth century at the Cape we see a settlement, backward and almost stagnant, with little promise of future development. Compared with the growth of the North American colonies, or with that later of Australia and New Zealand, the growth of the Cape as a colony of Europe was extremely slow. By the end of the century, 150 years after its establishment, the free burgher population numbered only 16,000; there were 17,000 slaves and an unknown number of Hottentots, Bushmen, and half-breeds—possibly 20,000 in all—giving a total of about 53,000 men, women, and children within the borders of the colony. During roughly the same period the population of European settlement in North America had grown to more than six million, and New York, founded (as New Amsterdam) a few years before Cape Town, was a thriving city that could have accommodated the total population of the Cape four or five times over.

The population of Cape Town itself consisted of Company's officials, free burghers, and slaves. Officials were paid poor salaries, and in spite of prohibitions and heavy punishments, indulged in private trade and in bribery and corruption to eke out a livelihood. Free burghers made a living as shopkeepers and artisans, and all, whether genuine merchants or not, engaged in the great eighteenth-century industry of smuggling. The Company had a monopoly of importing and exporting, but when the fleet was in harbour officers and ordinary sailors knew that any burgher in Cape Town would be anxious to buy whatever could be smuggled ashore, either secretly or by bribing an official. From the richest to the poorest, everyone in Cape Town took in lodgers from passing ships and was usually well content to accept goods in settlement of the excessive prices charged for board and bed. Cape Town, the Tavern of the Seas, was notorious for this; but sailors who have been at sea for three months are apt to forget about previous overchargings, and so the Cape Town 'merchants' flourished.

When no ships were in harbour, masons, bricklayers, carpenters, bakers, bootmakers, tailors, and smiths went back to their normal occupations. Not that these were physically arduous, because they almost all employed slaves who did the hard manual work, and who in time became the real skilled workmen of the Cape. It was a precarious livelihood that depended on the number of ships that touched at the Cape; and while that number steadily increased with ocean-going traffic, it fluctuated from year to year and varied with war and peace in Europe. During the Seven Years War (1756–63) for example, when Britain and France were at war in Europe, America, and India, British and French ships at first avoided the Cape; since at that time already about twice as many foreign as Dutch ships called, there was a trade depression. Then both British and French found it convenient to put in at a neutral port, and trade boomed to such an extent that Governor Tulbagh introduced sumptuary laws to prevent people from living 'beyond their means'.

Even in good years only about 160 ships called at the Cape, and it is no wonder that the citizens of Cape Town were delighted when, in 1781, a French fleet entered Table Bay and landed troops to occupy the Cape. Britain's North American colonies were, under George Washington, fighting their War of Independence, and France seized the opportunity of Britain's embarrassment to build up a European alliance against her. Holland had joined this alliance in 1780, and it was to stop Britain from occupying the Cape that France did. For four years Cape Town, and the colony generally, enjoyed their last boom under the Dutch East India Company and, so gay a place had it become, Cape Town was nicknamed 'Little Paris'. Not only French money, but French manners and dances took hold of the Cape to the delight of the young ladies and, we may imagine, the chagrin of the young men whose noses were put out of joint by their more elegant rivals. When the French departed in 1784 the Cape was a sadder and very much poorer place.

Life in eighteenth-century Cape Town, when the 'giddy and godless French' were not there, was a much more pedestrian affair. An afternoon stroll in the Company's Gardens, still a favourite spot with Capetonians; a drive by carriage, with the number of horses determined by rank; an auction sale; an occasional execution; weddings and funerals, after both of which large amounts of food and wine were served—such were the out-of-home amusements. There was no horse racing until the end of the century, and no theatre until the beginning of the nineteenth. There was plenty of indoor amusement—cards, billiards, backgammon, music on the spinet or harp, and dancing for which old and young had a passion; but few people read books, and there was no bookshop in Cape Town. Wealthier people visited one another at night to smoke churchwarden pipes, drink wine, gossip and play cards; the poorer classes, with less elegant homes, found their amusement at 'The Last Penny', 'The Red Ox', 'The Blue Anchor', or one of the many other taverns where soldiers and sailors and workmen usually had too much to drink, and on their way home fell into holes in the unpaved streets.

All males between sixteen and sixty had to enrol in the burgher militia, and part of their duty was to take turns at patrolling the streets by night to keep order and prevent crime. At nine o'clock a gun was fired, after which all good citizens retired and the burgher watch and the nightwatchmen paraded for duty, the latter setting off in couples, like Dogberry and Verges. They were known as the Rattle Watch because they carried a rattle which they sprang at every hour from ten onwards, shouting aloud the hour as they did so. Other duties were to test that doors were locked, to arrest slaves who were out without permission or failed to carry a lantern, to stop people from smoking, and to prevent disorderliness in taverns. In this latter task their success may be judged from the fact that they frequently joined in the tippling.

The prohibition against smoking in the streets at night was not moral; it was to prevent fire. Most of the buildings had thatched roofs, and with a south-east wind blowing sparks were dangerous; if a fire did break out, the volunteer fire wardens with their small manual engine were ill equipped to deal with it, and, in fact, their main job was to prevent the lookers-on from pilfering goods that might be carried out from the burning building.

Cape Town being what it was, a small town whose inhabitants normally had insufficient occupation and depended on periodic visits from ships for news of the world, it is not surprising that various visitors noted that the staple product of the Cape was gossip. The true citizen of Cape Town was rarely as happy as when sitting on his stoep to exchange rumours or to spin tall yarns to visitors about his 'experiences' in the wild interior which he had, in fact, never visited. Since sailors are themselves fond of spinning a tale, some surprising adventures must have been swapped when a sailor from the fabulous East was entertained by an imaginative Capetonian.

Nor is it surprising that 'precedence' played such a large part in the lives of officials and townsmen. There was no hereditary aristocracy at the Cape, and class distinctions, as they were known in Europe, did not exist; but their place was taken by an order of precedence laid down by the Company, which decided who should sit where in church or at social functions, who should have places of honour at funerals and weddings, and how each rank should be addressed. As the ruling caste in government, church and society, high Company's officials and their wives naturally came first; after them came ministers of religion, members of the Court of Justice, officers in the burgher militia, deacons of the church, and so on, down to attorneys and sextons. Everybody (and his wife) had set places, and the innumerable petitions, court cases, appeals to the governor, and general quarrelling that took place over alleged infringements of precedence show that it was a matter of deep concern to the inhabitants of Cape Town. Precedence could rock society in Cape Town in the eighteenth century as a royal scandal could that of the capitals of Europe in the nineteenth.

All power at the Cape resided in the Governor, who was himself subject to instructions both from the Chamber of Seventeen in Amsterdam, and, sometimes contradicting these, from the Council of Batavia. To assist him there was a Council of Policy consisting of seven officials, which carried out instructions from overseas and made local regulations called *placaaten*; seven members of the Council, together with three prominent burghers appointed by the Governor, formed the Council of Justice, the highest court in the colony, from which appeal lay to Batavia. A matrimonial court regulated marriage laws, and no marriage could take place legally without its consent; an Orphan Chamber looked after the estates of minors, and acted as a loan bank; a court of commissioners tried petty cases in Cape Town only; and, finally, a Burgher Council, later called the Burgher Senate, was appointed by the governor to fulfil the functions of a modern town council: it controlled the burgher watch and fire wardens, laid the grievances of the citizens before the government, and since it had very little money to spend, had perforce to allow streets to fall into a dangerous state of disrepair.

Government regulated life pretty thoroughly, even down to the hours during which bakers might deliver bread. All trade, internal or external, was a Company monopoly, and it farmed out or leased the right to deal in different commodities; the lease was sold by annual auction and the maximum retail price of the commodity was fixed by the Company. The right to supply the Company with the produce it needed was also sold by auction, and again the price was fixed beforehand. The only right to really free marketing at the Cape was the permission to sell produce to ships after they had been in harbour for three days.

Other matters besides trade were regulated. Whether or not a lady might wear a train or have silk and satin dresses; which ladies were allowed to use an umbrella or sunshade; how much money might be spent on a funeral or a bridal bed; how many servants people of different rank might employ and whether the coachman might wear livery—all these delicate matters were at one time or another the subject of regulation during the eighteenth century at the Cape.

The picture of the settlement at Cape Town in the eighteenth century is one of a commercial society, precisely and strictly regulated by a government whose concern was trade, not colonization; a society in which physical labour was as far as possible left to slaves and intellectual effort was uncalled for; in which private initiative was too frequently limited to evading regulations and outwitting officials. The Calvinist religion, the only form tolerated except, late in the century, for a small Lutheran community, had grown formal, and the religious indifference which was prevalent in Europe was a marked feature of Cape Town. Unbelief and religious ignorance were such that one contemporary observer described the people as 'a collection of heathen rather than a colony of Europeans and Christians'.

Education was provided by a few privately run institutions at which younger children were taught the elements of the three R's. Two attempts to establish a high school failed for want of support, and only a few of the wealthiest burghers could afford to send their children to Holland for further education. Early in the nineteenth century a commissioner from Holland reported that young people at the Cape had an intense dislike of mental activity and avoided it as much as possible. Another visitor remarked that the people of the Cape were, in their ignorance, so vain that if they were told about some of the glories of Europe they were apt to retort: 'Why didn't you stay there?'

In spite of this unflattering picture there is no need to think of the citizens of Cape Town as abnormally suppressed or devoid of all civilized virtues. As for suppression and lack of freedom, most people overcame the first and hardly noticed the second. Smuggling was carried to such lengths that, as one Commissioner said, it practically amounted to free trade; and penalties for a breach of regulations could frequently be avoided by currying favour or by bribery. In such ways people avoided the worst unpleasantness of despotic government, but they did so by breaking laws. The citizens of Cape Town, unlike the Pilgrim Fathers, had not left their homeland for the sake of religious freedom; and there was nothing in the environment of their adopted land to make them cling to religion in what was, in Europe, an irreligious—often miscalled tolerant—century. Slavery, unnecessary and hampering laws, the presence of a primitive race, and the superficial cosmopolitanism of a seaport tended to relax moral and religious standards.

As for the civilized virtues, it is difficult to measure these. Wealthier people in Cape Town built fine houses and surrounded themselves with beautiful stinkwood furniture, much sought after by collectors to-day; they enjoyed music and social intercourse; they treated their slaves in a kindly fashion as long as they obeyed, and punished disobedience with the savage brutality common to the century; they dressed with dignity and taste; they and their poorer fellow citizens lived leisurely, healthy family lives and brought up large families with most of the outward forms of civilized life as it was then understood in Europe. In all the circumstances, more could not have been expected of them, and more should not be attributed to them.

Within a radius of sixty miles from Cape Town lived the wine and corn farmers clustered round the village of Stellenbosch and the churches at Roodezand and Zwartland, which are the present towns of Tulbagh, Malmesbury, and Drakenstein. A farm was usually about 60 morgen (126 acres) in extent and formed a small community of its own with its gabled and thatched homestead, outbuildings and workshops and slave quarters, the whole surrounded by a low white-washed wall. There was a condition in title deeds to land that oak trees should be planted; and though the condition was not rigidly observed because, as farmers complained, the land was too small, most farms had trees round the homestead or as boundaries to their vineyards.

These farmers were comparatively well-to-do. They produced their own food and wine and were close enough to Cape Town to be able to market the surplus and buy sugar, tea, coffee, spices, clothes, furniture, crockery, and other items of necessity or luxury. Their hospitable homes presented an air of solid comfort, ease, and stability that was lacking in Cape Town. They were the squires, the landed gentry of the colony, and their attitude towards the parson, the official, and the flighty townsman was one of distrust mixed with slight contempt. By the end of the eighteenth century this immediate hinterland of Cape Town had been tamed and the inhabitants no longer feared marauding Bushmen. The life of the farmer had settled down to the routine of ploughing, sowing, reaping and threshing; to pruning his vines, attending to the vineyard, harvesting the grapes, and pressing them into wine. This routine was interrupted by an occasional visit to Cape Town and a more frequent one to Stellenbosch; by friendly and informal calls on neighbours; by hunting and by the week's compulsory military exercises once a year; by weddings and funerals; and, most popular of all, by auction sales. Advertised well ahead of time these auction sales were great social gathering places and people travelled many miles to attend them. Free drink and food were provided by the auctioneer, and sometimes a dance was arranged for the evening, all of which no doubt helped to keep the bidding brisk.

Local government for this whole area centred in the

village of Stellenbosch. The chief government official was the *landdrost* who was assisted by a district secretary and an unpaid board of *heemraden* to administer the district, try petty cases, collect taxes, register wills and notarial deeds, pay out 'lion and tiger money' as a reward for the destruction of wild animals, and organize and control the burgher militia. In this latter task the *landdrost* was assisted by a field cornet who, in the nature of his position, had to be a man of means and leisure whom the burghers would respect.

In the village of Stellenbosch itself the *heemraden* performed the duties of a modern town council, like the burgher council in Cape Town, and formed a link between the free burgher population and the government at Cape Town. One of their local duties was to regulate water rights. The old houses of Stellenbosch front practically on to the street much as some of the houses in London squares do, and have large gardens at the back. The gardens are irrigated by water that flows in furrows on both sides of the street, and it is the duty of the present-day town council, as it was of the eighteenth-century *heemraden*, to regulate the hours for leading water in such a way that everyone has a fair share. It was, and is, a delicate task, for people who have water rights are tenacious of their privilege.

The public buildings at Stellenbosch were the *drostdy* which was both official residence and office of the *landdrost*, the church, and the parsonage. The Dutch Reformed Church was an established church and the *predikant*, or minister, was an official of the Company, appointed, paid and pensioned like any other official; apart from preaching inordinately long sermons, as the custom was, he spent much of his time on *huisbesoek*, that is, on visiting his parishioners in their distant homes. Once in three months *Nagmaal*, or Holy Communion, was celebrated, and farmers and their families and retainers came from distant corners of the district in wagons, arriving on Thursday and leaving at dawn on Monday; for it was a social and business, as well as a religious occasion, when produce was bartered for three months' supplies of groceries. At such times the open square on which the church stood was not unlike the fairgrounds in Europe.

Although the church was an official organ of government, elders and deacons had a considerable say in its control. They were burghers appointed by the governor from a double list submitted by the church council, a system of appointment used generally by the Company for those institutions in which burghers were associated in the administration. *Heemraden* and field cornets were appointed in the same way, and this gave citizens some voice in the management of local affairs and established a valuable tradition of unpaid public service. It was not strictly voluntary service, for those who were nominated might not refuse; but, generally, nominees were proud of the honour and pleased to devote time to running local affairs.

There was a difference between the wine and corn farming community of Stellenbosch and the commercially minded burghers of Cape Town, separated as they were by thirty miles of sandy flats. It was the difference between a restless, unstable urban society and a less volatile but more firmly based society of landowners. Nevertheless Cape Town and Stellenbosch formed a community of people, living in a Mediterranean climate and having common social and economic interests. Across the mountains, eastward along the coast or into the Little Karroo, and north-east over more mountains, on to the Great Karroo, there trekked and lived a new breed of burgher, the trekboer, the nomadic cattleman; and, always in advance of the cattleman, the hunter. These were the third and fourth generation of the people who had, by the close of the seventeenth century, moved away from the western Cape because cattle barter was more profitable than producing corn and wine for a restricted and limited market. Their economic problems were different from those of the west, and their response to those problems produced a society that had little in common, socially or politically, with the settled west.

The word 'society' is perhaps misleading. An aggregate of large family units would be a more accurate description. Men and women married early, usually in their teens, and families of twelve or thirteen children were common, and people were grandparents at forty. Moreover, since eligible young men and women were scarce, many families were connected by marriage, and the polite custom that still exists in South Africa of addressing older men and women as *oom* and *tante* (uncle and aunt), and younger ones as *neef* and *niggie* (cousin) dates from a time when to do so was as likely as not to be strictly accurate. These large and interconnected families helped to hold together a dispersing people.

Somebody once suggested that South Africa should erect a monument to the ox for the part it played in opening up the country. All transport was by ox-wagon, a long, four-wheeled, tented wagon made of hard indigenous wood and held together by leather thongs rather than by bolts and screws; this method of construction gave greater flexibility, made repairs easier, and enabled the trekker to take the wagon to pieces to be carried over a difficult mountain pass. Half-inch iron bands gave strength to the wheels which had often to be locked when going down a steep or slippery decline. The usual 'span' of oxen was from twelve to sixteen, and each ox was trained to know its place in the team; the strongest and steadiest pair was at the rear, on either side of a single shaft, and the rest were yoked to a long chain leading from the shaft, the most experienced pair being leaders. Someone usually walked in front of the team, leading it, and the driver walked alongside or stood on the box at the front of the wagon; he knew every ox by name and was expert at wielding his fifteen-foot two-hand whip. It was a matter of pride with the young frontiersman to collect a well-matched team of red-and-white or black-and-white oxen, and to be able to control them by an accurate flick of his whip.

The large 6,000-acre farms that were 'loaned' to the cattle

farmers by the Company were easily acquired and easily left, abandoned or unofficially sold. When the grazing became poor, the drought too severe, or neighbours too many, the trekboer moved on. Then all the family belongings were packed on to the wagon, cattle, sheep and horses were rounded up, and a new trek was on. It has been pointed out that this trekking was a reversal of the usual progress from nomadism to settled agriculture. For many of the trekboers, however, it was a temporary reversal, and when it seemed possible to do so they settled down permanently, not, indeed, to the intensive cultivation of Europe for that was climatically impossible, but to stock and sheep farming and to as much cultivation as climatic conditions allowed. Thus it was that, as the cattlemen and hunters moved east and north-east, they left behind them a thin trail of cattle farms, isolated little settlements of white people and their Hottentot servants.

The Company's government at the ever-receding Castle in Cape Town disliked this dispersal of burghers because it imposed an impossible administrative task—impossible, that is, to a Company whose main concern was to cut down expenditure. It was the Company's contradictory economic policies that were largely responsible for the dispersal; and once it had begun, the Company was really powerless to stop it. It was with the utmost reluctance that the government in Cape Town could be induced to provide administrative machinery for its distant subjects, and this explains why, in a century and a half, only three districts outside of Cape Town were proclaimed: Stellenbosch was the first; Swellendam followed in 1746, and Graaff-Reinet in 1786. As at Stellenbosch, Swellendam and Graaff-Reinet each had its *landdrost* and *drostdy*, church and minister, *heemraden* and field cornets, the latter being more necessary there than at Stellenbosch, because when Graaff-Reinet was established the first open clash between black and white cattle farmers had already occurred—the first of many.

The social life of stock farmers, trekboers, and hunters

was, by Stellenbosch and Cape Town standards, rough, hard and uncouth. For the trekker and hunter, the ox-wagon was home; on stock farms houses were built but these were rough timber, stone, and thatch affairs with mud floors, not the fine, gabled houses of Drakenstein for which bricks, tiles, glass, timber, nails and screws had been imported from Holland. For beds, a straw mattress was placed over leather thongs stretched across wooden frames, or otherwise a mat on the ground would serve; a table consisted of boards placed over stakes driven into the mud floors, and chairs and stools were home-made. An important item of furniture was the wooden chest containing the neatly folded clothes for best wear; and above the rafters one might find a coffin, kept in case of emergency and used meanwhile for storing clothes or dried fruit and biscuits. As the eighteenth century wore on better houses were built; but good furniture, crockery, cutlery, and even kitchen utensils remained exceptional.

It was the same with clothing. There were no tailors or shoemakers, and clothes were home-made from rolls of cloth brought from distant Cape Town or bought from a pedlar; leather was skilfully used to make coats and trousers and the strong, comfortable *velskoen*. The trekboer or his wife made most of the things the family needed—soap, candles, grease for the wagons, and bullets. There was plenty of food though the diet was monotonous. Meat was always available even without slaughtering precious sheep or cattle, for the country teemed with game and every man was an expert with his smooth-bore flintlock; he had to be, for his own and his family's safety depended on it. Vegetables were scarce, and meal for bread not always available; when it was, women baked boer-meal rusks to be dried and stored against a rainy day or for the next trek. Though tea and coffee, nicknamed 'Boer's comfort', were usually to be had, many of the refinements and luxuries that made Cape cooking famous were either lacking or rare once the mountains had been crossed. Trekboers were content to do without spices and sugar, wine and brandy, just as they managed without doctors and apothecaries.

While Cape Town could boast a few private elementary schools, and Stellenbosch had a parish clerk who taught the young reading, writing, arithmetic, the psalms, and the catechism, trekboers and frontiersmen lacked even those limited facilities. Sometimes a retired or runaway soldier wandered from farm to farm, spending two to three months at each place teaching the children to read and write. For the rest, mothers taught their children to read and to memorize the Bible, and it was not unknown for a boy to be able to repeat all the psalms from memory. Children learnt enough to be admitted as members of the church, and their contact with the printed word was limited to the Bible and the hymn book.

Such were the cattle farmers, the pioneers who trekked over and beyond the mountains, away from the western Cape which was the gateway to Europe. What contact they had with the west was intermittent; they were neglected, almost abandoned, by Church and State; they lived hard, self-reliant, self-sufficient lives; they became strong, even fanatical, individualists and resented government, when at last it caught up with them, as 'interference'. By the last quarter of the eighteenth century their isolation was as complete as it had been in the first quarter; their ideas, their outlook on life, and their religion were those of their great-grandfathers. For them, the seventeenth century had wandered on into the eighteenth. And their isolation was not only from the Cape and Europe. Meeting perhaps once a year at *Nagmaal*, or in smaller groups at weddings and funerals, they were isolated from one another. In time it became an isolation from which they would not escape if they could.

And yet this scattered aggregate of family units never quite lost its sense of being a society. The bonds that bound them to one another became stretched to breaking point, but somehow they never snapped; and in the next century history was to strengthen those bonds until, in due course, it became possible to speak of a new Afrikaner nation. The bonds did not snap because, in the first place, the extensive clanship, the fact that so many trekboers were related by marriage, gave cohesion, however loose, to the dispersing population. Women played a notable part in maintaining this tenuous cohesion. Men might trek, and hunt, and make war; it was the women who brought up the large families and kept them together. Their courage and resourcefulness, and their keener sense of the decencies of life which they, more than their menfolk, missed, imbued them with the determination not to let things slide. Left to themselves the men might have degenerated into 'poor white trash'; it was largely owing to the women that such degeneration was arrested.

The second factor that helped the trekboers to maintain cohesion was religion. Towards the end of the eighteenth century the people of Cape Town and, to a lesser extent, Stellenbosch, were noted as being irreligious, or at best, indifferent. The religion that the trekboers took with them was the religion of the seventeenth century, not the religious indifference of the eighteenth. It was the religion of Calvin, stern, harsh, and unbending in spite of—or is it because of?—its comfortable doctrine of predestination that enabled white men so easily to regard black as inferior. The trekboers upheld the old custom of family prayers at which the Bible was read and psalms sung. They read the Bible and little else, and knew parts of it by heart; their ideas, their language and their conversation tended to be biblical, and they gave their children biblical names. In due course they came to identify themselves with the people of the Old Testament, a chosen people, a nomadic people whom God would lead to the promised land. The Calvinism of Swellendam and Graaff-Reinet was not that of Europe where it had been sternly disciplined by persecution. In South Africa it easily turned into an undisciplined and almost lawless individualism. Nevertheless, it gave its adherents a community of ideas which prevented them from falling apart.

The third factor that helped to keep this nomadic society together was war. The Hottentots had been the first people of Africa to dispute ownership of the land with European invaders, but after two short fights they had given up the struggle and recognized the inevitable. Thereafter they steadily bartered cattle, drank too much of the white man's liquor, and were ravaged by smallpox and other imported diseases. By the middle of the eighteenth century their clans had practically ceased to exist, and the landless remnants took service with Europeans, rode with them to hunt or to war against Bushmen, and continued to intermarry with slaves and with Europeans to produce the present Coloured population.

The Bushmen put up a much more determined and protracted resistance. Corn farmers in the north-west of the extended Stellenbosch district, and trekboers who crossed the mountains, were constantly harassed by Bushmen raiders who killed or maimed what cattle they could not drive off, and murdered such European and Hottentot herdsmen as they could lay their hands on. The Bushman hunter, to whom the idea that one man could 'own' a large piece of land was utterly foreign, was defending his ancient hunting grounds and water holes by making life intolerable for the newcomer; and he brought to the task all his considerable skill, cunning and tenacity. The response of the European was to organize commandos and unofficial hunting parties which shot down as many adults as they could, and took children prisoner for domestic service or as herd boys. And it was from this situation that the commando system, famous in South African history, was born.

Under the commando system every male burgher between sixteen and sixty was liable for military service and could be called on to defend the colony alongside regular soldiers. Military exercises were held for a week once a year; but these were not important except as social gatherings, for soldiers cannot be trained in a week. What was important was that their way of living made most burghers excellent shots and first-class horsemen with an intimate knowledge of terrain. For the kind of warfare in which they were called upon to take part they were admirably equipped, and all that was needed was an easy and rapid method of mobilization.

This was supplied by the commando system. When a raid was threatened or a counter-raid had to be made, the commandant (usually the *landdrost*) instructed the field cornets, who told all burghers in their area to report with 'horse, saddle and bridle, and three days' rations', which meant that each burgher took *biltong* (dried meat) and dried boer-meal rusks to last him and his Hottentot groom for three days, after which government would be responsible for rations, as it was for powder and ammunition. In this way a commando of several hundred men could be fully mobilized within ten hours. To an unmounted enemy, armed with bows and arrows or assegais, it was a formidable striking force, and it succeeded during the latter half of the eighteenth and the first half of the nineteenth century, in driving the Bushmen that had not been exterminated to the semi-desert lands of the north-west Cape, and beyond the Orange River, where their descendants live to-day.

The wars against African tribes must be reserved for a later chapter. Here, it is relevant to note that wars against common enemies, Bushman or African, helped to maintain and to strengthen the cohesion of the trekboers. Even against an ill-armed enemy, wars are arduous and dangerous, no less for the women who stay behind on lonely farms than for their husbands and sons on commando. Indeed, women had the harder part, for going on commando had advantages to offset hardships and danger. It provided excitement in the monotony of a cattleman's life, and danger added spice to excitement; it was an escape from the crowded family life of small houses to the exhilarating open-air life among old friends; no drill-sergeant maintained discipline, and officers were personal friends chosen by the burghers themselves; and the opportunity to exercise skill and daring with rifle and horse is always attractive to men who possess those qualities.

When the war or the raid was over, if luck held, there was the pleasure of riding home to waiting womenfolk, and taking along looted cattle, more than enough to compensate for previous losses by enemy raids. There was the retrospective pleasure of shared adventures and dangers, and the pride of having served under a fearless and skilful commandant; and there were plenty of good stories to be told. In short, and without minimising the dangers, frontier wars contained a good deal of what Sir Ian Hamilton called 'the champaign of war', and the commando played a considerable part in attaching men's loyalties to units larger than the family or the clan. The system was to play that part, to an increasing extent, in the nineteenth century and beyond.

Chapter Five

BRITAIN TAKES OVER

While the settlement at the Cape was pursuing its unhurried course, quietly and unconsciously storing up problems for future generations, new ideas were stirring and fermenting in Europe. By the end of the eighteenth century these ideas had started two revolutions, social and political, and had set Europe on the far from quiet road that led to the modern age.

Between 1750 and 1800, Benjamin Franklin flew a kite and attracted lightning to his conductor; Black discovered carbonic acid gas and latent heat; oxygen was discovered by Cavendish and hydrogen by Priestley; the Montgolfier brothers raised balloons by filling them with hot air; the Italian physicists Volta and Galvani added their names to the English language; and Jenner inoculated a boy with cow-pox. D'Alembert, Euler, Lagrange, Lavoisier, Herschel, Hunter, Brown, Linnaeus, Laplace, Coulomb—these were some of the scientists who were experimenting, measuring, and recording on a scale and with an accuracy not seen before, and forging the mathematical and scientific tools of the new age.

In the same period, Roebuck erected blast furnaces using coal only; Hargreaves, Cartwright, Kay and Compton invented improved spinning and weaving machines; and, most important of all, James Watt successfully harnessed steam to pump water from coal-mines and to work the new machines. The age of iron and steel which we call the Industrial Revolution had begun. Her climate and geographical position, her navigable rivers and the position of her coal and iron fields, and the long start that her inventors gave her, enabled Britain to defeat Napoleon and to establish herself as the greatest industrial, naval and colonial power of the nineteenth century. And, as an incident in that development, it took Britain to the Cape.

While scientific ideas and inventions were revolutionizing the economic basis of man's existence, other and equally potent ideas were at work in the realms of politics, art, literature, economic thought, education, and social life. In 1751 Diderot, Voltaire, Turgot, and others published the first two volumes of the *Encyclopédie* in France; and in England Hume was condemning restrictions on commerce in terms which, had they been able to read them, would have endeared him to the burghers of the Cape. During the next fifty years books were published that profoundly affected the intellectual climate of Europe: Rousseau's *Contrat Social*, Tom Paine's *Common Sense* and *Rights of Man*, Adam Smith's *Wealth of Nations*, Godwin's *Political Justice*. In England, Locke, Hume and Bentham, and the physiocrats in France, attacked accepted commercial and economic theories and practices; in Germany, Kant, Lessing, Schiller and Fichte applied reason to philosophy and natural science. In England Gibbon's *Decline and Fall* set a new standard in urbane irreverence towards pious but irrational beliefs; Johnson, Blake, Burns and Wordsworth, each in his own way, rebelled against the meek acceptance of authority; Mary Wollstonecraft propounded heretical views on women and marriage; and Gilray and Rowlandson caricatured and satirized English manners and customs. Most prolific of all, Voltaire turned his mocking laughter and withering scorn on all the superstitious follies and injustices whose existence had come to be regarded as inevitable. Everywhere the frontiers of irrationality were being pushed back.

Changes so far-reaching as to be called revolutionary are not the result of sudden impulses. They are the growth of many years during which the foundations of the established order are being undermined by new ideas and by subtle changes in economic processes; during this period those who advocate the new ideas are usually reviled as cranks and persecuted as dangerous and subversive, because the upholders of established order do not like change. The history of the abolition of slavery is a good example of this. Modern Europe began to trade in slaves in the sixteenth century. In 1700 the first recorded protest against slavery was made by a man called Sewell, in America, and from then onwards, and particularly after 1760, more and more people wrote and spoke against it; in 1772 Lord Mansfield ruled that no slave might be held in England itself, and in 1786 Clarkson published his *Essay on Slavery and Commerce of Human Species* which convinced Wilberforce that slavery was wrong and decided him to devote his life to its abolition. In 1807 Wilberforce persuaded the British Parliament to prohibit the slave trade, but it was only in 1833 that slavery was abolished in the British Empire. In the United States of America it was abolished, during a bitter civil war, in 1863, more than a century and a half after Sewell had first protested against it.

Although great changes are not the result of sudden impulses their actual arrival may be startlingly sudden. For more than a century philosophers, poets, scientists and inventors had been undermining the building which was the established order of eighteenth-century Europe. And then, within a few short years, the whole building was toppled down. In 1789, Louis XVI was advised that France was bankrupt and that, after two bad harvests, people were starving. He called together the States General which had not met for 175 years, and this gave the middle classes in France the opportunity to demand reforms which Louis and his aristocratic advisers resisted. From this situation developed the French Revolution which smashed the old order in Europe. The centuries-old feudal system was abolished and the doctrine of liberty, equality and fraternity proclaimed, not only for France but for Europe and the world.

The old order resisted, and for the best part of twenty-two years Europe was at war. When Napoleon was defeated at Waterloo in 1815, and the Bourbons were restored to the throne of France, it may have seemed as if the building of the old order had been restored; but it was not the same building. The eighteenth century had gone for good. Europe had tasted the wine of individual liberty, of equality and fraternity, and would never again be satisfied for long with substitutes. The Declaration of the Rights of Man and of the Citizen, proclaimed by the French National Assembly in 1789, did not so much note an achievement as announce a programme to which future generations, interpreting it in their own idiom, were to return again and again.

Across the Atlantic, another revolution had taken place. In 1776 the thirteen American colonies rebelled against their mother country because she tried to rule them without their freely given consent. It was a different kind of revolution from that in France: the American colonists revolted in defence of their ancient liberty as Englishmen, that there should be no taxation without representation; the French revolted in order to establish the same principle as a new liberty; but in both cases it was a revolt against arbitrary authority. By 1783 the Americans had won the struggle, and had set their feet on the road that was to lead them, in our own day, to a position of world dominance.

It used to be said that the provinces in France got their revolutions by post from Paris. In the same way South Africa got her revolution at the end of the eighteenth century from Europe. The corn and wine farmers of Stellenbosch and the cattle farmers and frontiersmen of Swellendam and Graaff-Reinet were but faintly stirred by the great events in Europe, and like the large mass of people in Europe itself, were unconscious of the underlying revolution in ideas. Yet those events and ideas altered the course of history for South Africa and wrenched the Cape settlement, not so much from the eighteenth century, as straight from the seventeenth into the nineteenth.

There were at the Cape, in the last quarter of the eighteenth century, two fairly distinct European societies, those of the east and the west. Each had its own problems, and the Company's government at Cape Town was able to deal effectively with neither. That government was soon to be replaced and it is convenient to examine what the problems were and how the Company in its dying days attempted to deal with them; by doing so we shall be in a better position to understand what sort of a colony it was that Holland left to Britain. From the point of view of the expansion of Europe in southern Africa, the east was more important than the west, though the burghers of Stellenbosch and Cape Town would have laughed at the idea that anything about the wild frontiersmen, whom they regarded as more than half-savage, could be important. But it was in the eastern Cape that Europe and the real Africa first met.

The Bantu-speaking tribes on the eastern frontiers of the Cape were the advance guard of the last and most formidable obstacle to the total conquest of southern Africa; and when, after more than a century, they were defeated, they retained their racial identity. So far from disappearing into some convenient and semi-desert lands, as the Bushman did, or being absorbed into the Coloured population, as the Hottentot was, the African remained to form two-thirds of the present population of South Africa.

While we know a great deal about the European frontiersmen, we know very little about the Xhosa and Tembu, the tribes that had come farthest south. They were the African frontiersmen, and though one must avoid pushing the comparison too far, there were some striking similarities in the economic situation of black and white. Both were cattle farmers first and agriculturalists second; being subject to the same climatic and geographic conditions, both required ever more land for their herds, which suffered equally in periods of drought; something like the same economic causes were moving both to extend their frontiers, the one northwards and the other south; and in both cases hunting parties were always in advance of the main body.

The differences were, however, more significant than the similarities, and nowhere so much as in the interpretation of land ownership. Private ownership of, and rights in, land was a conception deeply embedded in European custom and law; to the African it was alien. In African custom, land was owned by the tribe, not by the individual. The chief allocated fields for cultivation to individuals, but he did so as representative of the tribe and not because the land was presumed to belong to him; and the individual occupied the land and did not own it in the European sense of the word. Europeans and Africans were alike ignorant of each other's customs and, throughout the nineteenth century, this led to misunderstanding and injustice: European governments made treaties by which they believed they had *acquired* land from an African chief, while the chief thought he was merely giving them the right to *use* the land. Another source of misunderstanding was the fact that there were many clans and minor chiefs within a tribe, and in ignorance of this, Europeans made treaties with minor chiefs only to find that other members of the same tribe were not bound by them.

Early in the eighteenth century African hunters came into contact with European hunters and cattle traders. Since such contacts frequently led to quarrelling, the Company tried to prevent them by prohibiting trade with Kaffirs, as Africans were generally called; but such instructions were useless because the Company was unable to enforce them, and trekboers and Xhosa drifted steadily towards each other in search of more grazing land. When Governor van Plettenberg visited the eastern 'frontier' in 1778 he found that, in fact, no real frontier was recognized either by Europeans or by Xhosa; cattle trading, cattle raiding, and cattle grazing by black and white frontiersmen were taking place on both sides of the Great Fish River. He persuaded a few minor chiefs to agree to that river as a boundary; but in the next year the Xhosa, possibly in revenge for the killing of one of their men by a frontiersman called Marthinus Prinsloo, raided across the new boundary, killed some Hottentot herdsmen, and drove off European cattle. An unofficial commando was at once formed to retaliate, and the Company followed this up by appointing van Jaarsveld as commandant of an official commando, which drove the Xhosa back across the Fish River and captured more than 5,000 head of cattle to be shared among the burghers. This was the first Kaffir War.

In 1786 the Company appointed a *landdrost* at Graaff-Reinet with instructions to keep the peace and to prevent burghers from crossing the frontier into Kaffirland, an impossible task since he had no police force or soldiers with which to do it. Trading and raiding went on freely, and three years later the Xhosa chief, Ndlambi, crossed the boundary and drove the Europeans off their farms. The *landdrost* called up a commando, but the Governor at Cape Town, anxious to avoid war because of the expense, replaced him by a man called Maynier with instructions to come to terms with the Xhosa. Maynier, like many other officials at the Cape, believed that most of the fault lay with the white frontiersmen and he was determined to stop unofficial commandos from crossing the frontier to retrieve stolen cattle plus booty. Like his predecessor, however, he lacked the force to maintain the peace, and conditions on the frontier deteriorated. White freebooters, such as Buijs and Bezuidenhout, were living across the border and taking Xhosa wives, and they stirred up trouble among the tribes for their own benefit. Serious drought in 1791 and 1792 denuded the veld on both sides of the border, and European farmers crossed into Kaffirland in search of grazing; and a farmer named Lindeque, defying instructions, raised a private commando to raid cattle. The result was that the Xhosa once more invaded European territory and Maynier was forced to call out a commando to expel the invaders. Having done so, he came to terms with the Xhosa but failed to do what the frontiersmen wanted: demand cattle in recompense for their losses.

By this time Maynier and the Company's government in Cape Town were thoroughly unpopular with the frontiersmen. As they saw it, the Company did nothing to protect them; it believed that they were responsible for their own troubles and that they provoked the Kaffirs, and it appointed officials who shared these views; also, it would not allow them to do what they had always done: take the law into their own hands. Early in 1795 Commandant van Jaarsveld and forty burghers entered Graaff-Reinet, expelled Maynier, and set up a republican government; and Swellendam followed suit. But the days of the Company against which they had rebelled were numbered, and it was the British government that was left to deal with the situation.

The problems of the eastern Cape Colony were the social, economic, and political problems that arose from the conflict between European and African for land. The problems of the west were less complicated and arose largely from the bad government of the Dutch East India Company which was rapidly declining into bankruptcy. The mighty East India Company had reached the height of its power in the seventeenth century and from then both Holland and the Company declined relatively to France and England. But the decline was not only relative. Holland was involved in all the major European wars of the seventeenth and eighteenth centuries and was, as a consequence, weakened. In 1702 the office of Stadtholder, held by the House of Orange, was abolished, and Holland was ruled by a republican oligarchy; in 1747 the House of Orange was restored but the democratic opposition was still strong, and Holland was further weakened by these internal dissensions. In 1787 the democratic Patriot party was sufficiently strong to expel the Stadtholder, William V, from his capital at The Hague, and he was only restored when Prussia, at the instigation of Britain, invaded Holland and occupied Amsterdam. Holland was, thus, thoroughly divided politically and her commerce suffered accordingly.

The Dutch East India Company was weakened by the

decline of Dutch sea power and by internal political quarrels in Holland. Even so, it might have survived had its economic policies not been thoroughly unsound. Inadequate reserves were kept; the demand for high dividends led to poor salaries and to bribery and corruption; capital was used to pay dividends; the size of the Company's staff—over 20,000—made it difficult to supervise; and its monopolistic policies led it into the economic fallacy of restricting trade and destroying 'surplus' stocks in order to keep prices high. In 1792 the Company paid its last dividend, and in 1794 went bankrupt.

During the dying years of the Company the burghers of the western Cape tried to gain more political and economic freedom. In 1779 at a secret meeting in Cape Town four men were chosen to go to Holland with a petition signed by about 400 burghers who, following the democratic party in Holland, called themselves Patriots. They asked for seven seats on the Council of Policy and half the seats on the High Court; they demanded the right to appeal to Holland rather than to Batavia and to report regularly to the Chamber of Seventeen. They complained bitterly of the corruption of officials and asked for relief from certain taxes, for improved prices, and for freedom of trade. They also asked for freedom to flog their slaves without official interference.

War with England and the stationing of a French regiment at Cape Town in 1781 brought about a temporary economic boom and distracted attention from the burgher petition and from grievances. When the war was over the Company agreed to a few minor reforms, and the Patriots, not satisfied, again appealed—this time not to the Chamber of Seventeen but to the States General of Holland, a sure sign that they no longer expected anything from the Company. The Seventeen hastily sent out a new governor, van der Graaff, to grant further reforms, and since the political situation in Europe seemed precarious, to look to the defences of the Cape. He did his best, and spent large sums of money which the Company could not afford. The Cape was costing them more than all their East India possessions together, and in a desperate last-minute effort to put affairs on a sound economic footing, van der Graaff was recalled, and in 1792 Commissioners Nederburgh and Freykenius arrived on their way to the East.

The two commissioners cut down expenditure and increased taxation, measures that were, of course, thoroughly unpopular. But whatever they had done would, in any case, have been too late. When they left Europe the Girondins had compelled Louis XVI to declare war on Austria; while they were on the water, Frenchmen were beginning to sing the new national anthem, the Marseillaise; and in the month in which they arrived at the Cape (July) France declared war on Prussia. The threatening and high-handed attitude of Austria and Prussia gave Danton, Robespierre, and Marat the opportunity to seize power and to rule France by the dictatorship of the Reign of Terror. By the beginning of 1793 France declared war against Holland and England and began to carry revolutionary doctrines into the rest of Europe.

The Dutch, like many other peoples in Europe, were divided on the question of the Revolution. Royalty and aristocracy detested it and were determined to smash it; democrats welcomed it as the beginning of a new era of freedom. The Orange Party in Holland, like Burke in England, saw revolution as a threat to established order, while the republicans, like Wordsworth in England, saw it as a movement of liberation. In 1794 the French invaded Holland, and early in 1795 Pichegru galloped his cavalry over the frozen Texel to capture the Dutch fleet. William of Orange fled to England to form a government in exile, and Holland became the Batavian Republic, an ally of revolutionary France. Britain, in alliance with the exiled Prince of Orange, decided to occupy the Cape so as to prevent the French from doing so. Thus it was that, 143 years after Jan van Riebeeck had landed in Table Bay, and while the burghers of Graaff-Reinet and Swellendam were rebelling against the Company's government, Admiral Elphinstone and General Craig entered False Bay and landed troops where the present seaside resort of Muizenberg stands. After a few minor skirmishes the Dutch commander, Sluysken, surrendered and the rule of the Dutch East Company at the Cape had come to an end.

The first British occupation of the Cape lasted eight years, and the British government, knowing the occupation to be temporary, regarded itself as a caretaker government whose job it was to keep the place in order and change as little as possible. The old Council of Policy ceased to exist, its place being taken by the governor with supreme authority. But apart from that and a few minor changes, local and central government and the legal system were left untouched; senior officials who were not pro-French were retained at increased salaries. Since government was now a real government and not, like the Company, primarily interested in trade and dividends, all monopolies and trade restrictions were abolished. Government was generous, too, in the matter of remitting arrears of land rents, and when an increased brandy tax proved unpopular it was removed. Money was spent freely and good salaries paid, and the presence of a garrison and the frequent visits of British ships helped to revive trade. In Cape Town and Stellenbosch, therefore, the new government was by no means unpopular.

In making itself agreeable to the inhabitants the government had a great asset in Lady Anne Barnard, wife of the government secretary. She kept a diary and wrote long letters to Henry Dundas, Secretary of State for War and Colonies, from which we get a lively picture of life at the Cape during the first British occupation. While Lord Macartney, whose wife had remained in England, was governor, Lady Anne acted as official hostess and was highly successful in overcoming the natural hesitation of Dutch citizens of Cape Town and in persuading them to come to official receptions and dances to meet British officers and officials. She travelled with her husband to Stellenbosch, Paarl, Drakenstein, and other country places, staying with the *landdrost* or minister, visiting farms, being interested in what the farmers and their wives did, and enjoying their excellent cooking. By her natural and charming manners she endeared herself to all with whom she came in contact. Lady Anne entered with zest into everything she did. She insisted on climbing Table Mountain, a most unusual exercise at the time; she praised and, what was more important, insisted on using Cape wines in preference to French; she made candles and syrup; she persuaded a high Dutch official to salt, 'with his own hands', a rump of Cape beef which she sent to Dundas; and she also sent the Secretary of State for War and Colonies a box of ostrich eggs with precise instructions for use.

While life at Cape Town had much of novelty and amusement for British occupiers and Dutch inhabitants, things were different on the frontiers, north and east. On the northern frontier near the Orange River, runaway slaves, Hottentots, half-breeds and outlaws made life difficult for farmers, and unofficial commandos were still being organized against Bushmen. The Graaff-Reinet and Swellendam rebels, whom the British had inherited from the Company, accepted the new régime with reluctance; and the frontier districts continued to be as disturbed as could be expected when there was, on neither side of the disregarded 'boundary', an authority sufficiently strong to keep the peace. A new *landdrost*, Bresler, was sent to Graaff-Reinet with a few dragoons, and when in 1799 he arrested van Jaarsveld on a charge of forgery, another rebellion broke out among some of the discontented frontiersmen. It was by no means a popular rising. Most of the farmers refused to take part and the rebels consisted chiefly of van Jaarsveld's personal friends, a few deserters from the British Army, and the swashbuckling outlaw, Coenraad Buijs, who thought he had, through his numerous Xhosa wives, sufficient influence to promise help from the Kaffirs. Landdrost Bresler was expelled and Prinsloo became head of the new 'government'.

The government in Cape Town acted promptly and sent General Vanderleur with dragoons, infantry and Hottentot soldiers, a corps that had been raised by the Dutch East India Company. The rebellion was soon squashed for it had no popular basis. Prinsloo and his hundred followers surrendered, and he and van Jaarsveld, with eighteen others, were sent to Cape Town for trial.

No sooner was the rebellion over, however, than a quarrel between two chiefs, Gaika and his uncle Ndlambi, resulted in an invasion by Xhosa of what was considered European territory. It was, in fact, the third Kaffir War. General Dundas, nephew of Henry Dundas, was Acting Governor and he at once went to the frontier with a strong commando of burghers, chiefly from Stellenbosch and Swellendam. He did not effect much, and left the unpopular Maynier as commissioner over the frontier districts. Maynier did his best to maintain the rule of law: he tried to come to friendly terms with the Xhosa chief, Gaika; he forbade private commandos to make reprisal raids against the Xhosa; he made regulations for the registration and better treatment of Hottentots who, of late, had got into the habit of leaving their employers and either marauding on their own or joining the Xhosa. But these things were not what the frontiersmen wanted or needed. What they wanted was a government that would issue plenty of ammunition and leave them alone to deal with the Kaffirs; what they needed was a strong border force, and magistrates and police to enforce order within the border. And so, under threat of yet another rebellion, Maynier was recalled.

By 1802 the frontier war had simmered down, rather than ended, much as was happening in Europe, where Britain and France signed the Treaty of Amiens which was nothing more than a truce. By this treaty the Cape was to be handed back to France's ally, the Batavian Republic; and early in 1803 General Dundas handed over the government to the

Dutch officials, Commissioner de Mist and Governor Janssens. The eastern frontier was still in the restless and almost chaotic state in which it had been for thirty years, and was to remain for many more. Lady Anne Barnard, who left before the Cape was returned to France's ally, noted in her journal: 'I left with them a benediction—praying heaven to avert from the land the ills which French principles and French rapacity might pour over it in greater volume than clouds from the hills——' During the century and a half to come it was not French principles that troubled South Africa. Rapacity, not specifically a French vice, there was; but it is possible that a greater application of French principles of liberty might well have reduced the volume of ills that poured over the land.

The Europe that de Mist left in 1803 was strongly under the influence of French ideas. Everywhere liberals and republicans had welcomed French soldiers and regarded General Buonaparte as the heir to the Revolution, the bearer of its principles, and the liberator of Europe. In Vienna, Beethoven had inscribed his Eroïca Symphony 'Beethoven à Buonaparte'. In 1804 Buonaparte became the Emperor Napoleon, republicanism was thrown to the winds, and liberals in Europe began to realize that they were no longer to be governed according to the enlightened principles of the Revolution, but so as to suit the overpowering ambition of a tyrant. Beethoven crossed off his dedication and wrote: 'To the *memory* of a great man.'

De Mist, a young barrister with liberal and republican views, was in sympathy with French ideas of government. Even Napoleon, who held that power came from the top and confidence from below, had used these ideas for his own advantage; equality in the eyes of the law and before the tax-gatherer; no privileges; careers open to talents; an efficient civil service; separation of church and state and religious toleration; the responsibility of the state for education. Liberty, equality, and fraternity were no longer in the foreground, but they were not dead. No one had yet had the experience of applying these ideas in a multi-racial society such as the Cape was then and South Africa is now, and so no one had any idea of how complicated such an application could be. The frontiersmen of the eastern Cape knew nothing of these ideas, and the wine farmers in the west had only the sketchiest contact with them. It was through the government of the Batavian Republic that these nineteenth-century winds first began to blow on South Africa.

De Mist at once instituted the 'sweeping reforms' that he regarded as necessary: the High Court was thenceforth to be independent of the executive and to consist of professional lawyers only, and a qualified attorney-general replaced the old all-purposes and corrupt Fiscal; two new districts, Tulbagh and Uitenhage, were constituted; all districts were sub-divided into wards, each under a field cornet, and a weekly post between the *drostdys* instituted; the powers and duties of *landdrosts* and *heemraden* were clearly defined; trade was to be free.

So far, the colonists might all have approved. But there were other reforms: an employer might hire a Hottentot servant only on a written contract signed before official witnesses; though the Dutch Reformed Church continued to be state-supported, the right of public worship was granted to all creeds; civil marriage was instituted; and, probably the worst shock of all, a Board of Education was set up with the avowed purpose of making education secular. Most of the colonists had been untouched by the eighteenth-century intellectual revolution. To them, religion and education were so closely associated as to be practically the same thing; and as for tolerating other creeds, Calvinism was an intolerant religion. To such people de Mist's new-fangled ideas from Europe must have seemed sacrilegious.

The new government with its revolutionary ideas had hardly taken over at the Cape when the truce in Europe was broken. In May 1803 England reopened the war against France, and there followed the years during which Napoleon conquered the whole of Europe except for a small portion of the Iberian Peninsula where Britain had an uneasy foothold. It soon became obvious that, to break the power of the 'nation of shopkeepers', Napoleon would have to invade England or starve her by preventing her trade. Nelson foiled his plans for invasion by defeating the French fleet at Trafalgar and thus denying Napoleon control over the English Channel; and it was to prevent his ally, Holland,

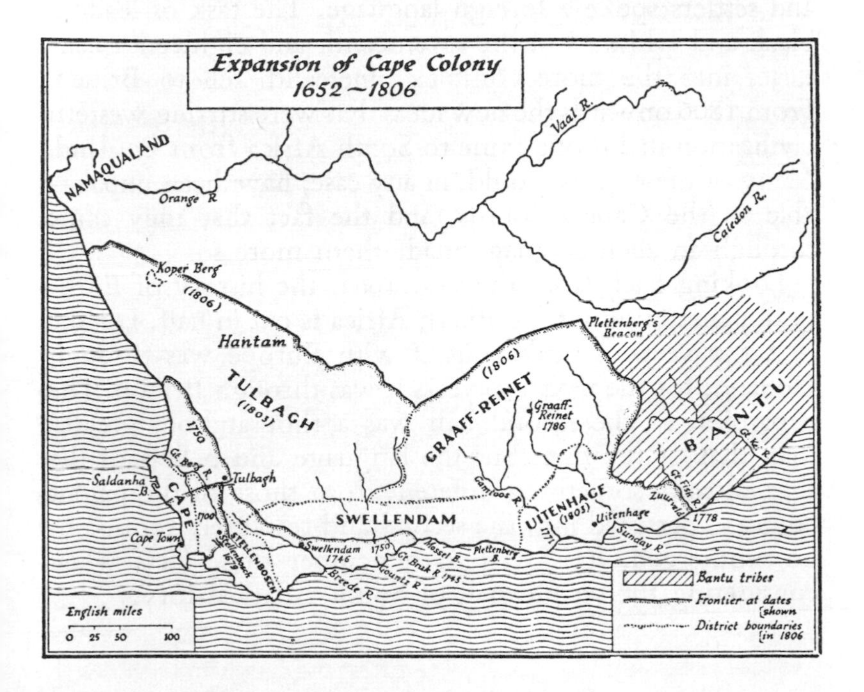

from interfering with British trade that Castlereagh sent a fleet of sixty-one ships with General Baird and 6,700 soldiers to take the Cape. De Mist had left the Cape in 1804 while Janssens remained in charge; and, with the inadequate forces at his command, the Dutch governor was unable to offer more than a token resistance to Baird.

The second British occupation was permanent, though the final cession was only ratified by treaty in 1814. Thus the

Cape, dependent as always on events in Europe, became a colony of Britain, a country whose language, habits, and traditions were different from those of Holland, the first mother country. Those differences, altering their shape and form, were to persist to the present day and be responsible for much of South African history. Problems created, but not solved, by the Dutch East India Company had now to be tackled by a different kind of government whose officials and settlers spoke a foreign language. The task of leading black and white from the seventeenth and eighteenth centuries into the more complex nineteenth fell to Britain. From 1806 onwards the new ideas that were stirring western civilization in Europe came to South Africa from England. Many of these ideas would, in any case, have been unpalatable to the Cape colonists, and the fact that they came through an alien language made them more so.

Looking back from the year 1963, the history of European penetration into southern Africa is cut in half. For the first 150 years Africa's contact with Europe was through Holland; for the next 150 years it was through Britain. The expansion of the second half was a thousandfold greater than that of the first; but the language and beliefs of the first, already something different from those of the parent country, persisted into the second and resolutely refused to be submerged. It is well to remember these facts when considering the second half of South Africa's story.

Chapter Six

BLACK AND WHITE

The colony that Britain took over in 1806 was a sprawling, thinly-populated, loosely-knit territory. Politically, socially and economically it was backward: its only definite boundary was the southern ocean, for to the north and east, the borderlands were vague and in constant dispute by Bushmen and African tribes. Apart from the more settled west, the legal status of the majority of the inhabitants was as vague as the boundaries. Of the total population of, possibly, 75,000, only the 25,000 Europeans were freemen; there were 30,000 slaves and the balance consisted of Hottentots, half-breeds, and freed or runaway slaves whose legal status had never been clearly defined. No one knew whether they had been Dutch subjects and were now British subjects with the same rights as Europeans, and their position as servants placed them entirely at the mercy of their European masters. In the eastern districts even title to land occupied by Europeans was vague and insecure; many of the loan farms were unregistered and none were properly surveyed, and apart from the actual buildings the farmers had no legal right to sell or bequeath the farms they were supposed to own.

The laws and their administration were equally indefinite and uncertain, especially in the frontier districts. Many of the *placaats* issued by the Company or the Batavian Republic were simply disregarded; *heemraden* who assisted *landdrosts* to administer law in petty cases were untrained and were personal friends of the farmers, and thus by no means impartial judges; the High Court sat at Cape Town only and it required a particularly conscientious *landdrost* to go to the trouble of remitting a case to a court sitting five or six hundred miles away.

Economically the country was backward. It had no staple export, and east and west depended on the fickle market at Cape Town. The currency was chaotic, and even Suez or Port Said in normal times could not show such a variety of coins in circulation: Spanish dollars, English guineas and shillings, ducats, ducatons, piastres, rupees, doubloons, gulden, rix-dollars and other Dutch coins—all these and more circulated and their value varied with supply and with public confidence. Paper money, in various denominations of the Cape rix-dollar, had been issued since 1782, and because the various governments that occupied the Cape since then had printed money freely, its value dropped steadily. Above all, slave labour and the existence of a landless half-breed population made the economy of the Cape fundamentally unsound.

It was, thus, a rather untidy mess that Britain took over from Holland, and before discussing the attempts she made to clear up the mess it would be well to look at Britain herself, the new mother country through whom the ideas that had swept Europe would enter South Africa. Nowhere would those ideas be put to a severer test and nowhere did their full impact have such far-reaching result. Britain was to be the medium for introducing South Africa to the nineteenth century. What was Britain like?

The French historian, Halévy, in his great work, *A History of the English People in* 1815, considers that it was to the Evangelical revival that England owed 'the extraordinary stability which English Society was destined to enjoy throughout the period of revolutions and crisis; what we may truly term the miracle of modern England, anarchist but orderly, practical and businesslike, but religious, and even pietist'.[1] During the eighteenth century, while new philosophical ideas both in England and on the Continent were

[1] Elie Halévy, *op. cit.*, Vol. III, pp. 11 and 12.

undermining the established order and preparing Europe for revolution, England alone experienced a religious movement which had no counterpart on the Continent. It began in the first half of the century when John Wesley and George Whitefield set out to regenerate the Anglican Church and founded Methodism; and it spread to the nonconformist churches and, eventually, to the Anglican Church itself where the group became known as the Evangelicals or 'the Saints'.

The large mass of nonconformists belonged to the working class or to the new and rising middle class, and the Evangelicals formed an all-important link between them and the ruling class which was mainly Anglican. The influence of this religious movement was felt in all ranks of society, and it is owing to this influence that most of the great nineteenth-century reforms were achieved. The Evangelicals usually inspired or initiated the reforms and combined with liberal Whigs, radicals, and nonconformists who provided the popular support necessary to compel Parliament to act. The abolition of the slave trade in 1807, and of slavery in the British Empire in 1833, was largely the work of the Evangelicals. Both these acts had a deep influence on South Africa.

Humanitarian reform in England was one of the results of the Evangelical movement, and foreign missions were another. Until late in the eighteenth century there were no Protestant missionaries anywhere in the world except a small band of Germans known as the Moravian Brethren who had established a mission to the Hottentots at Baviaan's Kloof. In 1776 the Evangelicals established the Society for Missions in Africa and the East, which later became the Church Missionary Society. In 1787 the Methodists, and in 1792 the Baptists, founded mission societies, and in 1795 the Evangelicals founded the London Missionary Society in which all orthodox Christian denominations could join; in course of time, as other churches established their own missions, it became almost entirely a Congregationalist mission.

The London Missionary Society was the first British society to send missionaries to South Africa—Dr. van der Kemp in 1799, Robert Moffat in 1817, Dr. Philip in 1819, and later, Livingstone, were four of the many who worked among Hottentots and Africans, and all four left an indelible mark on South African history.

Other things of importance to South Africa were happening in Britain between 1806 and 1836, the period during which the transition from Dutch to British government was taking place at the Cape. The works of Wordsworth, Coleridge, Jane Austen, the Lambs, Shelley, Keats, Byron and Scott were being published, to become under British rule and education part of the literary heritage of South Africans of all colours. The elder Mill was learning from Bentham some of the political and economic theories which, in the hands of his more famous son, were to influence British political thought throughout the century; Ricardo was writing against the danger of over-issuing paper money; Malthus was developing his theory of population that was to be discredited in the nineteenth century and revived in our own day; and Cobbett's *Political Register* was taking economic and political theories to the masses.

In 1820 the Atlantic was crossed by steamboat and five years later the first steamboat arrived in Table Bay. In the same year Stephenson constructed a steam railway from Stockton to Darlington; and Faraday was experimenting with electricity which was, in due course, to link South Africa more closely with Europe and the world. Finally, in 1828, Thomas Arnold became headmaster of Rugby where, five years earlier, South Africa's national sport was born when William Webb Ellis 'with a fine disregard for the rules of football as played in his time first took the ball in his arms and ran with it thus originating the distinctive feature of the Rugby game'.[1]

Politically, Britain was still in the grip of Tory reaction, and the unreformed parliament represented landowners

[1] From the inscription on the tablet at Rugby commemorating Ellis.

whose main concern was to keep the price of corn high and ruthlessly to suppress anything that looked even remotely like radicalism or Jacobinism. Those were the days of harsh game laws, of corn laws, and of hanging or deporting for sheep-stealing. In the days of depression, after Waterloo, the Tories passed laws to protect their own pockets at the cost of the people's food, and tens of thousands of Britons emigrated to the United States and the colonies. When a large open-air meeting was held at Manchester to demand reform it was broken up by the military at the Peterloo Massacre, and Parliament passed the Six Acts to deal with 'agitation'. Writing in 1819, Shelley described the government of England and spoke about

Rulers who neither feel nor see nor know,
But leech-like to their fainting country cling.

With the death of Castlereagh in 1822, however, the worst of the Tory reaction was over. Younger Tories, such as Canning, Huskinson and Peel, saw the need for social and political reform. The Combination Acts against trade unions were repealed and many trade restrictions were removed; the death penalty on more than a hundred crimes was abolished; and in 1829 the Catholic Emancipation Act was passed. In 1830 the Whigs came to power under Lord Grey and, two years later, the Great Reform Act became law, the foundation of the social and political reforms of the next hundred years.

By 1830 Britain had gone far in the process of changing from farmyard to factory. In 1750, 40,000 men were engaged in cotton manufacture and about 3,000,000 lb. of cotton were imported; by 1830 the figures were 800,000 men and 200,000,000 lb. The same story can be told in the coal, iron and steel, and other industries, and this tremendous growth necessitated better means of communication. Telford and Macadam built new roads, Stephenson began constructing railroads, and by 1830 thousands of miles of navigable canals had been made. Between 1750 and 1830 the population of Britain increased from 5½ million to close on 20 million, and the weight of population had shifted from the rural to the urban areas, and from the south to the Midlands and the north. Slums, periodic unemployment, and grinding poverty were among the earliest fruits of the Industrial Revolution in Britain; conditions of labour were unregulated and children of four and five were employed in coal mines and in cotton mills for sixteen hours a day. No wonder that Thomas Hood wrote, in *The Song of the Shirt*:

> *Oh God! that bread should be so dear*
> *And flesh and blood so cheap.*

There was plenty of work for the Evangelicals and the humanitarian reformers to do in England. By 1806 the first Factory Act had been passed, but in 1836 conditions of employment were still appalling, and it took much agitation and many strikes before working conditions in Britain were made tolerable.

Such were the people, the ideas, and the movements in Britain during the all-important first thirty years of her administration of the Cape. The ideas and movements were not all consciously for export, but they were brought to South Africa by administrators, settlers, and missionaries, and their impact was immense. Not only at the Cape, but throughout the whole territory that was to be South Africa, it was the missionaries rather than the administrators and settlers whose influence was to be the greatest. The missionaries had influential and vigorous contacts in Britain to whom they could appeal. In South Africa their influence was felt and resisted by the Europeans who reacted against the new ideas; but it was also felt by the Africans who were to constitute the large majority of the population. English and Scottish missionaries brought Christianity and Western civilization to the Africans and so began the process by which tribalism was fatally undermined, as the old order in Europe had been. That is the most significant fact of nineteenth- and twentieth-century southern Africa.

Missionaries from Britain were not the first to preach the Gospel to the heathen of South Africa. From the earliest days of the settlement the Company was concerned to christianize slaves and Hottentots, and though, during the eighteenth century, there was much religious indifference, there were always individual ministers of the Dutch Reformed Church who possessed the missionary spirit and tried to foster it in their European flock. In the last twenty years of the century two ministers, van Lier and Vos, did a great deal to persuade masters and employers to release their slaves and Hottentot servants for regular religious instruction; and by the end of the century missionary work was being done in most of the parishes of the western Cape.

The first missionary from overseas was George Schmidt, of the Moravian Brethren, who established a station for Hottentots at Baviaan's Kloof in 1737. He quarrelled with the Dutch authorities, however, over the question of whether he or a minister of the Dutch Reformed Church should baptize a converted Hottentot, and he left in 1744. The station remained closed until 1792 when three Brethren came to restart it, and it has flourished ever since, the work of the Brethren being extended to other centres.

Dr. J. T. van der Kemp and Dr. John Philip were two missionaries of the London Missionary Society, and their life and work at the Cape illustrate clearly the important part played by missionary societies in South African history. Van der Kemp was born in Rotterdam and studied medicine at Leyden but left to join the army before he had qualified. He subsequently described the next sixteen years of his life as years during which he was 'a slave to vice and ungodliness'. When he left the army he went to Edinburgh where he qualified as a doctor and returned to Holland to practise. Shortly after, his wife and only child were drowned in a boating accident and he himself was only just rescued, and as a result of this personal tragedy he became converted, and a few years later, wrote to the London Missionary Society offering his services. He went to London to be interviewed by the Board and was accepted, and on a final visit to Holland before sailing for the Cape, helped to establish the Netherlands Missionary Society.

Dr. van der Kemp and three others, a Hollander and two Englishmen, arrived at the Cape early in 1799 and were warmly greeted by Christians, such as the minister Vos, whom he helped to found the first truly South African missionary society. He intended working beyond the borders of the colony among the Xhosa, but after a lengthy visit he found that the chief, Gaika, would give him no facilities and he withdrew to the colony where, after various attempts, he was given permission to establish a station for Hottentots at Bethelsdorp, near the present Port Elizabeth. Here he worked from 1802 until his death in 1811, and during that time he became what he has remained to this day: a controversial figure in South African history. To-day, when Afrikaans-speaking South Africans wish to point to the evils that may result from foreign missionaries who do not understand local conditions, they quote Dr. van der Kemp and Dr. Philip.

And yet van der Kemp was an intelligent, pious and devoted man. He was, it is true, eccentric and believed that to teach and preach to Hottentots it was essential to live their life; he was a follower of Jean Jacques Rousseau and believed with him that the life of the savage is simple and perfect; he married the coloured daughter of a slave woman; he was unpractical and failed to do what so many later missionaries did: teach their converts to build good houses, to farm scientifically, and to learn trades. But it is doubtful whether it was these views and habits of van der Kemp that angered the frontier farmers and so many of their descendants. Much more important was the undeniable fact that he regarded Hottentots as free men who should not be compelled to work and who had civil rights that could be defended in a court of law, against their employers if need be.

When the British took the Cape in 1806 the status of Hottentots and half-breeds was undefined. In 1809 the governor, Caledon, tried to remedy this, and at the same time provide more labour, by a Hottentot Proclamation that brought them under colonial law and compelled them to remain in one district unless they had writen permission, called a pass, to move. Cradock, who succeeded Caledon, issued a further proclamation to the effect that Hottentot children, born on an employer's farm and living there for eight years, were to be apprenticed for a further ten years to that employer. Some restriction was probably necessary to counteract idleness and vagrancy which were partly inherent and partly the result of the white man's brandy and the loss of land. Nevertheless, the Hottentots, not unnaturally, disliked these restrictions, and many of them preferred to live at van der Kemp's Bethelsdorp or at one of the other L.M.S. stations, or even to cross the border into Kaffirland. This did not relieve the shortage of labour which had become worse when the slave trade was abolished in 1807, and soon the frontiersmen began to complain that the missionaries, and particularly Dr. van der Kemp, were stealing their labour and 'spoiling' the Hottentots.

Matters were not improved when Dr. van der Kemp's colleague, Read, wrote a lengthy report to the Society in London accusing farmers of cruelty to their Hottentot servants and of withholding wages. The Society was influential enough to make a fuss, and the Governor ordered the newly-instituted circuit court of 1812 to try the cases. Though van der Kemp had died in 1811, he and Read had been responsible for the accusations, many of which could not be proved, and the full rage of the frontier fell on the missionaries. Fifty farmers were accused and close on a thousand witnesses were called, and the whole district of Graaff-Reinet was in a ferment over such proceedings. Though none of the murder charges was proved, and though many of the others were baseless, the actual number of convictions was high, especially when it is remembered that evidence was difficult to collect because the cases ranged over a wide area and a large number of years, and that Hottentot witnesses were ignorant of legal procedure and often afraid to give evidence against their masters. Ignorance and fear on the part of non-European accused or witnesses still operate in South Africa and sometimes prevent justice from being done.

It was for such reasons that van der Kemp's name was reviled by trekboers and even by officials at the Cape who, in 1812, were Tories with little sympathy for landless Hottentots or missionaries with Jacobin views. Dr. Philip, who arrived in 1819, became even more notorious than van der Kemp, and for much the same reasons. John Philip was the son of a Kirkcaldy weaver, and for a time followed his father's trade. Having great eloquence, he was sent to London where he trained as a minister of the Congregational church; he returned to Aberdeen and ministered to a congregation for ten years before going to the Cape as superintendent of the London Missionary Society. He was a man of great intellect and ability, with a powerful personality that attracted devoted followers and created bitter enemies; he was frequently tactless, always fearless, and had a restless energy that led him into readily undertaking great tasks. For almost thirty years he was continuously in the limelight, and few men in South African history have attracted more attention.

When Philip arrived, the L.M.S. had thirteen stations in South Africa, most of them beyond the borders of the Cape Colony. His area thus included Hottentot subjects of Great Britain, and Griqua (or half-breed) and African tribes that lay outside British jurisdiction. He, too, found, what many mission societies and churches have since found, that it was impossible to keep out of political affairs, particularly in a country with a ruling class and a subservient working class of a different colour. Caledon and Cradock had placed the Hottentots in an inferior position by binding them to their employers. Philip determined to free them. He attacked the governor, Lord Charles Somerset, and other officials; he reported in vigorous, and not always accurate, terms to his

Society in London; and he paid a visit to England to rouse the Evangelicals and the Nonconformists. By 1828 he had succeeded, and in that year an ordinance was passed, known as the Hottentot Charter. It repealed the proclamations of Caledon and Cradock and placed Hottentots on an equal footing with Europeans. This famous ordinance had far-reaching results, for it established the principle that, in the Cape Colony, there was no legal colour bar. When, many years later, the Cape received representative government, Europeans and non-Europeans were enfranchised on the same terms.

The ordinance made Philip the best-hated man among the white colonists. Freeing the Hottentots aggravated the labour shortage and led to vagrancy and crime; and the hatred for Philip was increased by the publication, in the same year, of his *Researches in South Africa* in which he championed Hottentots and Africans and roundly condemned colonists and officials. But, much as he was disliked by white colonists at the Cape, he was admired, and his opinions highly regarded, in those circles in London that were able to influence political decisions.

Philip now turned his attention to African and Griqua tribes beyond the borders of the Cape Colony. He was a thoroughgoing segregationist, that is, he believed that it was better for white and black to live in separate states, because the blacks could not yet compete with the whites. Africans were ignorant and backward, and if they were to live in the same territory as the Europeans they would, like the Hottentots, be exploited. Philip was, therefore, strongly opposed to the annexation of any African areas and he advised the Secretary of State for Colonies to make treaties with African and Griqua chiefs to safeguard their land. Frontiersmen, on the other hand, wanted more land and regarded Philip as the arch-devil chiefly responsible for persuading the British Government not to let them have it.

There were, by 1836, many other devoted missionaries of the L.M.S. and of other societies, but van der Kemp and

Philip have been singled out because their careers illustrate a number of important points. In the first place, they illustrate the tremendous impact that nineteenth-century ideas, coming through the humanitarian movement in Britain, made on the Dutch inhabitants of the Cape. Had those ideas come from Europe rather than from Britain they would still have caused a strong reaction; the Moravian Brethren found that the farmers of Swellendam regarded their station at Baviaan's Kloof much as those of Graaff-Reinet did Bethelsdorp, and in the rebellion of 1795 a group of rebels from Swellendam attacked their station and compelled them to flee for safety. The frontiersmen were bound to react against the kind of idea that the missionaries brought from Europe, and the fact that British missionaries spoke a foreign language added resentment to the reaction.

The careers of van der Kemp and Philip also illustrate the way in which, in a society with marked class distinctions, the economic interests of the ruling class may clash with its religious tenets. That was true in England during the nineteenth century when the Established Church frequently opposed reforms that would have benefited the working class, but might have been detrimental to landowning interests. When, as at the Cape, class distinctions happen to coincide with difference of colour the clash is even greater.

Finally, the career of the two missionaries gives us a clue as to why the Dutch Reformed Churches and the English-speaking Churches, to this day, have different approaches to missionary work. It will be remembered that van der Kemp was warmly welcomed at the Cape and helped a Dutch Reformed Church minister to establish a South African Missionary Society. That warm feeling lasted for several years and then gradually cooled off. The Dutch Reformed Church sent its own missionaries across the borders, though not on the eastern frontier, and in later years established stations as far to the north as the Sudan and Nigeria. Outside of South Africa those missionaries have always co-operated heartily with missionaries of other denominations; inside South Africa the co-operation is less whole-hearted.

The reason for this lies chiefly in the fact that missionaries from overseas depended for their financial and moral support on people living in Britain, far away from daily contact with Hottentots and Africans. Missionaries of the Dutch Reformed Church at the Cape depended for their support on their European parishioners, the very people who employed Hottentots and fought against Africans. Philip and his brother missionaries had the fullest support from Britain when they stood up for Hottentot freedom and African rights; local missionaries could not count on such support, and, in many ways, theirs was the harder task. The Dutch Reformed Church was in a position analogous to that of the Established Church in England, and those men and women who, despite opposition, did mission work, deserve the title of 'Saints' by which the Evangelicals inside the Church of England were known.

Missionaries and officials, who were likely to be transferred or to return to Britain when their tour of duty was done, were not the only Britons to come to South Africa. Economic depression, unemployment, and high cost of living followed on the Napoleonic wars, and many people from Britain emigrated to Canada and the United States of America. In 1817, Benjamin Moodie successfully took 300 Scottish artisans to the Cape, and the attention of the authorities in Britain began to be drawn to the possibilities of relieving distress in Britain by assisting emigration to the Cape. When asked for his opinion, the governor, Lord Charles Somerset, welcomed the idea chiefly because he hoped to settle the immigrants on the Fish River boundary as a cheap form of defence, just as the Dutch East India Company had, 140 years earlier, encouraged immigration for the same reason.

The British Parliament voted £50,000 for the project and advertised a scheme whereby intending immigrants paid a small deposit and made themselves up into parties under leaders; on arrival at the Cape, each head of a family was to be given 100 acres in the Zuurveld, the area just west of the Fish River. Immigrants were not carefully selected, and in most cases the 'leader' was a retired naval or army officer, or someone with capital, who took the initiative in forming a party and coming to private terms with the members. The agricultural possibilities of the Cape were painted in glowing but unreal terms; 100 acres sounded like a large estate to land-hungry British ears, though the trekkers regarded anything less than 6,000 as too small. Few of the immigrants knew anything about agriculture anyway, and some of them were London Cockneys who, when they got down to it, planted onions upside down.

Fifty-seven parties, and a number of individual immigrants who paid their own expenses, eventually set sail for the promised land—about 5,000 in all—in twenty-four small vessels which sailed at intervals from various ports in December-January of 1819–20. Organization was poor: many of the immigrants arrived before their ship was ready to sail, only to find that there were no blankets or food for them; the weather conspired against them and froze the Thames so that ships departing from London were delayed by as much as a month. A sea voyage in those days was crowded, uncomfortable, and hazardous, and with such a mixed bag of passengers it is little wonder that discontent and quarrelling broke out. On board the *Northampton*, for example, an Irish party under one Mahoney was so obstreperous that the captain had to put two members in chains for a couple of days; on another vessel the Mutiny Act had to be read; and whooping-cough, measles, and even smallpox broke out to add to the general depression.

When the settlers arrived at Algoa Bay, soon to be called Port Elizabeth after the wife of the acting governor, Sir Rufane Donkin, their real difficulties began. The parties were taken by ox-wagon over rough tracks to their locations, and dumped, as it were, in the middle of the veld to find out for themselves what farming meant in a country with not very fruitful soil, and with periodic droughts and floods. Even those who knew something about farming found conditions utterly unlike those in the British Isles, and it soon became clear that many of the settlers would not be able to make a living from the soil. Government supplied rations of flour, meat, candles, soap, tea, coffee and sugar, and debited the cost against the deposits that had been paid in Britain; those deposits were soon exhausted and many settlers fell into debt.

The original parties had no internal cohesion, consisting of collections of people with little in common; men of some education were in the same party as semi-literates, and few of the so-called leaders knew how to inspire their followers; and the process of finding their own level was hindered by a government regulation that no one might leave his party without written permission. The Dutch frontiersmen were, for the most part, friendly and helpful, but differences of language made communication difficult. It is no wonder that a settler, Gunning, wrote to his former employer: 'You told me true when you said I might as well blow out my brains as come upon this expedition: indeed I have totally ruined myself.'

It was haphazard state-aided emigration, but things gradually sorted themselves out. Artisans moved to the towns to set up as independent tradesmen, and many gravitated to Cape Town where they soon found employment; others engaged in commerce; and those who chose to remain on the land were given title deeds to much larger farms than the original 100 acres. Settler complaints tended to centre round the governor, Somerset, though he cannot fairly be blamed for everything that went wrong, and the complaints reached London where Wilberforce and the Evangelicals, egged on by Dr. Philip, were already urging a full inquiry into affairs at the Cape. In 1823 Parliament appointed a commission of enquiry from which, as we shall see, many reforms besides redresses of settler grievances resulted.

The 5,000 British settlers were a mere trickle compared to the great stream that left the British Isles during the nineteenth century, and it is important to know why there was so little immigration to South Africa. Between 1820 and 1860 probably 40,000 immigrants came to South Africa, and that includes the 1820 British settlers and some 12,000 German and British settlers between 1857 and 1862. During that period more than a million English, Scots and Irish left the British Isles for Canada, Australia, New Zealand, and the United States; and from then until the end of the Second World War the populations of those countries were swelled by emigrants from Italy, Germany, Poland and other European countries, while small numbers only came to South Africa. In 1963 the white population of South Africa was just over 3 million; Australia, which began to be settled a hundred years after the Huguenots arrived at the Cape, has a white population of 10¼ million; New Zealand, starting twenty years after the British settlers came to South Africa, has 2½ million; and Canada, which became a British colony a hundred years after van Riebeeck landed at the Cape, has 17¾ million white inhabitants.

Neither geographic nor climatic conditions alone are sufficient to explain these differences between South Africa and her sister Dominions. The real reason is the existence of a large indigenous population in South Africa. More than half those who emigrated from Britain were crofters and agricultural labourers, but in the Cape Colony, and later in South Africa, agricultural labour was performed by slaves, Hottentots, Coloured and Africans, at rates of pay too low to attract labourers from Europe. The other Dominions could attract a large number of landless labourers, whose only capital was skill and muscle, and offer them fair prospects at good wages and, what is more, the chance of becoming landowners. South Africa had room only for those who could immediately become members of the employing class, for her policies, ever since the early days of the settlement, had consistently created an increasing class of landless labour within her own borders. What South Africa has lost in this way can be judged by the gains that other Dominions made through the steady inflow of hard-working and intelligent people from Britain and western Europe.

There is another aspect of the matter. While the populations of the United States and the colonies were being increased by emigrants from Europe and Britain, the European population of South Africa was, as we shall see presently, expanding its territory rapidly until, by the end of the nineteenth century, Europeans ruled over what is to-day the Republic of South Africa. In conquering the territory, the white man conquered the black inhabitants, and the increase in population was, in fact, more rapid than appears at first sight. The population of South Africa in 1963 included 3 million whites; but the total population is 15¾ million, more, that is, than Australia and only slightly less than Canada. But there are two differences between South Africa and Australia or Canada: they acquired their populations by immigration, and their citizens are, with negligible exceptions, of European stock and enjoy equal rights of citizenship. South Africa acquired the bulk of her population by war and conquest, and they are not of European stock nor do they enjoy equal rights with their conquerors.

To return to the 1820 settlers: though they were few in number their coming had far-reaching effects on the Cape Colony. They constituted a significant proportion of the existing European population, possibly as much as one-sixth; they spoke English and brought with them British habits and ideas; though few of them were voters in the England of 1820, many, had they stayed at home, would have been enfranchised by the Reform Act of 1832, and, in any case, they were accustomed to parliamentary government and the rule of law, and were not the kind of people to suffer in silence when their rights were in question; and, finally, they had friends in Britain to whom they could write. The British government was, therefore, compelled to pay more attention to the needs of the colony, and particularly of the frontier districts. When, sixteen years later, the original Dutch frontiersmen trekked away to the north, the character of the frontier districts was changed. Albany, as the area was called, had become an English-speaking territory with Grahamstown as its capital, and villages with English names such as Bathurst, Cradock, King William's Town, and Queenstown. From then onwards men of British as well as of Dutch stock were involved in frontier wars against African tribes, and when many of the Dutch trekked it was as if the old garrison had moved and a new one was left to man the frontier.

Chapter Seven

CONFLICT OF IDEAS

The period we have been considering, 1806 to 1836, marks the transition of the Cape from a Dutch settlement, half colony half refreshment station, to a British colony, and the process was often painful. The period also marks the introduction of the Cape to the new ideas that stirred Europe at the end of the eighteenth and the beginning of the nineteenth centuries, and this process, too, was often painful; and it was not less so because the introducer was Britain, not Holland, the language English, not Dutch, and the most vigorous apostles of the ideas were missionaries of denominations different from that to which the Dutch colonists were accustomed. We have seen how these ideas brought about a radical change in the status of Hottentots and Coloured people from servitude to liberty and legal equality with white men, and we must now look at some of the other changes that took place during these vital first years of British administration.

Economically, the first fourteen years of British occupation were prosperous. A large garrison in Cape Town and freedom of trade stimulated production, particularly in the wine industry. During these years imports and exports were increased sixfold and the cattle population trebled; even the abolition of the slave trade worked to the advantage of slave owners, who were able to hire their slaves out at better rates. But the post-war depression in Europe hit the Cape, and from 1820 poverty and economic insecurity affected both eastern and western districts. During these years, too, Britain began a movement of currency reform throughout the Empire, which meant, at the Cape, substituting British for the chaotic coinage that existed and wiping out the fluctuating and inflated paper money. In the long run the Cape benefited from a stable currency, but, at the time, many individuals suffered hardship.

Despite economic depression, however, many reforms were initiated during the thirty years. Existing large districts were divided and new ones proclaimed, thus giving easier access to local authority; the construction of better roads was undertaken; and a beginning was made in reforming the system of landowning by substituting quit-rent and eventual ownership for the old 'loan farm' system. This reform was resented by frontiersmen because it put a stop to the easy and cheap acquisition of land to which they had been accustomed. In Cape Town pipe-borne water was laid on and streets were improved; a lighthouse was built at Green Point, and an Observatory, at which Herschel worked from 1834-8, was established; and a public library was started at which Thomas Pringle, poet and unsuccessful settler, became assistant librarian.

Lord Charles Somerset imported six schoolmasters from Scotland to run the elementary schools that he was establishing, and Pringle wrote to his friend Fairbairn in Scotland inviting him to come out and establish a high school in Cape Town. This Fairbairn did, bringing with him as equipment a copy of Euclid, elementary books in geography, French, Latin, Greek and arithmetic, a few small globes, and an atlas. The governor, who disliked Pringle and Fairbairn, set up an opposition Grammar School, and there was much rivalry and quarrelling until 1828 when Somerset left, and a public committee took the lead in establishing the Athenaeum, in which the two institutions merged. Public subscriptions and donations were called for, and in the following year the Athenaeum became the South African College, an institution for higher learning with real, though underpaid, professors who were not allowed to administer corporal punishment! In due course the South African College became a university institution and is, to-day, the University of Cape Town.

Pringle and Fairbairn were not interested in schools only. In 1823 they and Abraham Faure, a Dutch Reformed Church minister, asked the Governor for leave to produce a monthly magazine alternately in English and Dutch. Somerset, the high Tory, distrusted periodicals and newspapers as revolutionary and dangerous, and refused; but it was found that the law prohibited magazines, not newspapers, and so Pringle and Fairbairn started the *South African Commercial Advertiser* which Greig printed on a wooden press borrowed from Dr. Philip. Somerset acted quickly. When Greig refused to submit to censorship his press was seized and he was expelled from the country; but Greig went to London where, supported by the editors of *The Times* and the *Chronicle*, he succeeded in getting Somerset's decision reversed. Somerset also attacked Philip who, mistakenly, he thought was behind the whole affair, and so it came about that settler grievances, the agitation for a free press, and criticism by the London Missionary Society all centred on the governor. In 1826 he was recalled, and two years later the freedom of the press was established at the Cape.

The year 1828 saw another great change at the Cape: the establishment of the independence of the judiciary. Until then government had made several small changes in the judicial system in such matters as giving minor criminal jurisdiction to *landdrosts'* courts, and one major change when, in 1811, circuit courts, consisting of two judges, were instituted to visit the districts periodically. It was a much-needed reform, for justice should be 'easy of access'; but its use by the missionaries in the so-called Black Circuit of 1812 made it unpopular with frontiersmen, who were not accustomed to a legal system that interfered between them and their servants.

In 1815 the new administration of law became even more unpopular when it was associated with the Slachter's Nek

Rebellion. A frontiersman named Bezuidenhout, rather more lawless than most, was charged with ill-treating his Hottentot servant and refused to appear before the circuit court. The authorities sent an officer and twelve Hottentot soldiers to arrest him, and in resisting arrest he fired on the troops and was himself killed. At his graveside his brother and a few friends swore vengeance and attempted to get the help of the Xhosa chief, Gaika, in establishing a republic. Gaika refused, and they got little support from the burghers, and the rebellion was easily suppressed. A special commission of the High Court tried the rebels, banished thirty-two from the eastern frontier, and sentenced six to death, one of whom was subsequently reprieved. The remaining five were publicly hanged, in spite of appeals for mercy when the gallows broke at the first attempt.

Though the Slachter's Nek Rebellion has been used in modern times to show the 'harshness' of British administration and the spirit of independence of frontiersmen, it really represented nothing of the kind. As for independence, the vast majority of frontiersmen shewed no inclination to join Bezuidenhout and his friends; and as for the harshness, little else could have been expected in 1815. Nevertheless, though the rebellion had not been popular, the execution of the rebels roused considerable resentment and did nothing to popularize the administration of law.

The revolutionary change in the administration of justice in 1828 came as a result of the commission of inquiry that had been set up by the Secretary of State for Colonies five years earlier. The whole of the existing system, central and local, was abolished. A Supreme Court with a Chief Justice and two judges independent of the executive, was set up ; an Attorney-General replaced the old Fiscal; judges had to be trained lawyers, members of the British or Cape bars; and the jury system was instituted. In local administration, the post of *landdrost* was abolished and resident magistrates were appointed with limited jurisdiction in civil and criminal cases; and appeals lay from the circuit courts to the

Supreme Court in Cape Town, and from there to the Privy Council in England.

This thorough overhaul was highly necessary and it gave the Cape Colony a stable judicial system. It was, however, a pity that the government did not retain the familiar and popular *landdrost* and *heemraden* courts. Their functions could have been adjusted to fit the new system, and the titles could, with advantage, have been kept. To have done so would have made reforms more popular, and it was a piece of unnecessary tactlessness to abolish them. Even more important was the fact that, at the same time that the Charter of Justice was issued, the English language became the only official language at the Cape. This was part of Somerset's policy of anglicizing the Cape as quickly as possible, and in pursuance of that policy he had issued a proclamation in 1822 by which, after five years, English should be the only official language. In 1827 the coming into force of this proclamation was delayed for a year and so synchronized with the Charter of Justice. Subsequent history proved the language policy to have been a first-class blunder, and its association with the judicial reforms was unfortunate.

To further his anglicizing policy Somerset brought to the Cape Scots schoolmasters in 1822; he also brought out a number of ministers of the Established Church of Scotland whose religious tenets were similar to those of the Dutch Reformed Church. Some of these men had been sent to Holland for a year before coming to the Cape so that they should be able to preach in Dutch, but at the same time reconcile the Dutch colonists to English, and their earliest efforts in Dutch caused considerable quiet amusement at the Cape. They were men of sterling character and, wiser than Somerset, learnt Dutch rather than compel their parishioners to learn English. By 1837 more than half the ministers of the Dutch Reformed Church Synod were Scots, and they and their descendants had a profound effect on the religious and educational life of the Cape Colony, and later of South Africa. Andrew Murray, Colin Fraser, Morgan, Sutherland were some of the Scotsmen who came to South Africa in 1822. Without abating one jot of their love for Scotland and her traditions they identified themselves with the people to whom they ministered; they retained their belief that to love one language and country it was not necessary to hate another; many of their descendants—and they had large families—became ministers of the Dutch Reformed Church or missionaries to other African territories. By their contacts with Scotland and by sending their children to Scottish universities, they brought South Africa under the powerful influence of Scotland's traditional belief in the value of sound education.

The language policy started by Somerset persisted until the 1880's. When representative and responsible government were instituted, English was the only language recognized in Parliament, and it was only in 1882 that Dutch was admitted on an equal footing. Though the policy had incidental results of value to the Cape, it was a failure except among a minority of western Cape people who, in course of time, became more and more closely identified with English ways and traditions; and the policy left behind it a trail of resentment that has persisted to the present time. Afrikaners to-day talk with pride and a certain amount of bitterness about the futile attempt of 'old Lord Charles' to kill their language. Forty years before Somerset, the British were wiser when, in Canada, they placed French and English on an equal legal footing.

Actually, when Somerset began to interfere with the language rights of the colonists, the Dutch spoken at the Cape was already beginning to differ from the parent language in Holland. For almost a century longer it was the written language, taught in schools and used, after 1882, in official documents; it was the language of the Bible and the pulpit, spoken there in varying accents and degrees of grammatical correctness; and it became the official language of the Boer Republics. But during the nineteenth century the spoken language diverged steadily from written Dutch in grammar, construction, vocabulary, and the meaning of words. From 1875 a group of men at the Cape began to write this emerging language as it was spoken, and for the next forty years the protagonists of Dutch and the newer Afrikaans fought a bitter battle which Afrikaans won. The fruits of the tree planted by Lord Charles Somerset were, therefore, somewhat different from those he had expected.

The same commission of inquiry that had recommended judicial reforms was responsible for changes in the powers of the governor. Since 1806 he had had complete authority at the Cape subject only to the Secretary of State for the Colonies who was, of course, responsible to the British Parliament. In 1825 a Council of Advice was instituted, similar to the one that had recently been set up in Sydney: it consisted of the governor and four senior officials, and instead of proclamations issued by the governor alone, ordinances were henceforth to be made by the Council. It did not, however, act as much of a check on autocratic power, because the governor could still act independently in emergencies and could reject the advice of his council. Nevertheless it was the beginning of the long process of passing from the government by one man to parliamentary rule; and the officials whose advice had been rejected had the right to record that fact.

The commission of inquiry had recommended that there should be a legislative council to include non-official members, but there were two questions that had to be settled before the British government would consider representative institutions: the status of Hottentots and the abolition of slavery. By Ordinance 50 of 1828 Dr. Philip had secured the free status of Hottentots, but the question of slave liberation remained, and in 1830 the British government rejected petitions from Cape Town and Grahamstown asking for an elected assembly. Fairbairn, who had married Dr. Philip's daughter and was editor of the *Commercial Advertiser*, had taken a lead in demanding an assembly, but when he realized that it might retard slave liberation he dropped the agitation.

In England itself exciting things were happening as parliamentary reform approached. Across the Channel the July revolutions of 1830 were toppling crowns and causing those who managed to retain them, hastily to grant popular constitutions. England escaped actual revolution, though not riots, because she had a parliament that could make the necessary changes. For two years the battle round parliamentary reform raged until, on 30th March 1831, the Reform Bill passed the House of Commons amid scenes about which Macaulay said: 'If I should live fifty years the impression of it will be as fresh and sharp in my mind as if it had just taken place.' Lord Grey, realizing that the Bill would not pass the House of Lords, appealed to the country and received an increased majority which strengthened his hand in threatening to create more peers should the House of Lords reject the Bill. It was passed in 1832.

Meanwhile the movement for the abolition of slavery had gathered force. In 1822 an Anti-Slavery Committee was founded by Fowell Buxton and Wilberforce, and backed by the Evangelicals and Nonconformists, it procured a number of regulations to soften the lot of slaves and to reduce their owners' rights over them. Registrars and guardians were appointed in the nineteen slave-owning colonies, and punishment record books, open to inspection, had to be kept. Though the slave-owners at the Cape realized that, sooner or later, slavery would be abolished, and though they even made tentative suggestions for gradual abolition by, for example, liberating all female slaves, they were bitterly opposed to the slave regulations; a near-riot occurred at Stellenbosch when the authorities proposed to examine punishment record books, and in other places slave-owners talked about rebellion.

The reformed Parliament in England abolished slavery in the British Empire in 1833 and so set free something like 800,000 slaves, about 29,000 of them being at the Cape. As from December 1834 all slaves were to be apprenticed to their owners for four years, after which they were freed; and

Parliament voted £20,000,000 to compensate owners. The share allotted to the Cape was close on £3,000,000 but was subsequently reduced to £1,250,000; this was payable in London, partly in cash and partly in bonds. Abolition hit the slave-owners hard. Since they could not travel to London to collect compensation they had to cash their claims through banks or, in the country districts, sell them at a heavy discount to speculators. Many farmers had raised loans with their slaves as security, and some of them went bankrupt when the loans were called up. As so often happens, the abolition of slavery was a great reform poorly carried out. Nevertheless, it was the best thing that could have happened to the Cape Colony.

A year after abolition had been passed by the British Parliament, a legislative council was set up at the Cape and met for the first time on 2nd April 1834. It consisted of the governor and four senior officials and from five to seven citizens appointed by the governor. Its powers were limited, but it was a big advance on the old Council of Advice. It could discuss only what the governor chose to lay before it, but no ordinance might be passed without its consent; and an ordinance so passed could be set aside only by the King-in-Council. The governor and four officials constituted the executive council, so that, even though the elective principle was not yet adopted, the idea of a legislative and an executive branch of government had been established. Two years later, in 1836, an ordinance of the legislative council made provision for the establishment of elected municipal councils, thus providing for representative government in local affairs.

The changes introduced by the British government during the period 1806 to 1836 have been dealt with at some length because of their twofold importance: they laid down the pattern of development for the Cape Colony, and they were partly responsible for the break-up of the colony by the emigration of thousands of its citizens northwards. Those changes can, legitimately, be regarded as reforms; but there is a difference between early nineteenth-century reform at the Cape and reform as it is normally understood in Europe. Great reforms usually come about after a long period of agitation on the part of a few individuals who, eventually, succeed in persuading a sufficiently large body of their fellow-citizens to support them in demanding, either by peaceable or by violent means, that a change be made. When the reform arrives it is usually bitterly resented and opposed by some people, but those who favour it are stronger than those who oppose. The abolition of slavery, social reform in England in the nineteenth century, and the revolutionary reforms in Europe are all examples of this.

At the Cape there was no preceding popular agitation, though the agitation for a free press may perhaps be regarded as a partial exception. The introduction of circuit courts and the establishment of a sound judicial system; the freedom of Hottentots and the liberation of slaves; reforms in the system of land holding; and the beginnings of local and central representative government—all these were reforms that were brought to the Cape from outside. Indeed, any internal agitation was usually against these changes, because to the colonists they seemed to be restraints rather than reforms. Although Dr. Philip and others were prime movers in securing reforms they did not depend for support on public opinion at the Cape. That opinion was usually hostile, and the reforms were made in spite of it.

Nowhere was hostility to the changes greater than among the Dutch frontiersmen. To them the changes represented nothing but interference with their customary way of living: circuit courts and the strict application of the rule of law interfered between master and servant; freedom for Hottentots deprived frontiersmen of cheap and personally controllable labour; the new land laws and the decision, in 1832, that Crown lands should be sold by auction, prevented them from acquiring large farms for next to nothing; the substitution of magistrates for courts of *landdrosts* and *heemraden* deprived them of a privileged position in court where *heemraden* had been men like themselves, not impersonal officials. Worst of all, prevailing views in London on the rights of Africans beyond the borders of the Cape Colony clashed with those of the frontiersmen. It was the nineteenth century overtaking the seventeenth and eighteenth; and by 1836 the Dutch frontiersmen decided to trek away from the nineteenth century.

Before describing that dramatic and fateful trek, we must see what was happening beyond the borders of the Cape Colony. Our knowledge of the history of African tribes, hundreds of miles north of the Fish River boundary, is sketchy and depends on traditional African stories and on reports by missionaries, hunters and traders who crossed the Orange River in the early part of the nineteenth century. It seems clear that among the many tribes in what is to-day the Transkei, Pondoland, Basutoland, Natal, Zululand, the Orange Free State, Bechuanaland, and the Transvaal, the period 1806–36 was one of almost continuous war. It is impossible to say why this was so, for on the whole, and despite the strong belief among Europeans that Africans are 'always savage and warlike', African tribes were not perpetually at war. They had reached the transition stage from pastoralism to settled agriculture, and unless a serious shortage of land occurs, warlikeness is not a characteristic of settled agriculture.

In Roman times, the Germanic tribes immediately beyond the borders of Roman conquest were always in a state of unrest, and it is possible that something like that was happening in South Africa. However that may be, we do know something about one cause of the unrest among African tribes. In the last quarter of the eighteenth century, in what is to-day known as Zululand, a small and insignificant tribe called the Ama-Zulu existed and owed allegiance to the much more powerful Abatetwa. The chief of the Abatetwa was Dingiswayo who, as a boy, had run away from his father and come into contact, no one knows where, with a European hunter, possibly an outlaw, who told him tales of European warfare. In due course he returned to his tribe, mounted on a horse and armed with a gun, neither of which had ever been seen by his fellow-tribesmen. He stepped easily into the position of chieftainship, left vacant by his father's death, and began to introduce new ideas of military discipline and strategy.

Chaka, younger son of the chief of the subordinate Zulu tribe, was a man of great physical energy and mental ability. It is said that his father was jealous of him; at any rate, he incurred his father's anger and he, in turn, ran away and took refuge with Dingiswayo. Here his abilities were appreciated and he soon became a military leader, adopting and developing the new ideas of Dingiswayo. He became chief of the Ama-Zulu, and on the death of his patron, of the Abatetwa. This must have been about 1818, and within the next ten years he had raised the Zulu from an obscure tribe to a powerful and widely feared nation that conquered and spread devastation throughout the present Natal and Zululand.

Chaka's army was organized in regiments, or *impis*, and was subject to an iron discipline under which death was the penalty for insubordination or cowardice; he discarded traditional chiefs and sub-chiefs and appointed proved military leaders in their places; marriage was allowed only to those who had killed an enemy in battle; his soldiers were armed with stabbing assegais and ox-hide shields, and the fighting formation was the crescent shape, with plenty of reserves to be thrown in at any threatened spot. In ordinary tribal warfare such armies and tactics were irresistible, and Chaka used them with deadly effect to spread terror throughout the tribes. Whatever he himself may have been in earlier years, he became a cruel and bloodthirsty tyrant who murdered out of personal caprice, and he met a tyrant's death when, in 1828, he was murdered by his two brothers, one of whom, Dingaan, carried on the tyrant's tradition.

These wars in Natal and Zululand had repercussions far and wide. If the unrest in South Africa may be compared to the unrest beyond the confines of Roman conquest, the effect of Chaka's wars may be compared to that of the invasion of Western Europe by the Huns. Tribes and remnants of tribes fled before the conquering Zulu, across the Drakensberg and on to the high veld of the present Free State and Transvaal; into Basutoland where a wise man, Moshesh, formed them into a nation; northwards to the present Southern Rhodesia where Mzilikazi founded the Matabele nation; further north to Nyasaland; and southwards to the borders of the Cape Colony. If there were empty spaces, or plenty of room as on the high veld, the refugees settled down to a new home; otherwise they, in turn, provoked wars of defence and offence. Into the borderlands of the Cape Colony, where Xhosa and Europeans were already competing for land, refugee Tembu and Fingo, fleeing from Chaka or from Chaka's enemies, went to complicate the situation.

On the African side of the border, land-hunger was aggravated by Chaka's wars, on the European side by the impact of British policy on Dutch frontiersmen. In these circumstances frontier wars were inevitable. In 1811 the fourth Kaffir War took place; the Xhosa were driven back across the Fish River boundary and a line of block-houses (or forts) was established along the frontier. In 1818 a quarrel broke out between Gaika and Ndlambi which ended in Gaika's defeat. The Cape government persisted in regarding Gaika as paramount chief though Ndlambi and his followers would not recognize him as such; and when he appealed to the governor for help, troops and burghers were sent to punish Ndlambi, who took his revenge by attacking Grahamstown. This was the fifth Kaffir War, in 1819, and when it was over Somerset tried to settle the border problem by declaring a strip of territory between the Fish and Keiskama rivers as neutral—a futile policy, since it removed from occupation by both sides a large piece of land when scarcity of land was the fundamental trouble.

The peace that followed this war was precarious, for

pressure was mounting on both sides of the vague border and reached bursting point in 1834. For the six or seven years before the sixth Kaffir War broke out conditions on both sides of the border were confused. Between 1831 and 1834 prolonged droughts parched the land and dried up fountains and streams, and locusts devoured what grazing was left; farmers on both sides of the border watched their cattle die, or wandered with the enfeebled beasts to seek water and grazing.[1] When the rains came, cattle raids from both sides, followed by reprisals, were resumed; under pressure from the British settlers in Albany, permission to trade in Kaffirland had been granted, and English colonists and Dutch trekboers were trading or grazing their cattle deep in Kaffirland, beyond the Kei River. To the north-west, hunters and missionaries had crossed the Orange River boundary, and small Griqua states had got themselves established outside the Colony; and trekboers, still considering themselves as British subjects, were buying farms on Griqua land. In 1834, three so-called commission treks crossed the frontier to find out if there was vacant land further north, and on their return they reported that there was plenty of good open veld unoccupied.

What was in fact happening during these years between 1828 and 1834 was that the frontier situation had become uncontrollable with the meagre resources of men and money that the governor had at his disposal. The desire for more land was urging the trekboers northwards, and the desire of British settlers to trade was taking them into Kaffirland; and to prevent these things from happening government would

[1] There is an old Afrikaans doggerel verse that opens:

Die sprinkaan en die droogte
Is swaar in onse land.

(The locust and drought lie heavy on the land.) Locusts and drought have played a large part in shaping political events. The locust has been brought under control by co-operation with other governments in Africa—in itself a notable tribute to that plague. Droughts are still with us, and General Smuts is said to have remarked that a prolonged drought was the most serious enemy of any government.

have had to spend millions of pounds to maintain a firm boundary. The British government was unwilling to do this, and on the African side of the border, there was no one tribe with sufficient authority or strength either to prevent European penetration or to restrain Africans from cattle raids. There could be only one end to such conditions: the annexation of tribal lands by the Europeans. That was to come later.

Meanwhile, in 1834, the sixth Kaffir War took place, and when the Xhosa had been driven out of the Colony, Sir Benjamin D'Urban, the governor, annexed a large area of land and extended the boundary to the Kei River. This new area he called the Province of Queen Adelaide, and unwisely promised that it should be made available for settlement. When he found that he was unable to keep the Xhosa out, and after he had been severely criticized by Lord Glenelg, Secretary of State, who depended largely on Dr. Philip for advice, D'Urban modified his policy and the new territory was disannexed. This was in 1836.

Many of the Dutch frontiersmen had left the Colony in 1835, but many more were waiting to see whether the government would make more land available. When it became clear that, so far from annexing Xhosa land for European occupation, the government in London blamed the frontiersmen for the war and was embarking on a policy of making treaties with Kaffir chiefs, these frontiersmen decided to trek beyond the Orange River and found a new state. Thus it was that, at the end of the first thirty years of British rule at the Cape, the Colony was disrupted and a good proportion of Dutch frontiersmen, British subjects by conquest, trekked away from the Colony in the hope of throwing off British rule. This is the movement that is known as the Great Trek.

Chapter Eight

THE GREAT TREK

On 4th July 1776 the American colonists published their Declaration of Independence which began: 'When in the course of human events, it becomes necessary for one people to dissolve the political bonds which have connected them one with another, and to assume among the powers of the earth the separate and equal station to which the laws of Nature and of Nature's God entitle them, a decent respect to the opinions of mankind requires that they should declare the causes which impel them to separation.'

On 2nd February 1837, the year in which Queen Victoria ascended the throne, the *Grahamstown Journal* published a document signed by Piet Retief, leader of one of the groups of trekboers who had decided to emigrate from the Cape Colony. It said:

'. . . as we desire to stand high in the estimation of our brethren, and are anxious that they and the world at large should believe us incapable of severing that sacred tie which binds a Christian to his native soil, without the most sufficient reasons, we are induced to record the following summary of our motives for taking so important a step, and also our intentions respecting our proceedings towards the native tribes which we may meet with beyond the boundary.'

Though the circumstances and the causes that produced these two documents were different they have much in common. Both show a realization that an extraordinary step is being taken and that the world at large should be told why; both go on to list their grievances; and both state their determination to set up independent governments. When people can no longer endure the government they have, there is, in a parliamentary democracy, a remedy in the ballot box. When there is no parliament they have three courses open to them: they may submit; they may rebel; or they may trek away. Neither the American colonists nor the Boers[1] would submit. The Americans rebelled, and, for seven years, fought a successful war of independence. The Boers trekked away and, much later, fought for their independence, and lost.

Piet Retief's Manifesto complained about the evils that threatened the Colony because of vagrancy—a reference to the laws that gave freedom to Hottentots and Coloured people; it complained about the severe losses that arose from slave liberation and the lack of protection against 'Caffres' in the frontier districts; and it complained about the 'unjustifiable odium' which had been cast on the Boers by 'interested and dishonest persons under the cloak of religion' —a reference to the part played by missionaries in shaping frontier and Hottentot policy. The Manifesto went on to say that the Boers would not hold slaves but would 'preserve proper relations between master and servant; they will deprive no one of property, but will defend themselves if attacked; they will draw up a code of laws; they will endeavour to live on friendly terms with native tribes.' Paragraph 9 of the Manifesto reads: 'We quit this colony under the full assurance that the English Government has nothing more to require of us, and will allow us to govern ourselves without its interference in future.' Finally, says the Manifesto, the emigrants are leaving their homes and 'entering a wild and dangerous territory', and they do so in firm reliance on God.

[1] It is not certain at what precise date the word Boer came to be commonly used for what we have called trekboer or frontiersmen. From now on it will be used when referring to the trekkers and to the white inhabitants of the republics they founded.

Retief put into words what many of the Boers were probably thinking; but as a statement of the causes of the Great Trek his Manifesto is inadequate. We have seen what the underlying causes were: land-hunger on both sides of the frontier; dislike of new ideas that were coming in from Europe and manifesting themselves as 'reforms', often unsympathetically carried out; and hatred of new ideas that regarded black and white as equal. Apart from these general causes there were, of course, many different reasons why individuals trekked. Reports on the high veld and Natal, brought back by those who had gone to spy out the land, were glowing, and the severe drought on the frontier in 1834–5 made the tall grass they spoke of sound more luscious; and the destruction of lives, cattle, and farm buildings during the sixth Kaffir War made the 'wide open spaces' farther north seem very attractive.

Some joined a party of trekkers because their neighbours or relatives did so and because they did not want to be left out of it; others joined, as their fathers and grandfathers had done, because they wanted more room; young bachelors joined for the sake of adventure and because the prospects seemed brighter farther north. Married men who had held back because of the hardship involved for their wives and children, found their womenfolk even more determined than they to quit a country where servants had equal rights with masters and their men were always in a state of political unrest. A few trekked because of difficulties with the law or because they could not pay their debts; and, after the first exodus, many who had stayed behind trekked to join relatives and friends in the new countries that had been opened up.

In time, the more personal reasons for emigrating were forgotten and became generalized in the form of 'respectable' motives. Human beings the world over seem to regard economic motives as 'sordid' and 'petty' and prefer to ascribe their own actions to more exalted and praiseworthy ideals. A man who joins the army during a war may do so because he knows his debtors will have no hold on him or because the pay may be better than in civil life; but he prefers to say that he is volunteering, at a financial sacrifice, for love of country or to fight for liberty. In the same way, men who trekked because they wanted more cheap land, or their hold over their labourers was threatened, or prospects seemed brighter elsewhere, came to believe that they had really trekked from more 'laudable' motives—love of independence and liberty and a desire to be rid of the British government just because it was 'foreign'.

This habit of rationalizing behaviour is a well-known characteristic of human beings; nevertheless, it is best to try to find out the truth. For one thing, in this particular case, it helps to explain why Dutch people from the settled western half of the Colony did not trek. They were as fond of their traditions and liberty as the frontiersmen. Yet, when the Great Trek was over, it will be found that those who emigrated constituted about 20 per cent of the Dutch-speaking population; and it would be a bold man who would regard the remaining 80 per cent as consisting chiefly of cowards and traitors.

There is no need to fall into the opposite error of thinking that the Voortrekkers were nothing but a set of irrational malcontents, moved only by selfish and personal considerations. For nearly all the emigrants, leaving the Colony meant leaving home and trekking into an unknown land. And leaving home meant selling, at glut prices, all the furniture and crockery that could not be loaded on to a wagon; it meant giving up a farm and a homestead, however primitive, where their children had been born and grown up; it meant, literally, uprooting themselves. As for the unknown promised land which they sought, there were plenty of hardships and dangers before they reached that, and plenty of situations that called for courage, endurance, self-sacrifice and faith. And these qualities were not called for in vain. It is no wonder, then, that the descendants of the trekkers think with pride of the achievements of their forefathers and regard the Great Trek as the Americans regard their War of Independence: a fight for freedom that laid the foundations of a nation.

The first two trek leaders to leave the Colony were Louis Trigardt and Janse van Rensburg, and it is from Trigardt's diary that we get a good picture of what a small trek was like. Trigardt's father had taken part in the Graaff-Reinet rebellion of 1799 and had been arrested by the British authorities. Since 1832, Louis had been living with his family and his herds in Kaffirland, across the frontier, and the government suspected him of intriguing with Xhosa chiefs against the Colony; there was a price on his head, and in 1835 he decided to move on. His trek travelled with nine wagons and consisted of six families, an old so-called 'schoolmaster', and seven or eight servants whom Trigardt calls 'Bushmen'; there were some saddle-horses, about 500 head of cattle, and about 3,000 sheep and goats. The total 'population' of the trek was about fifty, of whom thirty were children and nine were able to handle a gun.

How many miles a day could such a trek travel? Sixty years later, an Australian entomologist called Claude Fuller, who came to live in South Africa, was trying to reconstruct Trigardt's journey and remembered a verse from an Australian ballad by 'Banjo' Paterson:

Now this is the law of the Overland,
That all in the West obey,
A man must cover with travelling sheep
A six mile stage a day.[1]

Applying this rule, Fuller was able to plot the journey. Five to six miles a day was the pace, less when ewes were lambing or when there was good grazing and water.

The Voortrekkers did not travel on Sundays, though they were not always sure which day of the week it was, and they were strict observers of family prayers. There was no lack of employment on such a slow-moving trek: women

[1] Van Riebeeck Society publications, No. 13, p. XV.

attended to cooking, mending clothes, making soap and candles, and looking after the children; men had to give constant attention to their herds, their trek-gear and wagons, shooting for the pot, and mounting guard against African tribesmen; and the children took their share of herding cattle after they had had their early-morning lessons from the 'schoolmaster'.

Trigardt and van Rensburg moved in this leisurely fashion, and without adventure, over the Orange River, across the plains of the present Free State, over the Vaal River, and on to the Zoutpansberg in the north-eastern Transvaal. There the two leaders quarrelled, and van Rensburg went east to try to reach the Portuguese harbour of Delagoa Bay. He and his company were never heard of again. Trigardt stayed in the Zoutpansberg for more than a year, and his company built rough houses, laid out gardens and got ivory and skins from Africans by barter; but their supplies of coffee, tea and sugar, and—much more important—of lead and gunpowder began to run out, and they were much afflicted by malaria.

After two attempts to get a message to Lorenço Marques, Trigardt decided to trek over the Drakensberg to the coast. It was a desperately hard journey, cutting tracks, looking for a way through the mountains, taking the wagons to pieces to get them over the precipices; and when they had crossed the mountains into the tropical country below, they were attacked by fever and their cattle by tsetse fly. After eight months they reached Lorenço Marques and the Portuguese did their best for them; but all the men except Trigardt's eldest son, and many of the women and children, died, and the remnants of the party eventually reached Natal by sea in 1838.

Most of the trekking companies that left the Cape during 1836–7 were about the size of Trigardt's; but they tended to grow larger. In 1836 Andries Potgieter and Sarel Cilliers each led a larger trek consisting chiefly of neighbours and relations; Potgieter had about fifty wagons and forty men, including boys of sixteen and upwards, able to handle a rifle. Cilliers' trek was slightly smaller and included a boy of ten, Paul Kruger, who was to become the famous President of the Transvaal. Having crossed the Orange River the two parties joined hands and Potgieter was elected commandant with Cilliers as deputy; they moved northwards,

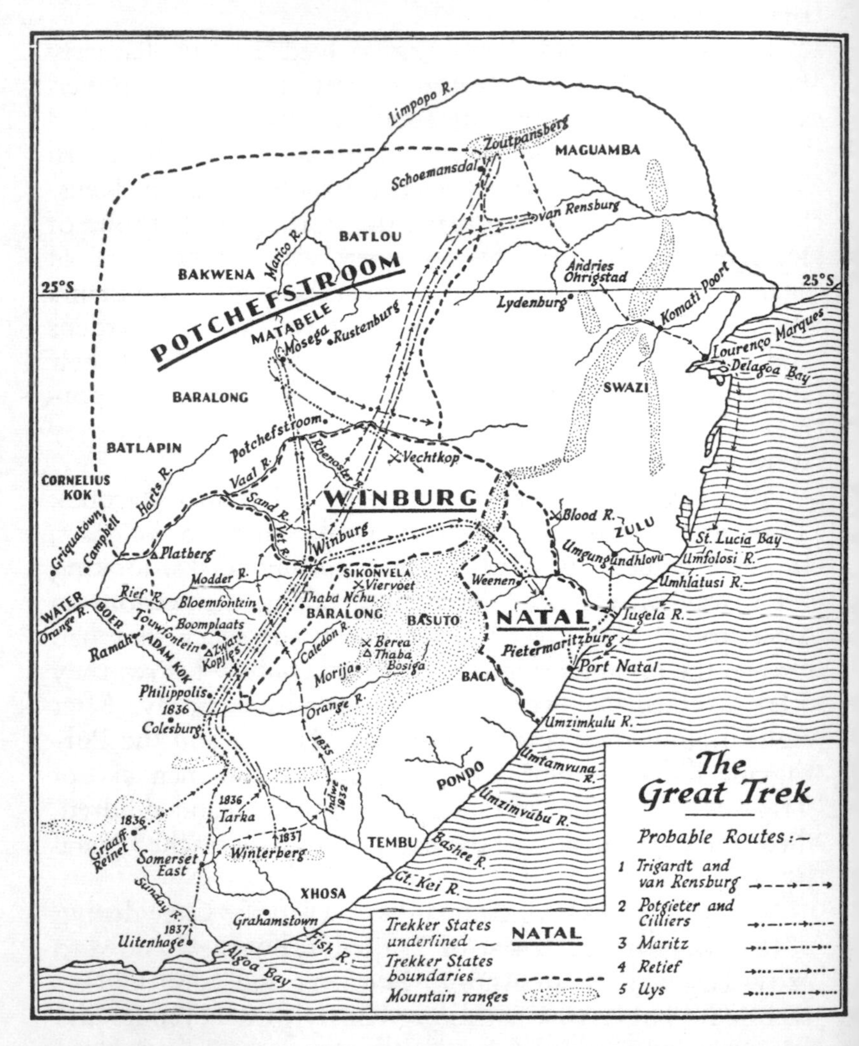

through the present central Orange Free State, and on the banks of the Vet River made a treaty with Makwana, chief of the Bataung, who 'gave' them land between the Vet and Vaal rivers. It was not his to give, but the Boers did not realize this.

While the leaders and a few followers rode east to spy out the land and to find out if there was access to the sea, the rest of the party, unwisely, moved forward towards the Vaal River. They tended to disperse instead of keeping in a compact body, and they failed to keep proper watch; and the dreaded Matabele attacked and killed two small parties. When Potgieter returned, in the nick of time, he gathered his company together at Vegkop (Hill of Battle) and there formed what the Boers called a *laager*. Wagons were lashed together to form a circle and the openings were plugged with thorn bush; in the middle of the laager four wagons were constructed into a shelter for women and children; horses were brought inside the laager but there was no room for cattle and sheep. Once the laager was drawn the Boers sat down to await the Matabele, and on 19th October 1836 the attack began.

The Boers were outnumbered by about a hundred to one, but, against that, they had guns with an effective range of 100 yards against the Matabele assegais' fifty yards; also, they had horses. What the Boers required more than anything else was cool nerves, and they had those. Riding out to meet the enemy they kept just out of assegai range and gradually lured the Matabele towards the laager, firing all the time. By the time the Boers were inside the laager the Matabele warriors' blood was up and they made mass attacks in vain attempts to break up the defences. From behind the wagons the Boers, with their wives reloading for them, poured round after round into the swarming Matabele until they withdrew. Once more Potgieter and his men rode out to draw the enemy, who once more attacked furiously and were driven off, this time for good; but they took with them the Boers' cattle and sheep, leaving their enemy victorious but without food or trek-oxen.

At Thaba Nchu, 150 miles south of Vegkop, lived the Barolong tribe under their chief, Moroko; they were enemies of the Matabele and friendly to the Boers, and to them Potgieter at once sent a messenger to ask for help. Moroko sent cattle to the distressed Boers, and Potgieter's messenger found that a strong trekker company, under Gerrit Maritz, was camping near Thaba Nchu. From this company relief was sent to bring the Potgieter-Cilliers party south again.

The three trek companies now combined and drew up a simple constitution which provided for a Volksraad (Council of the People) of seven elected members; the Volksraad was both legislature and court of law, and laws could also be made by a mass meeting of burghers. Potgeiter was elected commandant and chairman of the Krygsraad (Council of War) and Maritz was chosen as chairman of the Volksraad. However, there was no time for law-making. The Matabele had remained in possession of Boer wagons, cattle and sheep, and it was at once decided to send an expedition to recover these and teach the Matabele a lesson. Early in 1837 a well-armed party set out and defeated the Matabele, capturing over 7,000 head of cattle and recovering the lost wagons; they brought back with them, too, three American missionaries who had been working among the Matabele, and one of these, Daniel Lindley, devoted a great deal of the rest of his life in South Africa as pastor to the Boers.

There had been a general understanding that trekking parties, large or small, should cross the Orange River and then forgather at Blesberg, near Thaba Nchu, for consultation about future action. When the expedition to punish the Matabele returned to Blesberg they found that many more wagons had come in from the Cape Colony, and more were coming in almost daily. The trekker population had grown to over 1,000 and was becoming difficult to manage;

and, to make matters worse, Potgieter and Maritz were men of different temperament, the former silent, rugged, and conservative in religion, and the latter talkative, urbane and ambitious. They and their followers quarrelled about their respective official positions, about the division of cattle taken from the Matabele, and about religion. The Dutch Reformed Church at the Cape was strongly opposed to the Great Trek because it meant a dispersal of its members; and so the trekkers were without a minister. Maritz had brought with him Erasmus Smit, an unordained Hollander who had come to the Cape as a mission teacher under the London Missionary Society; but Potgieter and his followers would have nothing to do with Smit, preferring the ministrations of fully qualified Wesleyan missionaries.

In April 1837, when dissensions among the leaders had reached a critical stage, Piet Retief arrived on the scene with a large following. Retief was the ablest of the leaders of the Great Trek and was invited by a large majority of the trekkers to become governor and chief commandant of the united laagers. Older by twelve years than Potgieter, and by twenty than Maritz, Retief had experience not only of frontier life at the Cape but of the more settled western districts; he knew all about frontier wars, and he also knew something about the politics that accompanied them. To a great many trekkers the emigration meant simply a move to acquire a new farm; to Retief it meant establishing a new state that would rule over the new farms.

Retief was well equipped for leadership, but it would have required a superhuman being to hold the trekkers together. Shortly after Retief s arrival the united laagers consisted of about 2,000 trekkers together with Coloured and other servants; they were strung out in six camps between Thaba Nchu and the Vet River over an area of about fifty miles long and twenty broad. The whole body was daily growing by new arrivals and was slowly drifting northwards. Many of the trekkers were, for practical purposes, illiterate; they had no political or administrative experience and, in fact, disliked and distrusted an impartially administered legal system; growing up as frontiersmen they had no knowledge or experience of any kind of society other than that of pastoralism; they were self-reliant, and resented control; they were hospitable, and also suspicious; having lived isolated and individualistic lives they were quarrelsome when thrown together. The eighteenth-century trekboers, from whom the men of the Great Trek were descended, had known personal loyalty to the family or, at most, to the leader of a commando. They had never been loyal to a government or a State, and it is little wonder that when men nurtured in such traditions emigrated and were forced to establish their own State, they quarrelled and found difficulty in remaining loyal, in co-operating, or in submitting to discipline.

At the time that Piet Retief joined the Great Trek it can best be described as a rather loose and disorganized collection of trekker groups, on the march and in process of trying to become a nation. Retief saw the need for machinery of government, for discipline, and above all for an agreed plan as to where the new State should be. Simple machinery of government was set up in June 1837: Retief became governor and chief commandant while Maritz remained chairman of the Volksraad, and *landdrost* of the court, which consisted of the same men who constituted the Volksraad; Potgieter, to the annoyance of his personal following, held no high office. Commandants and field cornets were appointed; and a rudimentary constitution, known as the Nine Articles, was adopted and had to be accepted, under oath, by all trekkers, present and to come. For a couple of months it seemed as if Retief had succeeded in smoothing out the difficulties between the various groups. Then, in July, another trek arrived, under Piet Uys, and quarrelling broke out with renewed violence.

The real bone of contention was the direction that the united laagers should take. The country through which they were moving, the present central Orange Free State, was too near the Cape Colony and was much less fertile than Natal and the land beyond the Vaal River were reputed to be. Few trekkers, therefore, wanted to remain on the high veld. Retief proposed turning east, over the Drakensberg and down to the fertile Natal, where he could negotiate for land with the Zulu and have an outlet to the sea; Potgieter and his followers thought the land to the north, across the Vaal River, was better and was, in any case, further away from British rule. Uys supported Retief; so, on the whole, did Maritz. And so the Great Trek began to move eastwards towards the Drakensberg. But quarrelling did not cease. Potgieter always, and Maritz occasionally, grumbled about going to Natal; and in August 1837 Piet Uys and his followers declared their independence of the united laagers and refused to obey Retief and Maritz. Retief called a mass meeting of burghers in a final effort to reconcile differences, but in vain; and he and Maritz moved off to Natal, leaving Uys and Potgieter to their own devices.

The northern portion of the present Natal was, in 1837, occupied by the Zulu whose spectacular rise to power under Chaka was described earlier. Dingaan had murdered Chaka and succeeded him, and it was to Dingaan that Retief proposed to go for permission to settle in the 'empty spaces' that Chaka's wars had created. Port Natal, and a block of territory round it, was occupied by a small and miscellaneous collection of ivory-hunters, traders, runaway Zulu, and mixed European-Zulu people. Captain Gardiner, former Royal Naval officer and, by 1837, a missionary, was nominally the representative of the British government; in practice he had little authority, and Britain consistently turned down his suggestions that she should acquire the harbour by treaty with Dingaan. Gardiner had established the town of Durban and was on good terms with Dingaan, whom he had persuaded to accept a missionary, Francis Owen.

Near the present Van Reenen's pass, over which the road and railway run to-day, Retief and fifteen of his men managed to scramble down the precipitous Drakensberg range and to take four wagons with them, leaving the rest of his company on top of the pass. He rode on to Durban, through beautiful, fertile country that fully lived up to the favourable reports that had been brought back from it, and there found two young Englishmen who were prepared to accompany him as guides and interpreters to Umgungundhlovu, the capital of Dingaan, King of the Zulus.

Shortly before Retief and Dingaan met, a chief named Sikonyela had stolen some of Dingaan's cattle, and the King now agreed that if Retief would recapture his cattle and, if possible, bring Sikonyela himself, the Boers would be given land in Natal. Retief was well satisfied, and while he returned to Durban, sent messengers to tell the good news to the waiting trekkers. It was indeed good news. The trekkers had had a hard time since Retief left them: excessive rains, more lions than usual, and constant alarms that hostile tribes were about to attack—added to what they had already experienced—all these made them ready to receive with enthusiasm the news that here, at last, was the promised land. In spite of Retief's instructions to await his return, the trekkers began descending the passes into Natal. Women and children on foot, household goods tied securely to the wagons with leather thongs, the rear wheels of the wagons braked, and the two most sure-footed oxen drawing—so 1,000 wagons had come over the mountains within a month and were dangerously dispersed along the river banks of western Natal.

In disobeying Retief's instructions the trekkers had made a fatal mistake. Dingaan, whose spies reported the 'invasion' of Boers, was thoroughly alarmed. He had just heard that a small party of Boers, under Potgieter and Uys, had routed the Matabele at Marico in the northern Transvaal and had inflicted such a heavy defeat on them that they had left the Transvaal altogether and trekked north, to the present Southern Rhodesia. And the ease with which Retief and a small patrol recovered his cattle from Sikonyela served only to increase his alarm. The Boers with their horses and guns were dangerous to black men and it would be better to wipe them out before it was too late. Already they were occupying Zulu lands, even before Retief had fulfilled his side of the bargain. We know from Francis Owen, the missionary, and from traders at Port Natal, that Dingaan was profoundly disturbed and was scheming to get rid of the white wizards who so clearly threatened his country.

Back at the trekker camps Retief received various warnings, and Maritz and others tried to dissuade him from going to Dingaan's capital to claim his land. But Retief was self-confident and set out with seventy followers, thirty Hottentot servants, and an English interpreter, for Umgungundhlovu. The Boers were received with apparent friendliness by Dingaan, and after several days of talk and bargaining, during which Retief was again warned by Owen that the situation was dangerous, the King put his mark to a treaty granting all land between the Tugela and the Umzimvubu rivers to the Boers. He then suggested that, as a sign of friendly relations, the Boers should go unarmed into the royal kraal to watch a war dance and have a farewell feast with the King. Retief was anxious to avoid any sign that he and his men were suspicious, and agreed to the proposal. And, in the middle of the exciting Zulu war dance, Dingaan rose and shouted: 'Kill the wizards.' This was the signal for Zulu warriors, hidden in the surrounding huts, to slaughter the disarmed Boers.

This was on 6th February 1838, and during the following eleven months the trekkers suffered severely. Having killed Retief and his seventy followers, Dingaan sent his warriors to wipe out the rest of the white invaders. They fell on the unprepared laagers, slaughtered whomever they could find, and drove off Boer cattle. By the time the Boers were able to collect their scattered forces and form new laagers, 500 men, women, and children had been killed, and 20,000 head of cattle taken. News of the disasters reached the high veld, and Potgieter and Uys hurried to the assistance of the sorely tried trekkers in Natal. A commando of 350 men was formed to attack Dingaan; but it was badly organized and the old jealousy between Maritz, Uys, and Potgieter hampered effective co-operation. The commando was defeated at Italeni and Piet Uys was killed in action, despite the gallant efforts of his twelve-year-old son Dirk, who, seeing his father surrounded by Zulu, rushed to his help and was killed by his side. A small force of twenty Englishmen from Port Natal, and 1,000 Zulu retainers, mostly fugitives from Dingaan, made an attempt to invade Zulu country, but they were practically all killed.

Despite these reverses, and in spite of continuous threats of attack, shortage of supplies, heavy rains, and fever, most of the trekkers were determined to remain in Natal. Potgieter and his followers left; but by May the Boers had reorganized themselves into a semblance of the old united laagers and numbered about 3,500 men, women, and children. They began to build huts, to plough, and to sow. They drew up a constitution for the new State, which they had not yet secured, and established a township which they called Pietermaritzburg, after their two leaders, Pieter Retief and Gerrit Maritz. Erasmus Smit, the minister over whom Maritz and Potgieter had quarrelled, built a small school; and in October the first communion was celebrated on Natal soil.

In September Maritz died and the Natal trekkers were without a leader. Nevertheless hope had revived because news was received that Andries Pretorius, a frontier farmer from Graaff-Reinet, was organizing a large trek in the Colony to go to the help of the trekkers in Natal. In November Pretorius arrived, bringing with him a cannon, and preparations were at once made for a commando to attack Dingaan, for the Boers realized that their title to Natal would not be secure until the Zulu King was defeated. Early in December a force of 500 crossed the Tugela into Zululand and rode in the direction of Umgungundhlovu. On 9th December, a Sunday, a service was held at which

Sarel Cilliers vowed that, if God gave them victory, the trekkers would build a church as a memorial and would, ever after, remember the day.

A week later victory was granted. In a strong position, on the banks of Blood River, the Boers drew their laager and awaited the enemy. The Zulu attacked, wave after wave, and were driven back by devastating fire from the Boers. Then the Boers counter-attacked, and at last the demoralized Zulu fled. Pretorius and his men pushed on to the Zulu capital which they found deserted; and among the unburied skeletons of Retief and his followers they found, in Retief's leather knapsack, the treaty to which Dingaan had put his mark eleven months earlier.

The victory of 16th December 1838 is still celebrated in South Africa and, until 1952, the day was known as Dingaan's Day; in that year, however, it was given the more suitable title of the Day of the Covenant. The Voortrekkers kept their vow to build a church. This was erected at Pietermaritzburg, and though for several generations it was allowed to fall into disrepair and, at one time, served as a tea room, it has now been restored and is known as the Church of the Vow. Nor was this restoration the only act of piety. Recently more than a century after the event, the Dutch Reformed Church has established a mission station less than a mile from the spot where Retief and his men were slain. On this station, known as Dingaanstat, Afrikaner missionaries train Zulu evangelists and run an orphanage, a school, and a clinic for Zulu children.

News of the victory at Blood River was received with great rejoicing at the trekker camp under the Drakensberg, and trekkers at once began to move down towards Pietermaritzburg to stake out farms. But Pretorius and the Volksraad knew that Natal did not yet belong to them and that two obstacles still remained: there were British troops in Port Natal; and, though Dingaan had been heavily defeated, his power was not yet broken.

The Governor at the Cape, and the British Government

in London, had not known how to deal with the large-scale emigration from the Cape Colony. Sir Benjamin D'Urban had forbidden unauthorized trekking but was powerless to stop it; and in 1836 the British Parliament had passed the Cape of Good Hope Punishment Act which, in effect, declared that however far the emigrants might trek they would still remain British subjects. Sir George Napier, who succeeded D'Urban in 1838, tried to induce trekkers to return to the Colony but failed. He was afraid that war in Natal might, as it had done in the past, have repercussions right up to the eastern boundary of the Cape Colony, and so he persuaded the British government to allow him to occupy Port Natal as a precaution. Thus, while Pretorius was riding to Blood River, Major Charters and 100 troops of the 72nd Highlanders landed at Durban, where he installed Captain Jervis in command before returning to the Cape.

Jervis, whose mission was to try to maintain the peace between Boers and Zulus, persuaded both parties to meet in Durban to discuss terms. Here it was agreed that the Tugela River would be the boundary between Zululand and Natal, that neither side would cross the frontier, and that Dingaan would restore stolen guns, cattle, and horses. The Volksraad subsequently, unknown to Jervis, altered the boundary from the Tugela to the Black Umfulosi, which meant that Dingaan would lose half his country.

Dingaan was beginning to carry out his side of the bargain when an unexpected event altered the whole situation in favour of the Boers: Panda, Dingaan's half-brother, deserted him, and with a large following of Zulu, offered to assist the trekkers against Dingaan. The offer was accepted and a bargain struck: a Boer commando together with Panda's regiments would invade Zululand, depose Dingaan and make Panda king; in return, Panda would accept the treaty made with Dingaan and would pay an indemnity of 40,000 head of cattle, twice the number mentioned in that treaty.

Only one thing prevented the immediate execution of this plan: the presence of British troops; and that difficulty was removed in December 1839. Napier had failed to persuade the British government to annex Natal, and hearing of the agreement between the Boers and Panda, decided that it would be best not to involve British troops in any trouble between Boers and Zulu. He therefore recalled Jervis and the Highlanders. Thus it came about that, after two years of war and negotiation between Boers and Zulus, Dingaan's power was broken by a combined Boer and Zulu force. A trekker commando under Pretorius, and Zulu regiments under Nongalasa, Panda's general, invaded Zululand, put Dingaan to flight, proclaimed Panda king of the Zulu, took formal possession of half of Zululand, and captured 65,000 head of cattle and 1,000 Zulu children, who were to be apprenticed to trekkers. The Voortrekkers who had followed Piet Retief across the Drakensberg had achieved their state at last. But they were not to keep it for long.

Chapter Nine

THE WANDERERS

By the beginning of 1840 British troops had left Port Natal, Dingaan had been overthrown, and his successor, Panda, was a vassal of the Boers. It looked, therefore, as if the state of which Piet Retief had dreamed might at last take shape in the Republic of Natal. Within three years, however, British troops were back, and within six, Natal had been annexed by Great Britain. In 1840, incidentally, Britain acquired another colony in the southern hemisphere, when Captain Hobson signed the Treaty of Waitangi by which Maori chiefs agreed to become subjects of the Queen.

The annexation of Natal was not due simply to the supposed determination of Britain that her Voortrekker subjects should not escape her, as the Israelites had escaped Pharaoh. There were stronger reasons than that. Several ships, a few Dutch and one American, had put in to Port Natal to trade, and Cape merchants became anxious lest Durban, in foreign hands, should threaten Cape Town's commercial supremacy. Moreover, one of the Dutch ships contained Smellekamp, agent for a Dutch trading firm, who deluded Boers in Natal and on the high veld into believing that the Dutch King would come to their aid; the British Government took for granted that Smellekamp was a French agent. Finally, important in the new age of steam, coal had been discovered in Natal.

Even so it is doubtful whether, in the 1840's, these would have been sufficient reasons for annexation. The most important reason is to be found in the internal South African situation: a disturbed and always inflammable eastern frontier of the Cape Colony, and, behind the African tribes on that frontier, a Boer Republic whose policies and actions might easily set tribal and border wars in motion. That factor was always prominent in the minds of Governors at the Cape on whose advice the Secretary of State for Colonies depended. And it was the weakness rather than the strength of the Boer Republic that made its policies and actions dangerous. From the beginning the Republic suffered from internal weakness, while at the same time it was being called on to deal with problems that had defied governments at the Cape, and were to defy all future governments in South Africa.

There were many reasons for Natal's weakness. Most of the citizens of the Republic were skilled in border warfare but ignorant of the arts of establishing a State; they gave their loyalty to small units, the family or the clan, and this often involved disloyalty to a larger unit; their self-reliance and rugged individualism could, and frequently did, turn into anti-social behaviour. Inexperience in government showed itself in the inability to construct a constitution that was stable and could avert clashes between the Volksraad and the Commandant-General; this weakness bedevilled the Republic of Natal and was later to hamper the government of the Transvaal. Disloyalty was a constant bugbear to the leaders and took the form of splinter parties, desertion from commando, and refusal to obey orders. Anti-social behaviour showed itself in the unseemly scramble for cattle, for land, and even for African captive 'apprentices' after a campaign. The members of the Voortrekker Maatskappy (Company) were, in fact, what they and their fathers had been in the old Cape Colony, and it was to take many years before they were welded into a compact society. They were disunited on most things, even on whether or not to resist British annexation. What they had in common, as pastoralists, they had brought with them from the Cape: a desire for plenty of land, plenty of cattle, and cheap labour. By its very nature this common desire led to disunity. George Washington had had to deal with two of these weaknesses, disloyalty to the larger unit and anti-social behaviour; and, with Piet Retief gone, there was no one of similar calibre to lead the trekkers as Washington had led the American colonists.

Ignorance of political arithmetic and inability to cope with wayward subiects in the matter of land kept the Republic financially weak. Men who had grown up in the frontier tradition regarded plenty of land as a man's birthright, and when the Boers had conquered Natal their first action was to allocate land to burghers of the Republic, which meant any male over the age of fifteen; widows of those who had died in action were not forgotten, and Piet Retief's widow received three farms of the usual 6,000 acres each and a plot of land in the village of Pietermaritzburg. Most burghers got one farm, but many had two or three, and the Commandant-general had no fewer than ten. These farms were free grants in perpetuity on payment of a nominal annual fee of about one pound, and on condition that they were occupied, a condition that was seldom enforced. Further, since land-surveying was non-existent and the Volksraad at Pietermaritzburg too weak to enforce its own rules, a good deal of unauthorized land-grabbing and speculation took place.

Land, which was the main economic asset of the Republic, was thus recklessly squandered. What in a monarchy is called Crown land practically ceased to exist, and government had to depend on what small revenue it could collect from customs duties and fees and fines. The Volksraad did, indeed, have a scheme for gradual and rational occupation of vacant land; but it found itself in much the same position as the old government at the Cape with regard to the trekboers: neither the government at the Castle in Cape Town nor the Volksraad in Pietermaritzburg was able to control its more distant subjects. So the Volksraad was perpetually short of money, and the salary of the commandant-general, £75 a year, was normally in arrear.

It is possible that the Republic might, given time, have overcome these constitutional and financial difficulties. That it was not granted time was due to its other great weakness: the inability to deal with the problem of boundaries. Here again, the situation was not unlike the one they had left behind them in the Cape frontier districts. Dutch and British governments in Cape Town had been unable to prevent trekboers from trekking ever further afield until they came up against African tribes: and they had been unable to prevent their subjects from crossing boundaries to hunt, trade, recover stolen cattle, or raid for cattle. On the other side of the border, no African chief was strong enough to prevent his followers from doing the same.

It was the same story in Natal. The Volksraad in Pietermaritzburg and Panda in his royal kraal might issue decrees that no one was to cross the Tugela or the Umzimvubu; but frontiersmen were not accustomed to obey such laws, and Panda the Zulu had no more authority than Gaika the Xhosa. The Boers had, with some justification, laughed at British efforts to make treaties with Kaffir chiefs; but they themselves, in Natal and on the high veld, made many such treaties and found them equally useless for maintaining peace on the frontier. Cattle raids and hunting parties went on merrily. Worse still, there were raids from which Boers returned with Zulu orphans to be apprenticed. This system of so-called 'apprenticeship' was common in the days of raids on Bushmen in the Cape, and it was close to slavery. Knowing Britain's attitude to slavery, the Volksraad genuinely tried both to stop the raids and protect 'apprentices', but it lacked the strength to execute its own orders.

To complicate matters, thousands of Zulus poured into Natal to graze their cattle, as fugitives from Panda, or to work on Boer farms. By 1842 there were at least seven times as many Zulus as Boers in Natal proper, and the Volksraad was unable to cope with this problem except by the old and ineffective pass laws of the Cape Colony. Finally, though Panda had been put on his throne by a combined Boer and

Zulu force, and was a vassal of the Republic, there was always the danger of a Zulu invasion of Natal.

It was not from its northern boundary, however, that the Republic's chief difficulties came. The Boers claimed that, under the treaty between Retief and Dingaan, the Umzimvubu River was their southern boundary; and in accordance with their general policy that Africans not employed on European farms were not allowed to live in Natal, the Volksraad decided to push Pondo and Baca tribesmen south of the Umzimvubu. It was the usual border story. Complaints of cattle theft reached the Volksraad, and in December 1840 Pretorius led a strong commando south. On somewhat flimsy evidence he attacked a Baca chief, Ncapaai, killed thirty of his tribesmen and captured 3,000 head of cattle and seventeen orphan children to be apprenticed. Pretorius had gone beyond his instructions, as so many commandos in the Cape had done, but the Volksraad was unable to dismiss so popular a commandant-general. A year later, when the Boers were on the point of putting into force their policy of driving out Pondo and Baca who were not in employment, the Governor of the Cape Colony, Napier, told the Volksraad that since such action was likely to cause tribal wars and affect the eastern frontier, British troops would be landed at Durban.

In May 1842 the troops, under Captain Smith, arrived, and for the next three and a half years the Republic of Natal led an uneasy existence. The Boers had protested against the decision to send troops and against Napier's assumption that they were still British subjects, and they now prepared to resist. Pretorius established a camp at Congella, about four miles from the British camp near the harbour, and when Smith attacked him the Boers drove the British off with considerable loss. With great courtesy and humanity, not often seen in war, Pretorius did not follow up his advantage but allowed the British to bury their dead and tend their wounded, many of whom had been captured and returned to the British lines. A few days later a Boer patrol rushed the British sentries at the harbour, captured most of Smith's stores, including an 18-pounder, and took a number of prisoners.

Some hours before this last event a young Englishman and his Zulu servant, Dick King and Ndongeni, cut off on the Point, had swum their horses across to a small island in the bay from which they were able to reach the mainland. Hiding by day and travelling by night until they were out of Boer territory, they made for Grahamstown, 600 miles away. Ndongeni did not finish the journey, probably because, being a Zulu, he was afraid to enter Xhosa territory; but Dick King, with courage, skill and endurance, reached Grahamstown in nine days and raised the alarm. Troops from both Port Elizabeth and Cape Town were sent at once to relieve Smith, and the Boers were compelled to agree to a truce.

For another year there was an uneasy peace between the Boers and the British and uncertainty about the future of Natal. The British Government had not yet made up its mind to annex Natal, and among the Boers there was division between those who favoured complete surrender to Britain and those who, hoping for intervention from Holland and help from the high veld, wanted to resist. The administration of the Volksraad was rapidly disintegrating. Too poor and weak for effective government in times of peace, it was unable to face a prolonged war against Britain. Salaries remained unpaid; a few Boers had begun to trek back over the Drakensberg to the high veld, and those who remained were divided; the authority of the Volksraad and its officials was openly flouted; and the Zulu kept on coming into Natal.

At last, in July 1843, the Secretary of State for Colonies, Lord Stanley, decided on annexation and instructed Napier to send a commissioner to Natal to discuss with the Volksraad the future form of government. For more than two years the commissioner, Henry Cloete, negotiated with the Boers in the hopes of getting them to accept British rule.

He held public meetings, and private sessions with the dying Volksraad; he received private deputations and answered their questions; on one occasion he had a stormy interview with a deputation of women, led by the wife of Erasmus Smit the preacher, who told him that the Boer women would rather walk barefoot over the Drakensberg than submit once more to a British rule under which there was no distinction between black and white.

And so the Boer Republic of Natal, bravely begun in 1839, dragged to a pathetic close. The treasury was empty, the people were divided, and a Zulu invasion was held back only by the presence of the hated British troops. Those who had decided to stay in Natal hoped for some form of representative government and for secure title to their farms; those who were determined, if they could not resist, to leave, hoped to find a new home on the high veld. And each party called the other traitor. At length, in August 1845, the Republic was put out of its misery and Natal was formally annexed by Great Britain as a dependency of the Cape Colony, to be governed by a lieutenant-governor and an official executive council. Pretorius and many of the original Voortrekkers abandoned Natal and trekked back to the high veld to join their friends; but many of the Boers remained in Natal and became British subjects. And, as a sign that governments may change but the problems remain, one of the first despatches of the new lieutenant-governor asked for more troops to deal with increasing Zulu 'depredations'!

Back on the high veld, all trekkers belonged, in theory, to one Maatskappy or Company whose object was to establish one single republic. Actually there were a number of separate groups: one centred on the village of Potchefstroom, north of the Vaal River, where Hendrik Potgieter, who had refused to follow Retief into Natal, held sway; Winburg was the centre of another group whose territory lay between the Vet and Vaal rivers; and a third, rather nondescript, group lived just north of the Orange River boundary of the Cape Colony, and consisted of a few genuine trekkers together with a host of Boers who had simply settled there on land bought or hired from two Griqua chiefs, Adam Kok and Waterboer, with no idea of escaping from British rule. This area was known as Transorangia. In the south-east of the present Free State is the Caledon River, and beyond that Moshesh ruled the Basuto nation; and numbers of Boers had settled on the banks of the Caledon, on land claimed by Moshesh. The Barolong, under their chief Moroko, were at Thaba Nchu.

In 1840 Pretorius tried to bring Natal, Potchefstroom and Winburg under one authority. A treaty was made between Natal and Potchefstroom by which the Volksraad at Pietermaritzburg was recognized as supreme and an Adjunct-Raad at Potchefstroom was to be responsible under Natal for the high veld, though not tor Transorangia, an area of which genuine trekkers washed their hands. Having achieved this unity on paper the Volksraad opened negotiations with the Governor at the Cape for the recognition of their independence. As we know, this was withheld.

Conditions on the high veld were as chaotic as in Natal. Personal rivalries, indiscriminate occupation of farms, cattle raids on the borders, disputes with African and Griqua chiefs, a penniless government unable to enforce its own laws, uncertainty whether the British Government would acknowledge their independence, and, indeed, division as to whether they wanted that independence at all—all these were characteristic of the Voortrekker groups on the high veld. Having trekked from the Cape Colony they did indeed find more land; but they had not escaped the problems that arise from an unstable frontier society surrounded by African tribes.

Into this sea of troubles beyond the Orange River boundary the British Government ventured but gingerly. Natal was one thing, but the high veld with its scattered groups of Boers, Griqua, Basuto, Barolong, and other tribes was another. During the Natal negotiations Britain had made it clear that any agreement covered Natal only and not the high veld, where her policy was to make treaties with Griqua and African chiefs and to continue to regard all Boers as British subjects. The reply of the Boers, in April 1844, was to elect a Burgher Council at Potchefstroom, declare themselves independent, and promulgate a constitution known as the Thirty-Three Articles. Potgieter was

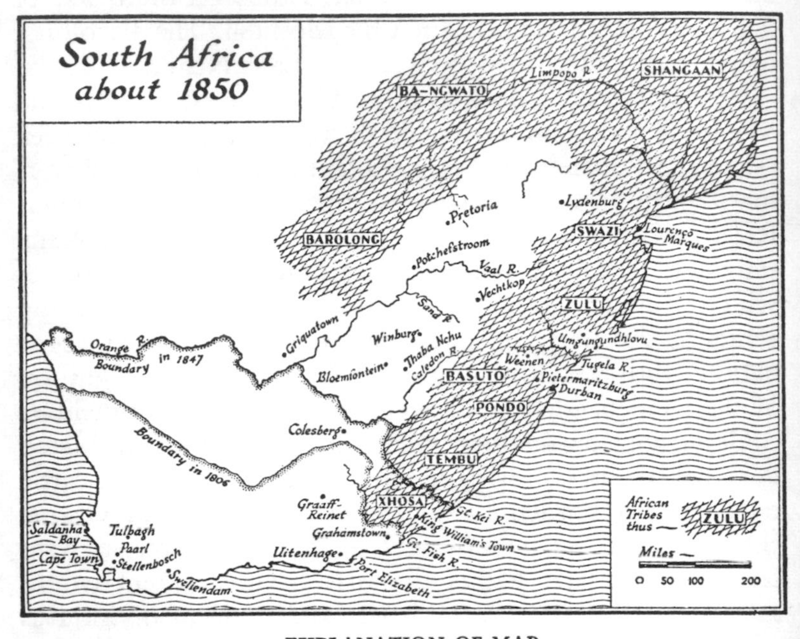

EXPLANATION OF MAP

This map shows South Africa in (about) 1850. The frontier of the Cape Colony had expanded to the Orange and Kei rivers. North of the Orange River there were scattered tribes and remnants of tribes from Chaka's wars. The high veld, frequently referred to in the description of the Great Trek, is (roughly) the area between the Orange River and a line running from Pretoria to Lydenburg. North of that line is low veld, and east of the Transvaal and Free State is the Drakensberg range which separates the high veld from Natal and the coast.

Commandant-general of this new Republic on the high veld to which many Natalians soon began to trek.

Britain's treaties with the Griqua chiefs, Adam Kok and Waterboer, virtually placed those Boers living on Griqua land under their jurisdiction. This was bound to lead to trouble, and in 1845 it did. Adam Kok sent a troop of Griqua to arrest a Boer called Krynauw who, disregarding Kok's authority, had had two African servants flogged. They could not find Krynauw but broke into his house and took guns and ammunition, and the immediate result was a fight between Boers and Griqua, and the despatch of troops by the Governor of the Cape, Maitland, to restore peace. So, for the first time, British troops appeared on the high veld, drawn thither by typical frontier troubles. Having restored peace, Maitland realized that it could not be permanent as long as Boers remained under Griqua authority, so he persuaded the chiefs to sell the land on which Boers were living and left Major Warden as resident commissioner in charge of the area, with headquarters on the site of the present Bloemfontein. Three years later the new Governor, Sir Harry Smith, proclaimed the whole territory between the Orange and Vaal rivers as a British sovereignty.

Meanwhile, Andries Pretorius, who had left Natal after the annexation, had been looking for a chance to assume leadership of the trekkers on the high veld. He now raised a commando, marched on Bloemfontein, and evicted Warden; but Sir Harry Smith soon returned with more troops, decisively defeated the Boers at Boomplaats, and restored Warden to authority.

Warden soon found, as Boers and Britons had found in Natal, and were to find throughout southern Africa, that frontier problems were always present. In drawing the boundary between the Orange River Sovereignty and Basutoland, he cut off from Basutoland several petty chiefs who owed allegiance to Moshesh. Trouble arose and Warden sent in a small detachment of troops to maintain British authority. The troops were defeated, and in 1852 Sir George

Cathcart, Governor of the Cape, arrived with 2,500 men to teach Moshesh a lesson. He failed to subdue the Basuto and was, in fact, himself on the verge of defeat, when the wise Moshesh sent him a diplomatic letter saying that Cathcart had shown how strong he was and should now be merciful and grant peace. Cathcart was glad to accept this opening to call off a war in which victory seemed doubtful.

Britain's belated and fitful entrance into high veld politics was not destined to last for long. Political changes in Britain had brought to power the Little Englanders who regarded imperialism as unprofitable, and it was soon clear that the British Government was anxious to withdraw from her commitments beyond the Orange River. The Voortrekkers on the high veld were a widely scattered community, poor except in land and cattle, difficult to tax and expensive to govern, and Britain decided to leave them to their own devices. Negotiations with Boer leaders were opened to this end, and in 1852 the Sand River Convention recognized Boer independence beyond the Vaal River, and in 1854 the Bloemfontein Convention did the same for Boers living between the Orange and the Vaal.

This was the end of the Great Trek, and the beginning of the two Boer republics that were to last for another fifty years before the descendants of the trekkers once more became British subjects. The Voortrekkers had hoped to establish one state; instead, they had established two, the Orange Free State and the Transvaal, whose official title was the South African Republic. Indeed, it was not until twelve years after Britain had withdrawn from the Transvaal that the trekkers in that area were able to compose their internal quarrels and establish a single state. The tendency of trekkers to give their personal loyalty to leaders rather than to the community was so strong in the Transvaal that, on two occasions at least, it led to a minor civil war. At one stage there were four little republics across the Vaal; and all attempts to unite the Transvaal and the Orange Free State failed.

The two-newly born republics were sparsely populated. The Free State had between fifteen and twenty thousand European inhabitants, men, women and children, and the Transvaal probably slightly more than twenty-five thousand; and it is impossible to estimate how many Africans there were within the borders of the republics. Much of the land occupied by the trekkers was vacant land which they held by treaties with African chiefs or by right of conquest. Where the Boers found tribes in actual occupation they usually left them undisturbed: but there can be no doubt that many thousands of Africans became landless as a result of Boer occupation. To the African the possession of land meant its use, and to the European it meant physical possession, the right to ownership; and many Africans who, under customary tribal law, had sound title to the land they were living on, lost that title under European law.

When Britain abandoned her authority over the trekkers most of them had, for almost twenty years, led a nomadic and uncertain existence. Even where they had settled and built primitive mud houses their tenure was insecure and their political future uncertain. Few men and women under thirty could recall a time when danger from wild animals, war against African tribes, quarrels over leadership, and talk of war against the British were not part of their daily lives. They had little if any education, and the parent Dutch Reformed Church of the Cape was only just beginning to catch up with them. And their experience of laws and administration was small.

The Voortrekkers carried the social and economic habits of the eighteenth century into the nineteenth. They were not progressive farmers determined to force the land to yield as much as possible. Land had been plentiful in eighteenth-century Cape Colony, and when it became scarce they trekked to where it was once more plentiful. They trekked away from the settled agriculture of the Cape and from contact with Western civilization; and the jump was so big that the lines of communication of those who trekked farthest north from the base of Western civilization in South Africa became unduly stretched.

In the Transvaal most of the political and economic weaknesses that could have been expected in such circumstances were to be found: rugged individualism amounting to a disregard for law and order: economic backwardness from which the Republic was rescued only by the discovery of gold; and a rigidness of outlook in religious, social, and political matters that was unable to adapt itself to nineteenth-century ideas. The Orange Free State was more fortunate in that it was closer to the Cape and in more continuous touch with the base of Western civilization. It drew many of its civil servants and judges, and its most statesmanlike President, from the Cape; and it attracted professional and commercial men, largely of British stock, to its towns and villages. The result was that the Free State became a settled state in a remarkably short time, while the Transvaal retained for many years much of the frontier mentality.

The results of the Great Trek were profound. By withdrawing about a quarter of the Dutch-speaking population from the Cape it gave British ideas and institutions a chance to become firmly established in the Colony. During a short period of twenty years it established three new States and opened up great tracts of land to European occupation. It brought large numbers of Africans under European control and deprived them of their customary land; it also, in due course, brought European law and order where there had been tribal warfare. It opened up southern Africa to Western civilization, with all its blessings and curses, and thus dealt a crippling blow to African tribal society. It established, in the two Republics, the principle that there would be no equality between black and white either in church or state.

Finally, the Great Trek and the policies followed towards it by Britain widened the gulf between Britain and her former Dutch subjects and brought into being a distinctive European nation, the Afrikaner people. Largely republican in outlook, speaking their own language which was derived from Dutch, and firmly wedded to their Calvinist church, the Afrikaner people took national root in the two republics; and when, at the end of the nineteenth century, they were conquered by Britain in the Anglo-Boer War, the roots were so firmly established that the nation survived even the shock of utter defeat.

By the middle of the nineteenth century the Great Trek had balkanized South Africa by establishing four distinct political entities and dividing the European population; and all this had happened in less than a generation. Instead of slow and steady expansion there had been one rapid jump; and a hundred years later South Africa has not yet recovered from the effects.

Chapter Ten

NEW POLICIES AT THE CAPE

Between the years 1830 and 1860 European civilization was spreading rapidly but painfully thinly over South Africa and was coming into contact with African tribalism on a far larger scale than on the eastern frontier of the Cape Colony. And while a new European nation was being born in South Africa, great changes were taking place in the Europe from which it had sprung. In 1830 Belgium, a future European power in Africa, became independent of Holland; and Louis Philippe's 'bankers' government' had been set up in France. In the first months of 1848 half the princes of Europe lost their crowns by revolution and the rest were compelled hastily to grant constitutions to their subjects; France entered, uneasily and by way of a republic, into the Second Empire of Napoleon III; across the Rhine, Bismarck began to plan German unity under Prussia and at the expense of France and Austria, and of political freedom; and across the Alps Mazzini, Garibaldi and Cavour had set their feet on the rough road to Italian unity. And everywhere railways and telegraph wires were ushering in a new and strident age.

Britain did not escape these revolutions: industrially she led them; and politically she managed in her own way to accomplish them without civil war. She became the asylum for exiled rulers and revolutionaries impartially; Karl Marx freely prepared in the British Museum the social dynamite that was later to be used on the Continent. But Britain paid the price, in slums and social misery, for industrial leadership, and during the first half of Queen Victoria's reign was taking the steps which were intended to correct the worst results of industrialization and which led, inevitably, to the modern welfare State. 'Investigate, report, legislate', was the Utilitarian motto enthusiastically adopted by reformers from the 1830's onwards, and it produced the Factory Acts and other great pieces of social legislation that justified the title of 'a century of reform'. Social reform by legislation requires an adequate and well-trained administrative service, and this too was beginning to take shape in early Victorian England. It was a public service that acquired a reputation for honesty and impartiality which made it the envy of Europe, and through the Colonial Office it was exported to British colonies. Next to parliamentary institutions this may well be regarded as Britain's greatest gift to her colonies.

Britain was, however, exporting more than a system of administration. It was Gibbon Wakefield who convinced Britons that planned emigration to the colonies was the remedy for over-population, and it is largely due to his inspiration and energy that hundreds of thousands of Britons settled in New Zealand, Australia, and Canada. During the years 1841 and 1842 alone, when Boers were leaving the Cape Colony in large numbers, 62,000 Britons emigrated to Canada, 80,000 to the United States, 18,600 to Australia and New Zealand, and 340 to the Cape.[1] Canadian wheat and New Zealand mutton found a ready market in Britain, and Australian wool, produced from merino sheep originally imported from the Cape by Macarthur, far outstripped the South African both in quality and quantity.

In the 1830's, too, British opinion towards colonies was changing. Until the American War of Independence colonies were regarded as useful only in so far as they served the mother country. The lessons which England drew from the successful revolt of her American colonies were that all colonies were a risky investment and that existing colonies should on no account be given freedom lest they abuse it in order to become independent. This was the prevailing view

[1] G. E. Cory, *The Rise of South Africa*, Vol. IV, p. 391 n.

in Britain when, in 1837, rebellions broke out in Upper and Lower Canada. The British government suspended the Canadian constitutions and sent Lord Durham, with Gibbon Wakefield as adviser, to Canada to investigate.

The Durham Report, published in 1839, laid the foundation for a new British colonial policy that has lasted to the present time. Durham pointed out that the American colonists revolted because they did not have enough freedom, not because they had too much, and the lesson to be drawn from that was that colonies should be given more freedom, not less. He advised that, as soon as possible, Canada be given full responsible government; and what was true for Canada was true for other colonies. Within twenty years of the Durham Report New Zealand, Tasmania, the Canadian colonies, and with the exception of the sparsely populated Western Australia, the Australian colonies, had all been granted responsible government.

For reasons that were discussed in Chapter Six, the main stream of emigration from Britain passed South Africa by. There were reasons, too, why the new colonial policy was slower to take effect at the Cape than in other British colonies. The population of the Cape was small, scattered, and lacked cohesion. Of the total of about 120,000 more than half consisted of recently liberated slaves or illiterate Coloured people; and the European population was divided into English and Dutch who had not yet learned to co-operate in public affairs and had little experience of representative institutions. There was discord between the west and the east, between Cape Town and Grahamstown; since the arrival of British settlers and the exodus of Boers, the eastern districts were largely English, but this did not alter the belief of the frontier districts that the government in Cape Town neither understood their difficulties nor cared about their interests.

The problem of a boundary between black and white had not been solved. Border raids and cattle thieving were still the order of the day and led, during the period we are considering, to two more Kaffir wars. British settlers were no less insistent than Boers that the fault lay with the African tribes, and that outright annexation was the best possible solution. A prominent settler, Bowker, said in a speech that just as the land had been cleared of springbuck to make room for sheep, it should be cleared of Kaffirs to make room for good farming. However much opinion in Britain had been influenced by the Durham Report, the British government would not approve such a policy. Meanwhile, the frontier had to be defended; and since the commando system had broken down, British troops, paid for by British taxpayers, were stationed in the frontier districts. Cape revenue that was too small to pay for its own defence was also too small as a basis for responsible government; and capital that flowed easily to other colonies was shy of the Cape.

These hindrances to constitutional development gradually disappeared. The establishment in 1836 of elected Boards of Commissioners to deal with local affairs, and a few years later of school committees and road boards, provided much-needed experience in working representative institutions. The habit, made popular in Britain by the Evangelicals, of holding public meetings, publishing pamphlets, and drawing up petitions, spread to the Cape, and aided by a vigorous press in Cape Town and Grahamstown, went to create that public opinion without which there can be no real representative government. A steady increase in the production and export of wool helped to improve revenue. And, finally, from 1847 the British Government began to abandon the policy of treaties with tribal chiefs, and annexed the land between the Fish and the Keiskama as the district of Victoria East, and between the Keiskama and the Kei as a separate colony called British Kaffraria. Into these areas magistrates were sent to govern the tribes.

Dutch and English colonists were learning to live and work together, and as if to strengthen co-operation and to test it, the British Government decided in 1849 to make the

Cape a penal settlement. There was an immediate uproar. Dutch and English combined to send protests to the Queen, to establish an Anti-Convict League, and to use public meetings and the press in an agitation such as the Cape had not seen before. Differences between east and west were, for the moment, forgotten. When the government persisted and sent out the *Neptune* with 282 convicts, chiefly Irish political prisoners, the agitation reached new heights. Farmers and shopkeepers boycotted the ship; four of the nominated members of the Legislative Council, and many officials, resigned; and when the Governor, Sir Harry Smith, appointed others in their place, rioting broke out in Cape Town and the Council was prevented from sitting. Eventually the British Government gave way and the *Neptune* sailed for Van Diemen's Land, while grateful Capetonians renamed their principal street after Adderley, the British M.P. who had successfully pleaded their cause in the House of Commons.

Even before the anti-convict agitation had provided such an impressive demonstration of the growth of public opinion at the Cape, petitions had from time to time been sent to London asking for representative government, and in 1846 Lord John Russell's Whig Government had accepted the principle. Various draft constitutions were put forward from the Cape, but a change of government in London and another Kaffir war delayed proceedings until 1853, when a constitution was finally approved. It provided for a House of Assembly and a Legislative Council, both elected by males, irrespective of colour, who earned £50 a year or owned property with a rentable value of £25 a year. The Governor had power to dissolve Parliament, to veto legislation, or to reserve it for the approval or disapproval of the Crown; and the Executive Council consisted of officials who were responsible, not to parliament, but to the governor.

This was representative and not responsible government. Under responsible government the Governor is titular head of the State and has no power to prevent legislation; and the executive, or cabinet, consists of members of Parliament who are responsible to Parliament and retain office as long as they have the support of the majority. The same reasons that delayed the granting of representative government at the Cape delayed the advent of full responsible government. Frontier problems still persisted obstinately; the Cape was not self-supporting but depended on Britain to cover deficits; and Britain was reluctant to institute responsible

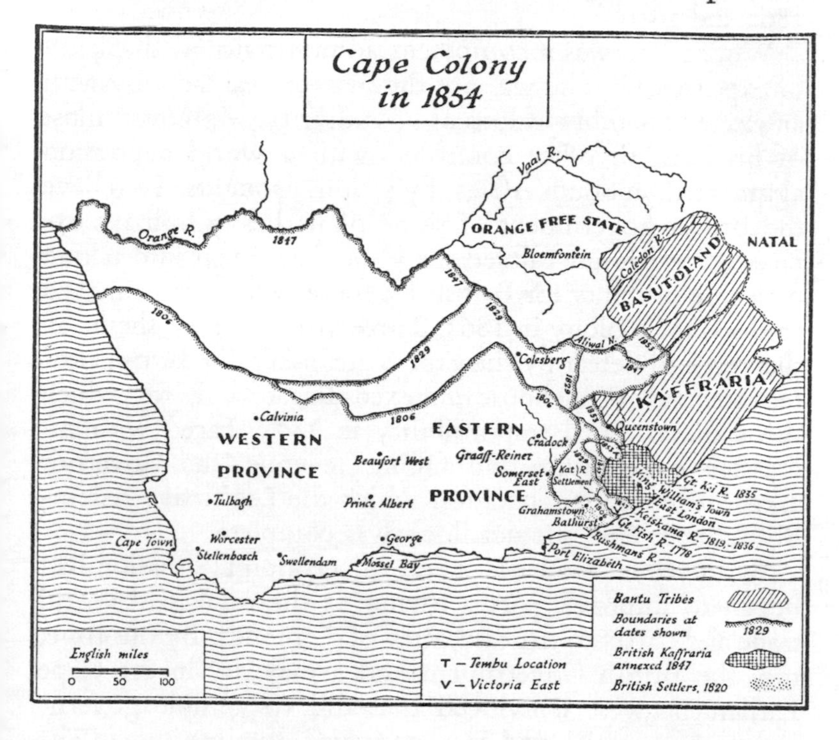

government in a colony where the numerically weaker Europeans were politically and economically so much stronger than the non-Europeans.

Nevertheless, it was only a matter of time before these difficulties would become less formidable or would, at any rate, appear so in comparison with the more serious difficulty of a clash between Parliament and the executive. Under representative government that clash was bound to come. As long as times were good, and the popular Sir George Grey was Governor, executive and legislative worked in reasonable harmony. But when a strong-minded governor disallows legislation passed by an elected parliament, and when that parliament in reply refuses to vote supplies, administration is brought to a standstill. This is what happened during the governorship of Sir Philip Wodehouse between 1862 and 1870.

Wodehouse was a competent administrator with plenty of experience but he was not the man to deal tactfully with an elected assembly jealous of its authority. Moreover, most of his term of office coincided with a world depression aggravated, in South Africa, by serious droughts. To relieve the British government of some of its heavy military expenses Wodehouse cajoled the Cape Parliament into taking over responsibility for British Kaffraria, which was annexed to the Cape Colony in 1865. Three years later Moshesh, on the verge of defeat by the Free State, asked for British protection, and Wodehouse annexed Basutoland, for which the Cape assumed responsibility in 1871. Faced with increasing expenditure and falling revenue, the Governor asked for additional taxation which the Legislative Assembly refused. And the deadlock was complete.

By the time Wodehouse left the economic situation had begun to improve, partly owing to the revival of world trade and partly to the discovery of diamonds. By this time, too, the British Government and a majority in the Cape Parliament were convinced that full responsible government was essential, and in 1872 it was duly instituted. The Cape Parliament was now master in its own house. The cabinet was responsible to parliament and the governor was bound to act on the advice of his ministers in all internal matters, as a constitutional monarch does. John (afterwards Sir John) Molteno, a farmer from the Beaufort West district who had for many years taken the lead in demanding responsible government, became the first Prime Minister at the Cape. The governor at the Cape was, at the same time, Her Majesty's High Commissioner for South Africa. This was a position of great and growing importance since the Cape's affairs with other South African states were conducted by the High Commissioner.

Through most of the nineteenth century Europeans everywhere in southern Africa were extending their political control and Africans were fighting to defend their tribal lands against the white invaders. The Boers had trekked away from the uneasy eastern frontier of the Cape only to establish many thousand more miles of boundary and to extend greatly the area in which black and white fought for possession of the land. And on the frontier the Boers had left behind them, the British government vainly tried to keep the peace by making treaties with African chiefs.

Drought, poor harvests, and a plague of locusts in 1845 prepared the way for the seventh Kaffir War. Cattle raids increased and became more daring, and in 1846 Colonel Hare and 1,500 men entered Xhosa territory to compel the chief, Sandili, to surrender some wanted men. Hare was ambushed and defeated, and the triumphant Xhosa invaded the Colony; but after some initial success in destroying farms and driving off cattle, they were expelled and compelled to come to terms. The Governor, Sir Harry Smith, was determined to make an end of the treaty system, and having annexed land as far as the Kei River, he summoned the chiefs and offered them the choice between the staff of peace and the staff of war. Sir Harry was always dramatic. A wagon-load of gunpowder had been prepared, and at a given signal was blown up before the eyes of the astonished chiefs. 'There go the treaties. Do you hear? No more treaties,' Sir Harry announced.

It was not quite the end of all treaties in South Africa; many more were to be made and broken. But it did begin a new policy of the eastern frontier, a policy that may be summed up as: annexation and a reduction of tribal land; magistrates, police, missionaries, and traders; the gradual decline of the authority of chiefs. In other words, it was a policy of ruling by peaceful means as an alternative to constant border wars.

The Xhosa were defeated for the moment only, and they could not have been expected to regard the new policy with enthusiasm even though it might be for their ultimate good. In 1850 the eighth Kaffir War broke out when a witch-doctor, Mlanjeni, assured the Xhosa that his charms would turn aside white bullets. It was the longest of all the Kaffir wars, and during it the troopship *Birkenhead* was wrecked on its way to East London with reinforcements. But despite this and other setbacks, including bad organization, the result was a foregone conclusion: by 1853 all the chiefs had surrendered.

Three years later witchcraft played an even more fatal part in tribal affairs. A tribal witch-doctor, Mhlakaza, lived on the banks of a small stream, the Gxara, which flows into the Kei River near its mouth. In this stream was a dark pool, set in a banana grove and constantly disturbed by the ocean tides; and next this pool Mhlakaza's niece, a young girl named Nongqause, sat by the hour seeing visions and hearing the prophecies of ancestral voices. These visions were interpreted by the witch-doctor, and the rumour began to spread that the dead chiefs were prophesying that, on a given day, they and their dead warriors would arise and help the black man to drive the white man out of the country. But first the black men must slaughter all their cattle and destroy their grain. When that condition was fulfilled the great day would arrive; a blood-red sun would arise and return to the east in the afternoon; a hurricane would sweep away the white man; and dead warriors, with plenty of fat cattle and grain, would arise to join their people.

These rumours came at a time when the morale of the African tribesmen was low. They had been defeated in war, their land had been taken from them, and to add to their misery, a cattle disease had decimated their herds. It is little wonder that a superstition-ridden people, in desperate straits, regarded these prophecies with both fear and hope. Chiefs sent their own witch-doctors to Nongqause to find out for themselves. Some of them reported that they had seen nothing in the pool but banana leaves disturbed by wind and tide; but most of them returned to their chiefs convinced of the truth of the prophecies. Efforts of missionaries and officials were successful in persuading individual sub-tribes and chiefs to pay no heed, but the majority of Xhosa and Tembu tribesmen slaughtered their cattle and scattered their grain. When the day arrived, in February 1857, it found a starving people unfit for war. Thousands of Xhosa poured into the Colony, not as invaders but seeking food and employment. It is estimated that, in spite of government efforts to provide food, 25,000 died of hunger, and the population of British Kaffraria was reduced from over 100,000 to 37,000.

The question naturally arises whether this national suicide of the Xhosa was purely a matter of supersitition or whether those behind it were following a deliberate policy. Superstition is not a matter of reason and it is never possible to say where it begins and ends; Hitler was superstitious, and no one can say for certain what exact part superstition and cool reasoning played in his decisions. Kreli, chief of the Xhosa, was himself deeply under the influence of witch-doctors. We know, too, that he had never been reconciled to the death of his father Hintza or to the loss of his lands, both at the hands of the white invaders, and that he hoped that if his soldiers were reduced to starvation they would fight all the more fiercely. There is strong evidence, too, that Moshesh, chief of the Basuto, was playing a deep game. Realizing that war between Basutoland and the Free State was likely, he was anxious to keep British troops fully occupied in the Cape Colony so that there could be no inconvenient interference between him and the Boers; he therefore sent messengers to egg on the cattle-killing madness.

It is probable that statecraft and witchcraft worked hand

in hand, the one using the other; but it is impossible to say which came first. J. H. Soga, himself an African, describing the incident in his book, *The South-Eastern Bantu*, says: 'It is not Kreli's fault that he was under the compulsion of these beliefs. They were those of his own people. It is hard for one who has been moulded in the spirit of faith in witchcraft, to extricate his mind from such beliefs.'[1]

Even before the cattle-killing episode, Sir George Grey, whose wise and honourable administration earned him such a high reputation in New Zealand, had begun to apply a more positive civilizing policy in British Kaffraria. Grey's reputation in South Africa is, if anything, higher than in New Zealand. He believed that there would be no peace or progress for the African or the European as long as witchcraft and superstition flourished, and he realized how close the alliance between tribal chiefs and witch-doctors was. He also believed that the wisest policy was not merely to annex African territory, but to encourage education, to build hospitals and roads, to promote better farming, and to build up a civil service which would gain the respect and trust of Africans. His was a policy of leading tribesmen from tribalism to Western civilization.

It was many years before this policy was fully carried out or bore fruit. The Kei River was now the eastern boundary, and beyond that, in the Transkei, lived Fingo, remnants of Xhosa tribes, and Tembu. Beyond them again, and on the coast, was Pondo territory; and between the Pondo and the Basutoland mountains were the Griqua under Adam Kok, who had trekked away from the southern Free State, over the precipitous Basutoland mountains, to found a new home for themselves. Beyond Griqualand East and Pondoland lay the British colony of Natal.

[1] Some African pupils believe that the story of Nongqause as told in the history textbooks used in South African schools, is a European invention. What really happened, they say, is that European officials inspired her to tell lies. There is no evidence for this belief and it is an interesting example of how an awakening nationalism can re-tell history to throw a more favourable light on its own past.

Among these tribes and clans there were frequent quarrels and petty tribal wars, but there was only one more serious war against the Cape—the ninth Kaffir War in 1877. Step by step the Cape Government extended its boundary and its authority north-eastwards, and when Pondoland was annexed in 1894, the gap between the Cape Colony and Natal had been closed. The frontier problem, so long the preoccupation of governments and people in the Cape Colony, and no less of the African tribes, had ceased to exist. The trekboers and British settlers had advocated annexation so as to give more land to Europeans; and as far as the Kei River, that policy had partially prevailed. But beyond the Kei a wiser and more liberal policy had been followed: the land was annexed and brought under white administration, but for the most part Africans continued to live on tribal lands, thenceforth known as Reserves. It was the policy of annexation, not in order to dispossess Africans but to bring them under European control.

Chapter Eleven

DISRUPTION AND DEPRESSION

There were times, between 1850 and 1870, when it seemed as if European civilization would not be able to maintain its precarious hold on the interior of South Africa. Everywhere there was internal disunity, or war between white and black, or both. In a dispatch of 1860 Sir George Grey pointed out that small and isolated States were a constant invitation to African tribes to attack; their revenues were too small to provide for adequate protection, for education, or for an efficient administration; trade and commerce were bound to languish, and life and property became insecure. 'South Africa', said Grey, 'appears to be drifting, by not very slow degrees, into disorder and barbarism. . . .' The picture was not overdrawn.

In 1852 Britain had recognized the independence of the Boers north of the Vaal River, and the two rival Voortrekker leaders, Pretorius and Potgieter, had been reconciled. A constitution which provided for an elected Volksraad, a President and an executive council, was drawn up, and Pretoria became the capital of the new South African Republic. But a year later the two veteran leaders died, and their sons reopened old quarrels. When the younger Pretorius was elected President, three of the four districts promptly withdrew from the Republic and formed their own independent States—Lydenburg, Utrecht, and Zoutpansberg—each with its little mud-house village as capital. The Volksraad met from time to time, either in Pretoria or elsewhere, and when it was not interrupted by war against African tribes or broken up by internal dissensions, passed resolutions which few obeyed. There was no civil service and no money to pay for one. The Transvaal was, in fact, a collection of clans and lacked any real form of central government.

Since there was no central authority capable of enforcing law or preventing raids, there was almost perpetual war with tribes on the ill-defined borders. One of the terms of the Sand River Convention had stipulated that there should be no slavery, but in spite of repeated resolutions by the Volksraad, Boers returned from the wars with African children as 'apprentices'. The President himself, Pretorius, wrote to the *landdrost* at Zoutpansberg asking him to 'buy him half a dozen little kaffirs'.[1]

Despite his failure to unite the Transvalers, Pretorius, attempted, in 1857, to claim authority over the Free State, and, supported by a few Free Staters, rode to Bloemfontein for that purpose. The Free State President, Boshof, ordered him to leave; he did, only to return with an invading commando; and the Free State and Transvaal commandos were restrained from fighting only by the moderating influence of Commandant Paul Kruger. Pretorius returned to the Transvaal where he and Kruger persuaded Zoutpansberg to join the South African Republic. Leydenburg and Utrecht remained independent until 1860.

In that year Pretorius, in another attempt to unite the Free State and Transvaal, stood for the Free State presidency and was elected. But during his absence from the Transvaal his personal enemies intrigued against him and persuaded a majority of the Volksraad that he could not be president of both States at the same time; whereupon his friends organized a public meeting, dismissed the Volksraad, and made arrangements for fresh elections. For two uneasy years Pretorius tried to sit on both presidential stools while the Transvaal drifted into civil war. In 1863 he resigned the presidency of the Free State and returned to contest that of the Transvaal; and when the rival candidate, van Rensburg, was

[1] See E. A. Walker, *A History of South Africa*, p. 292, n.

elected, the Pretorius party maintained that the voting papers had been tampered with, and civil war broke out. Paul Kruger, by this time Commandant-general and a staunch constitutionalist, first defeated Pretorius's men and then agreed to hold fresh elections. At these, Pretorius was elected and the Transvaal was, nominally, united.

Conditions in the Free State were, to start with, little better, though it found its feet more quickly than the Transvaal. Members of the Volksraad showed the same disposition to stalk out of the meeting when they were defeated; and in any case, they refused point blank to spend more than three weeks away from their farms to conduct the nation's affairs. Hoffman, the first President, was compelled to resign when his opponents in the Volksraad trained the guns from the Fort on his house; and when the Volksraad sent an official to the village of Harrismith to remove books and furniture from the local government office, which it could no longer afford, he had to use his bare fists against the local inhabitants before he could carry out his instructions.

These were minor growing pains, however, and soon disappeared. Though local sentiment remained strong, the Free State had little of the personal quarrels between leaders that plagued the Transvaal for so many years. Moreover, it had on its borders a strong African tribe, the Basuto, under an able leader, Moshesh; and in the ever-present fear of war with Basutoland, the Free State could not afford the luxury of internal strife. And there were other and more positive reasons why the Free State soon became recognizable as a State. On its southern border was the Cape Colony, the base of European civilization in southern Africa, and influences from there that hardly reached the 'wilds' of the Transvaal affected the nearer-by Free State. Probably the strongest of these was the Dutch Reformed Church, particularly in the person of Rev. Andrew Murray, the first pastor to be appointed to the Free State.

Murray's father, Rev. Andrew Murray, senior, was one of the Scottish ministers brought to the Cape in 1822 by

Lord Charles Somerset, and after spending ten months in Holland to learn Dutch he became minister of the Dutch Reformed Church at Graaff-Reinet. Two of his sons, John and Andrew, were sent to Aberdeen for their education, and thence for three years to Holland, and they returned as qualified ministers in 1848, just after Sir Harry Smith had proclaimed the Orange River Sovereignty. Appointment to the Church was, at that time, in the hands of the Governor, who interviewed the two brothers. To John he said: 'You are the elder and therefore I shall give you the charge at Burghersdorp.' To Andrew he said: 'And as you are the younger, I am afraid I shall have to send you to Bloemfontein.' It was a fortunate choice for the Free State.

Andrew Murray arrived in Bloemfontein in 1849, and shortly afterwards reported to his brother John that the officers of the garrison had shot nine lions outside the village! He was not quite twenty-one years of age and had the whole of the Free State for his parish, with occasional visits to the Transvaal. His first concern was, of course, the spiritual welfare of the people, and he visited every corner of his immense parish, preaching, baptizing children, catechizing and admitting new members to the Church, celebrating *nagmaal*, establishing new congregations and encouraging them to build churches.

But a man of Andrew Murray's personality, intellect, and abilities is usually active beyond the confines of his immediate work. He was deeply concerned at the lack of educational facilities and saw to it that elementary schools became part of the new churches that were being built. He arranged for teachers to be imported and persuaded the Volksraad to appoint itinerant teachers. When Sir George Grey gave the Volksraad £3,000 to establish a theological seminary, which subsequently became the Grey College, Andrew Murray was one of the three trustees; and since a rector could not immediately be found, he acted in that capacity for a while. That the Free State became conscious of the importance of an educational system was almost entirely due to Murray.

At the conferences that preceded the Sand River and Bloemfontein Conventions, Murray acted as interpreter. It was by the latter convention, in 1854, that the Free State became a republic, and the inhabitants were fairly evenly divided on whether they wanted independence. The party that opposed Britain's withdrawal sent Murray and a Dr. Frazer to London to try to persuade the British Government to retain control; but the mission failed, and Murray, who had been opposed to a republic, accepted it as an accomplished fact and worked as hard as ever for the new government. He was one of the few people with whom President Boshof was on intimate terms, and his contacts with the Cape and with Europe made him an invaluable adviser to the President of the young Republic.

Andrew Murray left the Free State in 1860 for the Cape Colony where he continued to work, on an increased scale, for the church and for education. He saw the need for Christian literature for his people and began to write books and tracts; and by the time of his death in 1917, at the age of 88, he had written 240 tracts and books, some of which were translated into fifteen languages. His influence was not confined to his own country, and his name became well known in Nonconformist circles throughout the world; but it is in southern Africa that the greatest impact of his work was felt. He came to be regarded as the spiritual leader of South Africa and as one whom statesmen were glad to consult. His work within his own Dutch Reformed Church, his contact with other religious denominations, his enthusiasm for education, and his fervour for missions left an indelible mark on South African history.

Another result of the close contact between the Free State and the Cape Colony was that, from 1848, English-speaking people settled in the Free State, particularly in the villages, where they started commercial and trading businesses or became estate agents and auctioneers; and banking companies from London and the Cape found it profitable to follow trade and commerce. These people identified themselves with the life of the Republic and played a considerable part in public affairs, particularly in local government. When all field cornets were summoned to Bloemfontein in 1854 to discuss the question of Britain's withdrawal, fifteen out of the ninety-seven were English-speaking; and early Free State records are scattered with the names of Englishmen—taking part in wars against the Basuto, signing petitions, becoming members of local bodies, organizing cricket, football, racing, and other social activities, and establishing that typically English institution, the 'Club'. They transacted a good deal of their business in English but they usually spoke English and Dutch; and soon they had their own churches, Anglican, Presbyterian, Methodist, and Roman Catholic. All these things counteracted isolationism and made for a more tolerant and progressive society than was possible across the Vaal River.

Sir George Grey's description of small states unable to defend themselves was applicable to the Free State in the 1850's; it was thinly populated with farmers who had little ready cash to pay taxes, and it was no match for its powerful Basuto neighbour. Grey, having come to South Africa from New Zealand where he had been responsible for federation, turned his attention to the possibilities of re-uniting some of the scattered elements in South Africa. In 1858 he suggested separating the eastern districts of the Cape Colony from the western, and then federating them with British Kaffraria, Natal, and the Orange Free State: he assumed that if this plan succeeded the Transvaal republics would eventually be forced to join. The Free State, though by no means unanimously, received the suggestion favourably, but the British Government vetoed the proposal and recalled Grey, thus losing what was probably the most favourable opportunity of repairing some of the damage of the Great Trek.

It was not only politically that South Africa was torn by division. The Dutch Reformed Church at the Cape, like the

British government, had frowned on the Great Trek, and when it eventually accepted the fact that many of its members had left the Cape for good, it found those members not unnaturally suspicious of its belated attempts to send them pastors. The personality and devotion of Andrew Murray and his colleagues managed to allay suspicions in the Free State, and though separate synods were established both there and in Natal, the connexion between the three churches remained close. But in the Transvaal Murray's efforts were only partially successful, for one section of the Transvalers had imported a minister, van der Hoff, from Holland and refused to recognize the Cape Synod; and yet another section hived off under Rev. Postma, also from Holland, to form a separatist church, the *Gereformeerde Kerk*. There were, thus, in all four states the *Nederduits Gereformeerde Kerk*—the original church of the Cape—each with its own synod, and in the Transvaal there were, in addition, the *Hervormde Kerk* which did not differ much in doctrine from the parent church, and the *Gereformeerde Kerk* of extreme Calvinists which, many years later, spread to the other states.

For both the Dutch Reformed Church and the Anglican Church the 1860's were trying times of schism. Not only was the former disrupted by political dissensions; it was torn internally by doctrinal division. Several of its ministers had, while studying in Holland, come under the influence of modernist teachings, then prevalent in German and Dutch universities, which were unorthodox on such matters as man's essential sinfulness. The Cape Synod decided to take action against these *Liberale*,[1] as the unorthodox were called, and expelled first Rev. Kotzé and then Rev. Thomas Burgers. The two ministers appealed to the courts against this expulsion and won their case, both in the Cape Supreme Court and before the Privy Council where Andrew Murray ably argued the case for the synod. But modernism, though it won its case on legal grounds and had a few brilliant exponents in South Africa, failed to find a real foothold among

[1] *Liberale* in this connexion meant 'latitudinarians'.

an essentially conservative people, and the *Liberale* movement died down. Orthodoxy was saved.

The Anglican community was rent by an even more bitter quarrel which involved both the doctrine and the legal position of the church in South Africa. Robert Gray had been appointed Bishop of Cape Town in 1848 and, five years later, Metropolitan of South Africa. Convinced that he was legally empowered to do so, he summoned a Synod in 1857 and, by doing so, raised a hornets' nest. Though the majority of Anglicans supported him, many held that the church in South Africa had no separate existence and that to summon a synod was tantamount to a declaration of independence from the Church of England. Five parishes refused to attend the synod, and the Rector of one, Rev. Long, was subsequently dismissed. He appealed to the Supreme Court and lost, but the decision was reversed by the Privy Council and Long had to be reinstated.

There was much worse to follow. In Natal, Bishop Colenso was beginning to exercise his considerable talents in a critical examination of the Old and New Testaments, and the results of his labours were to shake Britain as well as South Africa. As a boy, Colenso had a hard struggle against poverty. He won his way to Cambridge where he became Second Wrangler and was awarded a Fellowship at St. John's College; he resigned his Fellowship and accepted a living in Norfolk, and from there was appointed Bishop of Natal in 1853. As a missionary his work was outstanding and he will always be remembered for his stout and unceasing championship of the rights of Africans; as a bishop of the Church of England he became the most controversial figure of his day. In 1861 he published his *Commentary on the Epistle to the Romans*, which, in the next year, the English bishops condemned. Bishop Gray thereupon tried Colenso for heresy and deprived him of his diocese.

Colenso refused to submit, maintaining that he had been appointed by the Crown under Letters Patent and that Gray had no authority over him. He was upheld by the Privy

Council and, returning to Natal, was engaged for several years in a bitter and undignified quarrel. The Dean bolted the Cathedral at Pietermaritzburg against him, and Colenso and his friends forced an entry; when Gray sent the Bishop of Bloemfontein to try to settle matters, Colenso barred and picketed the Cathedral. The Bishop of Cape Town, as Metropolitan, consecrated another Bishop of Natal; but the quarrel could not be ended until, eventually, the Anglican community was legally recognized as the church of the Province of South Africa, a voluntary organization in communion with the Established Church of England. When that position was recognized, the Church of the Province of South Africa had, in effect, achieved union and dominion status, many years before those terms could be applied to the country itself.

Disruption in church and state, frontier wars, and bitter political quarrels were all signs that South Africa was having difficulty in adjusting herself to the rapid territorial expansion she had undergone: the small population had bitten off more than they could chew. In the 1860's these difficulties were aggravated by economic weakness and depression. Except in the western Cape Colony and the coast of Natal, capital was scarce; and even in those parts public loans were not readily subscribed on the London market under seven or eight per cent. In the Free State, and even more in the Transvaal, unsettled government and lack of sufficient revenue put public borrowing practically out of the question.

The American Civil War[1] began in 1861 and, within a year, cotton mills in England were closing down, trade slackened, and merchants and banks were refusing credit. When the Civil War ended in 1865 the wool market collapsed and real depression set in. The Free State, crippled by an exhausting and inconclusive war against the Basuto,

[1] The Civil War gave South Africa two songs: the first is the popular *Sarie Marais*, set to a Civil War tune. The second is a Cape Malay song connected with the *Alabama*, the Confederate ship that was allowed to leave the Mersey, to the intense anger of the North. The song is: *Daar Kom die Alabama* ('There comes the Alabama').

issued paper money which immediately declined in value, and the Cape just escaped a similar fate. The Transvaal was unable to pay its officials in money of any kind. From the Cape to the northern borders of the Transvaal farms were bonded, cash was short, and public revenue declined. Though the opening of the Suez Canal in 1869 had reduced the volume of traffic through the Cape ports and Durban, the Cape and Natal were better off than the Republics. But South Africa as a whole was barely subsisting and there was no money available for the roads and railways without which her economic position would not improve. It was obvious that something like a miracle was necessary to save South Africa from drifting into the 'disorder and barbarism' that Sir George Grey had foreseen in 1860. That miracle was the discovery of diamonds and gold.

Chapter Twelve

DIAMONDS AND GOLD

The first diamonds were picked up on the banks of the Orange River, near its junction with the Vaal, in 1867. A hunter named O'Reilly, and Schalk van Niekerk, a farmer, noticed an attractive, glittering stone among the pebbles with which the Jacobz children were playing, and when they expressed admiration and interest, Mrs. Jacobz gave it to van Niekerk who took it for analysis to a chemist in the village of Colesberg, more than a hundred miles away. The chemist pronounced it worthless, but van Niekerk was not satisfied and sent it to Dr. Atherstone at Grahamstown who reported that it was a first-class diamond. Two years later an African witch-doctor found a stone for which, to his astonishment, Schalk van Niekerk gave him 500 sheep. This was the famous 'Star of South Africa', which was sold for £11,000 and resold for £25,000. And the great diamond rush had begun.

The lands where the first diamonds were found lay on either side of the Vaal River for about a hundred miles before it enters the Orange. These were the alluvial diggings, where diamonds could be found in the gravel and sand, and could be worked by individual diggers using primitive equipment. The river diggings were soon exhausted, but by 1870 and 1871 more diamonds were picked up twenty-five miles east of the river at Dutoitspan, Bultfontein, De Beer's, and, most famous of all, Colesberg Kopje which was soon to be called Kimberley after the Secretary of State for Colonies. At these dry diggings, as they were called, diamonds could be found on the surface too; but it soon became clear that far more diamonds were to be found underneath the surface than on top.

Men came from all over the world to seek their fortunes in this flat and arid land: Boers from the Transvaal and Free State; clerks from Cape Town, Stellenbosch, and Wellington; artisans and shopkeepers from the coastal towns; Australian and American prospectors and miners; men from the cities of Europe and the British Isles; and, in their tens of thousands, Africans who came, not to seek great fortunes but to work for enough money to buy a rifle or more cattle. After the diggers came shopkeepers, publicans, traders, lawyers, land speculators and estate agents with little training, financiers and well-dressed diamond buyers from London and Paris. They came on foot and on horseback; from Cape Town they came by ox-wagon, taking three months over the journey, by mule-cart, or by horse-drawn post-cart if they could afford the £40 fare. They lived in wood and tin shanties or in tents; and they lived, worked, and drank hard —wine, whisky, Cape brandy, beer, and if a digger made a lucky strike, a case of champagne for him and his friends. The large majority of diggers made a bare living; but all were invincibly persuaded that they were just about to make their fortunes.

By 1871, four years after the first diamond had been picked up and only one year after the rush had begun, there were more Europeans on the diamond fields in and around Kimberley than had taken part in the Great Trek; and from the river diggings alone diamonds worth £300,000 had been taken, more than four times as much as the Transvaal national debt at that time. Kimberley had become the second biggest town in South Africa, only Cape Town being larger, and was a market for farm produce from hundreds of miles away; a dozen eggs or a pound of butter fetched a pound in hard cash at the barren diggings. The whole country shared in the economic fortune. Cape and Natal imports and exports, and revenue, rose steeply. On the diamond fields land values soared, and farms that had most likely been free grants were sold by Boer farmers to land-speculating companies for £6,000, to be sold four years later for £100,000.

Most important of all, capital for railway construction now became more easily available. Apart from seven miles of railway between Durban and the Point, there were, in 1871, sixty-three miles of railway in the whole of South Africa. This line, from Cape Town to Wellington, had been built by private capital in the 1860's, before the depression; and until diamonds were discovered the terminus remained Wellington, for there had been nothing to attract capital for the extension of the line. By 1873–4, however, the Cape government had bought out the private company and begun extending the line, while construction was started on lines from Port Elizabeth and East London. And with railway development went the rapid extension of telegraph wires and the construction of roads and bridges.

For a short while after the discovery of diamonds it was uncertain where the political control of this valuable new asset would lie. No one had worried about such poor agricultural land but there were plenty of claimants once diamonds were discovered. The Griqua chief, Waterboer, claimed it as Griqua territory; and President Brand claimed it for the Free State and sent police to enforce his claim and maintain order. But neither the diggers nor Great Britain would recognize the claim, and the police failed to maintain order. President Pretorius claimed it for the Transvaal and, in Transvaal fashion, gave three of his friends a monopoly to seek for diamonds! The response of the diggers at Klipdrift, on the Vaal, to this claim was swift; they declared themselves an independent Diggers' Republic and elected an ex-able-bodied seaman of the Royal Navy, the burly Stafford Parker, as President. The Cape Colony made no claim but urged Britain to annex the territory in the interests of law and order and, incidentally, of Cape revenue.

The diamond fields were, in truth, situated in no-man's-land and no claim was clear cut. Waterboer's claim was based on earlier occupation, but no European, digger or otherwise, would have submitted to Griqua rule. The Free State probably had the best claim, based on the fact that when the Free State was ruled by a British Resident, that rule had extended to the Vaal River and thus included Kimberley. The Transvaal claim was based on vague treaties and agreements with African chiefs. After much argument the Governor of the Cape, Barkly, who as British High Commissioner represented the strongest power in South Africa, persuaded the Transvaal, Waterboer, and two African chiefs whose boundaries were also in dispute, to agree to arbitration. The Lieut.-governor of Natal, Keate, was selected as arbitrator, and in 1871 he awarded the disputed diamond-fields area to Waterboer. Since Waterboer had, previously, asked to be taken over by Britain, Barkly annexed the whole area, known as Griqualand West, to the Cape Colony. Two years later it became a separate Crown Colony, but in 1880 it was once more part of the Cape Colony.

In the interests of the orderly development of South Africa as a whole this was probably the best solution to the diamond-fields dispute. What was needed was a strong power able to maintain law and order, and neither of the two Republics was able to do that effectively; and Waterboer certainly could not have done so. Nevertheless, the whole business savoured of sharp practice on the part of Great Britain; and the Boers maintained then, as many do to this day, that Britain 'stole' the diamond fields. The Free State had refused to submit to arbitration, but Brand very sensibly decided to make the best of a bad job and went to London to try to get compensation. The fact that Britain paid the Free State £90,000 to relinquish her claim seems to indicate that there may, after all, have been some justice in that claim.

A few of the fortune-seekers who came to the diamond fields were destined to play major roles in the economic and political life of southern Africa, and of these the most colourful was Barnett Isaacs, better known as Barney Barnato. The son of a Jewish shopkeeper, Barney had grown up in Whitechapel where his father had taught him to box; he had little schooling, and it was his ambition to become an actor. He arrived in Kimberley in 1873 to join his brother, who had gone out two years earlier; and he came with no money, with slight abilities as an actor, juggler, and acrobat—Barney's greatest source of pride was his ability to recite Hamlet's soliloquy standing on his hands!—and with boundless vitality and optimism.

Barney Barnato arrived in the middle of a slump. In the financial capitals of the world banks were failing and shares were crashing on the Stock Exchanges. Nobody wanted to buy diamonds, and many diggers were packing up; only the optimists and those who had made, and kept, a little money were able to hang on for better times. Barnato stayed on, doing anything that would earn him a few shillings a day: buying a few pocket knives or pencils or pairs of braces and selling them at a small profit; bartering for scribbling blocks the right to wash the gravel on a claim and thus picking up a few small diamonds which he was lucky enough to sell for a pound; or working as a clown in a circus. When times improved, he and a partner set up as small-scale diamond dealers, buying from the diggers on the spot and selling to merchants from Amsterdam and London.

By 1876 Barney Barnato had managed to collect a capital of £3,000. And now a new danger seemed to threaten the diamond industry. Everywhere else in the world where diamonds had been found they had been alluvial, and geologists and mining experts were practically unanimous in saying that diamonds could not be found in any other way. If they were correct, diamond digging at Kimberley would come to an end when the yellow ground in which they were found was exhausted; and by 1876 the diggers were coming to the blue ground that lay beneath the yellow. There were, however, one or two experts who thought that the blue ground might contain diamonds. One of these was an amateur geologist from Grahamstown, Dr. Atherstone, who had recognized as a diamond the first stone sent him by Schalk van Niekerk in 1867. Atherstone was convinced that the geological pipes of blue ground, deep down into the earth, would contain the real store of diamonds.

Barnato had no theoretical knowledge and very little practical experience. But he, too, believed in the blue ground, and he and his partner sank all their capital in buying up claims from diggers who, having exhausted the yellow ground, believed there were no more diamonds to be found. Atherstone and Barney Barnato were right. The blue ground contained the world's greatest store of diamonds, and by 1880 Barnato was making £1,800 a week, and investing his money in more and more claims. Within a few years he was a millionaire and one of the most important people in the diamond industry.

Closely associated with Barney Barnato, in diamond dealing if in no other way, was Cecil Rhodes. He was the son of the Vicar of Bishop's Stortford and had been sent, on account of his health, to his brother Herbert who was cotton farming in Natal. In 1871, at the age of eighteen, Rhodes went to Kimberley and was soon making enough money to enable him to go to Oxford, leaving his claims to be worked by his friend Rudd. But his thoughts were never far from Kimberley and Africa, and until 1881, when he finally succeeded in taking a pass degree, he divided his time between Kimberley and Oxford. A year earlier, Rhodes, already a wealthy man, was elected as Member of the Cape Parliament for the constituency of Barkly West.

Ever since the discovery that the blue ground contained diamonds, digging had become more and more chaotic. Alluvial diggings can be worked by individuals, but when the diamonds are hundreds of feet below the surface this becomes impossible. On the four big mines near Kimberley there were over 3,000 claims, some no bigger than seven square yards, and it may be imagined what confusion resulted when each individual claim holder tried to dig down hundreds of feet. Shaft walls subsided, accidents were frequent, and disputes even more so. To overcome these difficulties, groups of miners began to combine in limited liability companies to work their joint claims. But that was not enough; modern mining machinery and techniques were called for which groups of diggers could not afford. And it was here that Cecil Rhodes and Barney Barnato seized the chance to combine small companies into four large companies, one for each of the mines.

As a young man at Oxford Rhodes had drafted a will in which he expressed his dreams of extending the rule of Britain, not only in Africa. To carry out his ideas in southern Africa he needed plenty of money, and he knew that he would get it if he could consolidate the four mines and control both the production and the sale of diamonds. In 1887 he set about doing this, and his greatest rival was Barney Barnato who, at this time, had more money than Rhodes. For more than a year a great financial battle raged between these two men in their early thirties, the one a Jew from Whitechapel, the other a parson's son from Hertfordshire; the one a cheerful, quick-witted, flamboyant, lively little man who liked noise and excitement and plenty of people around him and who liked making money for its own sake; and the other a big, clumsy, reserved man who hated crowds and noise and who made money because of the power it gave him to carry out his imperial schemes.

Rhodes was unable to defeat Barnato by financial manœuvres so he came to terms. He flattered Barnato's vanity by getting him elected to the exclusive Kimberley club, whose members had been accustomed to refer to Barnato as 'a little Jew', and by persuading him to stand for Parliament;[1] and eventually Barney agreed to merge his interests with those of Rhodes in exchange for cash and a share in

[1] Barney Barnato did stand for Parliament and was elected in 1888. Always the actor, he carried out his election campaign dressed in a silver-grey coat and driving in a coach-and-four accompanied by six liveried horsemen dressed in green and gold. It was Kimberley's first election. Since 1888 that constituency has had many a less exciting, but never a more spectacular, election contest.

the new venture. With the signature by Rhodes of a cheque for £5,338,650 the De Beers Consolidated Mines came into being.

The final details of this great deal were arranged at a meeting that was dramatic and full of significance for the future of South Africa. Dr. Jameson, Rhodes's friend, was the host, and Rhodes, Beit, Barnato and his nephew, Woolf Joel, were the guests. Financial details had been settled and the real argument was now about the scope of the new company. Barnato said it was to dig and sell diamonds. But Cecil Rhodes spoke about Bechuanaland and the road to the north, about the Matabele and the Mashona, about lakes and rivers and peoples in Central Africa; and he had maps to show them what was in his mind. These were the things that De Beers might help to finance. Barney Barnato and Woolf Joel said these were dreams, and dreams did not pay dividends. 'No, my friend,' said Rhodes, 'they are not dreams. They are plans.' The meeting lasted for eighteen hours, Rhodes doing most of the talking, tirelessly urging and explaining and persuading, until Barnato gave way. Rhodes had queer ideas, said Barnato. Some people fancied this and some that, but he had a fancy for making an empire. 'You want the means to go north, if possible, so I suppose we must give it to you.' And so, at four o'clock in the morning in the country home of Dr. Jameson, Rhodes got his way—the means to go north.

After diamonds came gold. Even before diamonds were discovered it was known that there was gold in the Transvaal, and there had been several minor rushes. But it was not gold in payable quantities; and in spite of the Transvaal government's offer of £5,000 to anyone who found payable gold, it was only in 1884 that two brothers, Struben, established the fact that there was gold on the Witwatersrand. Two years later the main reef was discovered and the rush began.

The gold rush had some of the same features as the diamond rush, but on a much larger scale. Where thousands had gone to Kimberley, tens of thousands made for Johannesburg. Every boat that arrived at the ports deposited crowds of men from Britain and Europe, from Australia and America; young men from the Cape and Natal and the Free State made their way, by train as far as it went (soon it was to be Kimberley) and then on foot, by ox-wagon, or by mule or horse transport. And for every white man there were at least two black men, doing the rough and heavy work. Those men who had made money at Kimberley either went themselves or sent their agents to buy up any land in sight. Transport drivers reaped a rich harvest conveying people and goods to the gold fields, and, so lucrative was the business, objected strongly to railways being built through the Free State and Transvaal.

At Kimberley it had taken many years before the mines were consolidated and the individual digger excluded. On the Witwatersrand there was no alluvial gold. It was deep in the earth, embedded in solid rock which had to be hauled up and crushed to extract the gold. There was no room for individual diggers, and from the beginning companies were formed to buy land, prospect, and mine. Much money was needed, more than at Kimberley; and though a good deal came from the Kimberley millionaires, it was not enough. However, in a world in which men placed as much faith in the gold standard as in the Bible, money was readily available on the Stock Exchanges of London and New York to mine this mineral that was more precious than diamonds. It had taken a lot of talking by Rhodes to interest the Rothschilds in Kimberley; but no one needed to be persuaded to invest in gold or in any enterprise connected with it. The world wanted more gold with which to finance expanding world trade and was eager to invest the capital necessary to extract it.

The degree of technical knowledge and skill required for gold mining was, from the start, much higher than that needed for diamond mining. Shafts had to be sunk that were, eventually, to go more than a mile into the earth; and many miles of precisely calculated tunnels had to be constructed. From such depths the ore could not be raised by man-power, and here too South Africa was fortunate in that large resources of cheap coal were discovered next to the gold fields. The costs of deep-level mining were great, and the best-known method of extracting the gold from the ore yielded only 60 per cent. But once more fortune smiled on the Rand. The cyanide process of extraction which gave a 90-per-cent yield was discovered and began to be used in 1890.

Although there was no room for individual diggers, the same sort of chaos prevailed, in the early days, as at Kimberley. At one time there were no fewer than 450 mining companies on the Witwatersrand and there was much waste and inefficiency. Eventually, and by the same sort of process as at Kimberley, amalgamations into groups of mines that could pool resources and skill took place. Much later, the Transvaal Chamber of Mines was established to look after the interests of the whole industry and to ensure an adequate labour supply, both skilled and unskilled.

Within ten years after the discovery of the main reef, a city had arisen on what had been bare veld. It was a city that grew in a hurry, without planning, and it was peopled by mining magnates, technical engineers, skilled miners, unskilled African workers, and a host of people who made a living by supplying the wants of those engaged in mining, by speculating in shares, or by fraudulent company promoting. There was no place in Johannesburg for the individual digger of Kimberley who hoped to make his fortune by a lucky strike; but there was plenty of room for his equivalent, the speculator. At the height of his financial power Barney Barnato said that people in England were so eager to invest money on the Rand he could have floated a company to dig a tunnel from the Bank of England to Johannesburg and no one would have queried the project!

This piece of the Transvaal, hitherto isolated, was now (1894) connected by rail with Lorenço Marques, Durban,

East London, Port Elizabeth, and Cape Town. And forty miles north of this cosmopolitan industrial world lay Pretoria, the capital of the Boer Republic that held sway over the unruly Witwatersrand. The Boers were farmers and their country was a sleepy rural republic. Johannesburg was a noisy, intensely alive, money-grabbing, urban centre. The Boers spoke Afrikaans and read the Bible in Nederlands; Johannesburg spoke mostly English and seldom read anything that had no direct connection with gold mining and share pushing. To Paul Kruger, the man who was a boy on the Great Trek, and to his government, the people of Johannesburg were *Uitlanders*, 'outlanders' or foreigners. On one of the few occasions that he could be induced to visit Johannesburg he addressed a meeting as: 'Burghers, friends, murderers, thieves, and robbers,' and the crowd broke into 'Rule Britannia'.

In the experience of the Transvaal Republic, Johannesburg was indeed something utterly foreign. Its population soon outstripped that of the rest of the Transvaal, though not by a fraction as much as the wealth and taxability of Johannesburg exceeded that of the rest of the Republic. Towering over the Transvaal in economic strength, Johannesburg was subject to government from Pretoria, and Kruger was afraid to let any power out of Boer hands; in vain did the inhabitants of Johannesburg petition the President to institute municipal government for their city. The government taxed the mines, directly or by the sale of concessions granting monopolies; and concession hunting became a major activity in Johannesburg. Concessions for the sole right to supply dynamite and to manufacture cyanide affected gold mining most directly; but there were many others, including the right to manufacture jam. A visit to Pretoria, frequently followed by the bribing of an official whose salary was such that £1,000 represented wealth, and the flotation of a company to exploit the concession—that was the routine. So fantastic did the whole system become that Lord Randolph Churchill, visiting the Transvaal in

1895, reported a rumour that someone had applied for a concession to grant all other concessions!

It was certainly difficult to govern Johannesburg from Pretoria. It would have been difficult enough from Johannesburg, and the wonder is not that the attempt failed but that it was ever made. The get-rich-quick and cut-throat atmosphere of Johannesburg, the variety of its energetic population, the complications of a rapidly expanding city, and the intricacies of mining laws would have made Johannesburg a hard administrative nut for the most up-to-date government; and the Boer government was ill equipped to deal with the situation. Some of the laws enacted by the Transvaal Volksraad were good on paper and had been made in the interests of the mining industry. But the laws were poorly administered because the Transvaal civil service was unable to cope with the immense amount of work and soon became enmeshed in red tape. It took Pretoria two years to decide what the scale of cab fares in Johannesburg should be.

The effect on South Africa and on the whole of Africa of the discovery of diamonds and gold was immense. Kimberley and the Witwatersrand induced what were, in reality, the second and third Great Treks of South Africa, each of them far greater in scope, speed, and intensity than the original. The Great Trek had gone by ox-wagon, at the pace of the ox; the diamond and gold treks had begun with the ox and had drawn railways in their wake; and the railways had not followed the lines of grass and water, but of minerals. The Great Trek had enormously increased contact between Europeans and African tribes; the mineral treks drew Africans away from their tribes and brought them, as individuals, irrevocably into the industrial life of South Africa, so that tribal life, though it might linger on, was doomed. The Great Trek had spread pastoralism and agriculture on to the high veld; diamonds and gold gave birth to the industrial revolution.

The Great Trek had resulted in the establishment of two

Boer Republics: in the Free State, Britons had settled and become part of a society in which co-operation between Boer and Briton had ripened slowly and naturally; the Transvaal had remained largely Afrikaans until the gold trek pitchforked into its midst a noisy and turbulent community of Uitlanders who never really became part of the country and who made co-operation between Boer and Briton difficult. The Free State got its English-speaking citizens in small doses, commercial, professional, and farming folk who easily adapted themselves to the tempo of the Republic; the Transvaal had larger doses of a strident, get-rich-quick type which it found difficult to absorb. It has not yet done so. The Great Trek was an Afrikaner effort; the mineral treks were predominantly British.

The Great Trek had divided South Africa politically into British colonies, Boer Republics, and African tribal lands; it had caused Britain to withdraw south of the Orange River. The diamond and gold treks were largely responsible for reuniting South Africa, for eliminating independent African tribes, and for extending British control, not only to the northern borders of the Transvaal, but far beyond into the Rhodesias and Central Africa.

Finally, the Great Trek brought African tribesmen into armed conflict with Boer commandos; but after each local conflict the social life of the African was not greatly different from what it had been. He might lose some of his land, or he might be subjected to Boer rule; but he continued to live his simple tribal life. When he went to work on Boer farms he found the ways of the white man strange, but he continued to do the kind of things he had been accustomed to: he tended cattle and sheep, grew maize and vegetables, and lived the unhurried, seasonal life of a farm; he kept his social customs of initiation and marriage dowry; he ate his customary food and drank kaffir-corn beer brewed by his womenfolk. His Boer master knew his language and was good-naturedly tolerant of his ways. In spite of the vast and obvious differences between Christian white and heathen black, there was much in common between the Boer farmer and the African farm labourer, and each had the leisure to adapt himself to the other's habits. The relationship between the two was patriarchal and personal.

The mineral treks were far more catastrophic in their impact on the African. In Johannesburg, everything was noise and bustle, and there were no familiar cattle and sheep to herd—only to be slaughtered to feed the townsmen; no one had time to study African habits or learn a Bantu language, except as a soldier learns a few words in a foreign country; the Afrikaans saying, *Môre is nog 'n dag* (Tomorrow is another day), used on leisurely Boer farms, had no place in mining and industry where people work to the clock or to the sound of a steam whistle. A man's wife and family could be taken to a Boer farm and his children properly initiated and taught the good manners and customs of the tribe. But Kimberley and Johannesburg, in the last decades of the nineteenth century, were no places for women; and even later, when industrial towns began to draw African labour, men were at first hesitant to take their families with them to live in overcrowded slums where tribal dignity, good manners, and discipline withered. South Africa, black and white, is still painfully struggling to adjust herself to the social situations created by the mineral treks.

Chapter Thirteen

IMPERIAL EXPANSION

When diamonds and gold were discovered in South Africa, Britain and Europe were entering upon a new phase of history. In 1871 the German Empire, long nursed by Bismarck, came to maturity and Kaiser William I was crowned at Versailles; the France of Napoleon III had toppled, and Germany was soon to become Britain's most serious rival and the greatest menace to the balance of power in Europe. Germany came late into the industrial and colonial race, but she made up vigorously for lost time. By the late seventies and early eighties she was pushing, east and west, into southern Africa and making treaties with African tribes. The scramble for Africa had begun and was not to end until, with minor exceptions, Europe had conquered Africa and completed the process begun in the fifteenth and sixteenth centuries.

At the same time that Germany was becoming the strongest Power in Europe, Britain was entering upon the great imperialist phase of her history. The policy of withdrawing from further colonial commitments that was characteristic of the third, was reversed during the fourth quarter of the nineteenth century. By 1877, the year of the first annexation of the Transvaal, Disraeli had made his Queen Empress of India; and the mounting capital of the industrial age, the rivalry of France and Germany, and the superb self-confidence of Victorian nationalism led Britain on to the path of finance-imperialism that is called Empire Building. The discovery of diamonds and gold gave the financiers a chance to join hands with the imperialists, and the history of

South Africa from 1875 till the end of the century must be seen against this background.

The Cape had always been the port of entry for western civilization into southern Africa. It was the base from which that civilization had spread, carried by trekkers and missionaries, hunters and traders, diamond and gold seekers; and it now became the base of operations for imperialist expansion into southern Africa. The governor at the Cape was, at the same time, Her Majesty's High Commissioner in South Africa, the representative of the paramount Power, and it was natural that the Cape Parliament should, by association with Britain, become involved in the expansion of British rule. From 1880, the moving spirit in that expansion was Cecil Rhodes, a member of the Cape Parliament and, in 1890, Prime Minister. If it was difficult to separate the Governor from the representative of an imperial Power, it was more difficult to distinguish between Rhodes the Prime Minister and Rhodes the imperialist, or between either and Rhodes the millionaire.

The first sign that British policy was taking a new direction in South Africa came in 1875 when the Secretary of State for Colonies, Lord Carnarvon, proposed that a conference be held in South Africa to consider, among other matters, federating the different States and colonies. He sent J. A. Froude, the historian, to investigate and report, and Froude behaved tactlessly. The Cape had but recently achieved responsible government, and the cabinet was jealous of its powers and annoyed with Carnarvon for going over its head in proposing the conference and in nominating delegates from the Cape. Further, Carnarvon's proposals envisaged the separation of the eastern and western parts of the Cape Colony, a proposal that pleased the eastern separationists but was anathema to the Prime Minister, Molteno, and his Cabinet. Froude openly favoured the separationists and incurred the anger of the Government who looked upon him as an 'imperial agent' who was hampering them in the discharge of their duties.

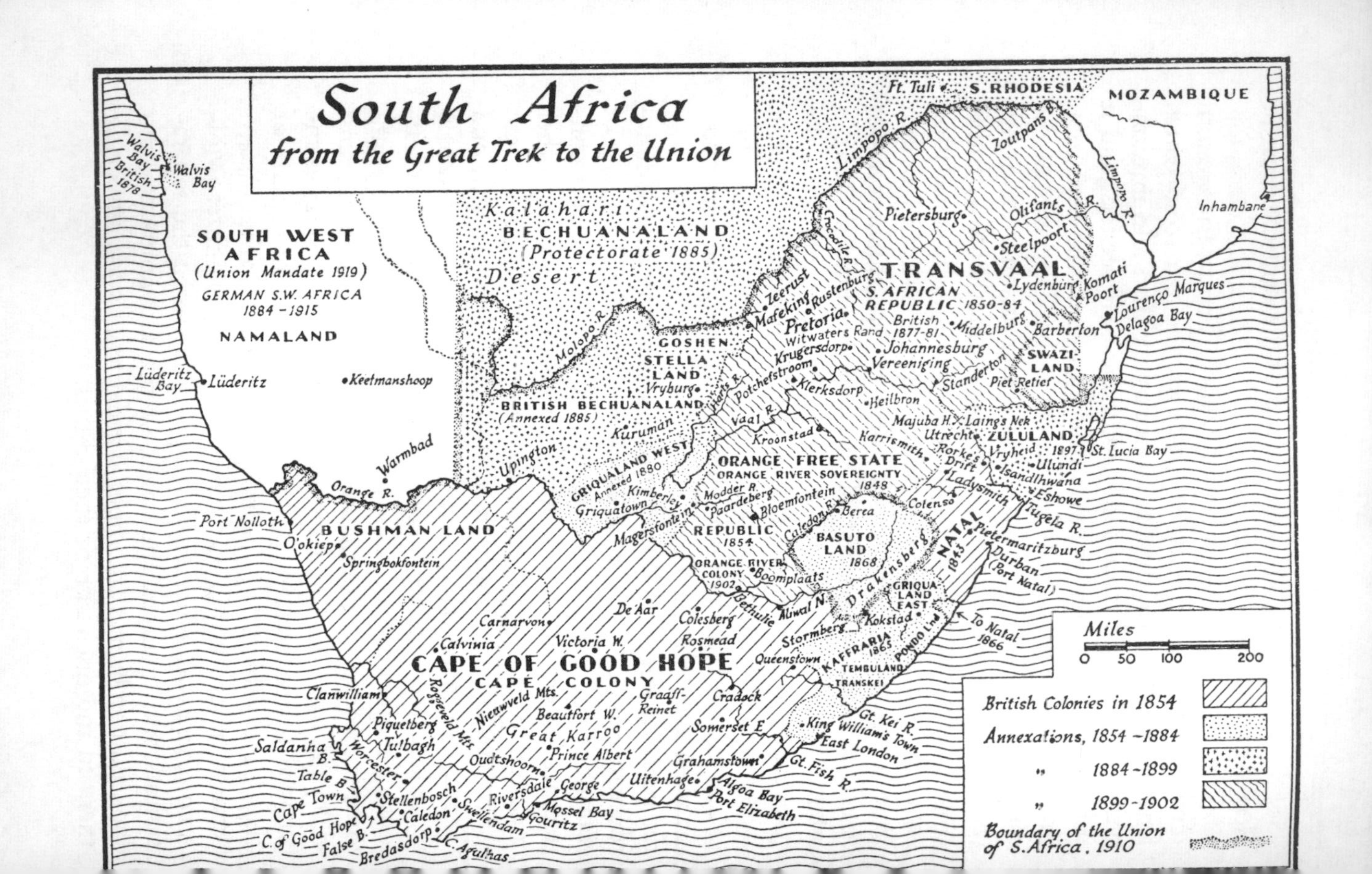

South Africa
from the Great Trek to the Union
SOUTH WEST AFRICA
(Union Mandate 1919)
GERMAN S.W. AFRICA 1884-1915
NAMALAND
Walvis Bay British 1878
Walvis Bay
Lüderitz Bay
Lüderitz
Keetmanshoop
Warmbad
Orange R.
Port Nolloth
O'okiep
Springbokfontein
BUSHMAN LAND
Kalahari
BECHUANALAND
(Protectorate 1885)
Desert
Molopo R.
GOSHEN
STELLA LAND
Vryburg
BRITISH BECHUANALAND
(Annexed 1885)
Kuruman
Upington
GRIQUALAND WEST
Annexed 1880
Kimberley
Griquatown
Magersfontein
Paardeberg
Modder R.
Bloemfontein
Caledon R.
Berea
ORANGE FREE STATE
ORANGE RIVER SOVEREIGNTY 1848
REPUBLIC 1854
ORANGE RIVER COLONY 1902
Boomplaats
Bethulie
Aliwal N.
Kroonstad
Vaal R.
Harts R.
Potchefstroom
Klerksdorp
Heilbron
Harrismith
BASUTO LAND 1868
Drakensberg
GRIQUA LAND EAST
Kokstad
Stormberg
KAFFRARIA 1865
TEMBULAND
TRANSKEI
PONDO Lnd
To Natal 1866
NATAL 1843
Pietermaritzburg
Durban (Port Natal)
Tugela R.
Colenso
Ladysmith
Rorke's Drift
Isandlhwana
Eshowe
Ulundi
Vryheid
1897
St. Lucia Bay
ZULULAND
Utrecht
Majuba H.
Laing's Nek
TRANSVAAL
S. AFRICAN REPUBLIC 1850-84
British 1877-81
Pretoria
Rustenburg
Zeerust
Mafeking
Witwaters Rand
Krugersdorp
Johannesburg
Vereeniging
Standerton
Piet Retief
SWAZI-LAND
Barberton
Middelburg
Lydenburg
Komati Poort
Steelpoort
Olifants R.
Pietersburg
Crocodile R.
Limpopo R.
Zoutpans B.
Ft. Tuli
S. RHODESIA
MOZAMBIQUE
Inhambane
Lourenço Marques
Delagoa Bay
CAPE OF GOOD HOPE
CAPE COLONY
Carnarvon
Calvinia
De Aar
Colesberg
Rosmead
Victoria W.
Clanwilliam
Roggeveld Mts.
Nieuwveld Mts.
Beaufort W.
Graaff-Reinet
Cradock
Queenstown
Great Karroo
Prince Albert
Somerset E.
Piquetberg
Tulbagh
Saldanha B.
Worcester
Table B.
Cape Town
C. of Good Hope
False B.
Stellenbosch
Caledon
Swellendam
Bredasdorp
C. Agulhas
Oudtshoorn
Riversdale
George
Mossel Bay
Gouritz
Grahamstown
Uitenhage
Algoa Bay
Port Elizabeth
Gt. Fish R.
East London
King William's Town
Gt. Kei R.
Miles
0 50 100 200
British Colonies in 1854
Annexations, 1854-1884
" 1884-1899
" 1899-1902
Boundary of the Union of S. Africa, 1910

Like Carnarvon, President Brand in the Free State and President Burgers in the Transvaal realized the need for some sort of common policy in South Africa; but the diamond-fields dispute was too recent in Boer minds to make federation under the British flag palatable. In the end, Carnarvon had his conference, in London and not in South Africa, and he had it without delegates from the principal States—the Cape Colony and the Republics. It had been a mistake—a mistake that was to be twice repeated in stronger measure—to attempt to impose unity on the South African States from without, and Carnarvon now aggravated the situation by deciding to annex the Transvaal. To this end he gave secret instructions to Shepstone, delegate from Natal to the London Conference. If the Cape was unwilling to be used as a springboard for expansion, Natal would serve.

In 1856 Natal had been separated from the Cape Colony and given a modified form of representative government under a lieutenant-governor. Boundaries were hopefully drawn and, as elsewhere in South Africa, failed to preserve the peace or keep Africans from flocking into Natal. Theophilus Shepstone, the son of a missionary from the Transkei, introduced a policy that was new in South Africa: he created reserves for those Africans who had come to live in Natal and attempted to restore the tribal system under European supervision. By wise administration and great personal influence with the tribesmen Shepstone managed to maintain peace for close on thirty years; but in 1873 relations between black and white were seriously disturbed when a Hlubi chief named Langalibalele rebelled against European rule. And in that same year Cetewayo became chief of the Zulu and began to revive the military traditions of Chaka and Dingaan, thus constituting a threat to both the Transvaal and Natal.

To complicate matters for Natal, and ultimately for South Africa, indentured Indian coolie labour was imported to work on the sugar plantations which the climate of Natal favoured and on which Africans could not be persuaded to work. Within a few years of the first arrivals in 1860 the Indian population of Natal exceeded the European. Most of the Indians remained in Natal after they had served their three-year indentures, and many of them moved into the towns where they became market gardeners, shopkeepers, or domestic servants; and much of the prosperity of Natal was built up on Indian labour. That prosperity brought more European immigrants, and still more Indians, until, in the twentieth century, the governments of India and South Africa put an end to indentured labour and free immigration of Indians. The Colony of Natal from which Shepstone set out to annex the Transvaal in 1877 had, thus, its fair share of typically South African problems.

There were plenty of excuses for interfering in Transvaal affairs. An exhausting and inconclusive war against the Bapedi had brought the Republic to bankruptcy; internal administration had, for all practical purposes, collapsed; Shepstone, the authority on the Zulu, warned everyone that they were preparing for a war, and though he may have exaggerated the facts in support of his policy of annexation, there was truth in his warnings. Throughout South Africa, including the Transvaal, unofficial voices were raised asking Britain to intervene in the interests of general peace. So divided was the Transvaal itself that, in 1877, Shepstone was able to go to Pretoria with a few soldiers, discuss matters at sherry parties with members of the Volksraad, promise that good (and responsible) government would be instituted, and hoist the British flag without overt opposition.

As an attempt to amalgamate the South African States, achieve a common Native policy, and unite Boer and Briton, the first annexation of the Transvaal was a failure. The suppression of one of the two Boer Republics by Britain roused Afrikaner sentiment everywhere, not least in the Cape Colony where Rev. S. J. du Toit had, two years earlier, founded a movement to encourage the speaking and writing of Afrikaans. The annexation gave strength to this movement, which in 1879 became the Afrikander[1] Bond, an anti-British movement that spread to the Free State and Transvaal. Vigorous protest came, too, from J. H. Hofmeyr who had opposed du Toit's movement and was, now and later, a supporter of federation under the British flag—but not a supporter of imperialist aggression.

In spite of arousing Afrikaner sentiment the annexation might have proved less of a failure had the Transvaal been well administered and had other conditions in South Africa been more favourable. But the administration tried to go too quickly, it flouted the Boer leaders, Kruger and Joubert, and it did not carry out Shepstone's promises; and in 1877 a three-year drought set in, as severe as any South Africa had experienced. In the same year the Cape Colony became involved in its last Kaffir War; a year later the Transvaal itself was once more at war with the Bapedi; and in 1879 the threatened Zulu war broke out, a war that included the Zulu victory at Isandhlwana; the famous battle of Rorke's Drift where the Zulu invasion of Natal was halted, and the death, in a minor skirmish, of the Prince Imperial of France who was serving on Lord Chelmsford's staff.[2] Imperialism was not doing well, and Gladstone made the most of its failures in his Midlothian campaign which swept the Liberal Party back into power in 1880.

Gladstone's Ministry, fully occupied with the Irish Land League and other difficulties, neglected the Transvaal; and at the end of 1880 the Boers took matters into their own hands, declared their independence, and besieged the small British garrisons in Pretoria, Potchefstroom, and Lydenburg. General Colley marched with troops from Natal but

[1] The word was so spelt in those days. Later the *d* was dropped and the correct spelling now is Afrikaner. In 1881 Hofmeyr captured the Afrikander Bond in the Cape and led it steadily away from its earlier, anti-British, policy.

[2] It was at this time that Disraeli remarked about the Zulus that they 'convert our Bishops, defeat our Generals, and put an end to our dynasties'. The Zulu were eventually defeated by Chelmsford at Ulundi, and Cetewayo was banished, only to be reinstated in 1883, a year before his death. In 1897 Zululand was annexed to Natal.

was defeated at Laing's Nek and, more seriously, at Majuba where Boer volunteers climbed the hill under continuous fire and captured it. Though the bravery of the Boers drew an admiring poem from *Punch*, the memory of the defeat at Majuba remained with the British, and 'avenge Majuba' became an easy cry to arouse patriotic sentiment.

Even before Majuba Gladstone had begun negotiations with the Boer leaders, Kruger, Joubert, and Pretorius; these negotiations continued, and the Pretoria Convention was signed in 1881 granting independence to the Transvaal subject to Britain's suzerainty, which meant that her foreign and Native policies were subject to British control. Three years later, at the London Convention, this was modified: the Transvaal was allowed to make treaties with the Free State, and Britain surrendered her right to veto Transvaal legislation affecting Africans. By this time Germany had entered the race for colonies and Britain refused to give up her control of Transvaal foreign policy because she was afraid the Republic might make an alliance with Germany.

By 1884 all attempts to join together what the Great Trek had put asunder had failed, and the policy of federation was no longer popular. Nevertheless, the desire for some form of union of the South African States did not die; it took new shapes, and after the discovery of diamonds and gold, burned more fiercely than ever. From Cape Town Rhodes, with his 'fancy for making an Empire', looked forward to a southern African union that went far beyond the schemes of Grey and Carnarvon. This was to be achieved by peaceful means if possible, by force if necessary, and in any event under the British flag. Paul Kruger and the majority of his burghers who still hoped for a united Boer republic, the dream of the early Voortrekkers, were implacably opposed to union under the British flag. Thus Rhodes and Kruger came to symbolize the two opposing forces: the late nineteenth century against the early eighteenth, industrialism against pastoralism.

In between these two policies there were many shades of

opinion. There were Transvaal burghers who favoured an arrangement with Britain, and there were Uitlanders who supported Kruger. In the Cape, Afrikaner sentiment was pulled in two opposing directions: J. H. Hofmeyr had captured the Bond and turned it from its anti-British aims; but he and his followers were opposed to imperial aggression against the Republics to whose burghers they were bound by ties of kinship, religion, and language. Hofmeyr and Cape statesmen such as Merriman, Schreiner, and Sauer supported Rhodes as long as his policy seemed to be one of peaceful expansion of the Empire with the ultimate hope of inducing the Republics to join hands with the Cape and Natal. But when Rhodes tried to force the pace they parted company with him and their sympathies became more and more deeply engaged with the Transvaal.

Between the Transvaal and the Cape lay, both in a physical and a political sense, the Free State. The citizens of that republic had strong cultural ties both with the Cape and with the Transvaal and were commercially dependent on the Cape ports and railways. Memories of past disagreements, going back to the Great Trek period, prevented the Free State from committing itself to Kruger's policy of a single Boer republic which would, inevitably, be dominated by the Transvaal; and it feared that such a policy would lead to war with Britain. Until 1896 the Free State acted as a bridge between opposing policies, and it was not before imperialism bared its teeth that Free Staters, somewhat reluctantly, threw in their lot with their kinsmen across the Vaal River.

Rhodes's plans for extending the Empire northwards depended on control of the territory on the western borders of the Transvaal, known as Bechuanaland, and inhabited by African tribes. The western boundary of the Transvaal had always been vague. When the Voortrekkers defeated the Matabele in 1837 they had claimed jurisdiction over all land and tribes that had been subject to the Matabele; but boundaries were never drawn, and the sparsely-populated borderlands between the Transvaal and Bechuanaland, in which constant raids from both sides occurred, had remained disputed territory. Missionaries of the London Mission Society had established stations along the so-called Missionary Road; Robert Moffat had been at Kuruman, and it was from that station that his famous son-in-law, Livingstone, set out to explore Central Africa. In the disputes between tribesmen and Boers, the missionaries took the side of the Africans and accused the Boers of attacking the tribesmen and of taking young Africans as 'apprentices'; and the missionaries, in particular Mackenzie, had consistently advocated taking Bechuanaland under British protection.

Matters came to a head in 1884. Germany had established herself on the west coast; Rhodes was straining to push northwards; and Kruger was threatening to incorporate two little Boer republics, Stellaland and Goshen, that had established themselves in the disputed area. These hard facts had their effect in Cape Town and London and achieved what the missionaries had vainly advocated. By 1886 the southern portion of Bechuanaland, south of the Molopo River, was annexed to the Cape Colony and a protectorate was proclaimed over the northern half, thus securing what was variously called the Missionary Road, the Suez Canal to the North, or the Road to the North. Rhodes now sent his agents to Lobengula, chief of the Matabele, to obtain a concession to dig for gold in Mashonaland, and he himself, not without serious opposition in Britain, eventually persuaded the British Government to give a Royal Charter to his British South Africa Company. The Charter was granted in 1889, and a year later the British flag was hoisted at Salisbury, the future capital of Southern Rhodesia, by Rhodes's chief lieutenant, Jameson.

In that same year Rhodes became Prime Minister at the Cape and was in a position to push forward his schemes vigorously. Those schemes included closer settlement of Rhodesia and the construction of railway and telegraph lines northwards from Kimberley, through Mafeking, and on to Bulawayo. He used his wealth and his authority, both as Prime Minister and as director of the Chartered Company, to forward his plans, and he had to play his cards with skill. In political and official circles in Britain he had to overcome a great deal of suspicion and reluctance on the part of those who regarded him as just another capitalist millionaire. In London he played on imperialist ambitions and fear of Germany; in Cape Town, to keep the co-operation of Hofmeyr, he played down what he called the 'Imperial factor' and gave no sign that he might contemplate the use of force against the Transvaal.

Indeed, in 1890 it is probable that Rhodes was thinking in terms, not of force, but of an economic federation with the Transvaal that might lead to political federation. But during the next few years he changed his mind. It is possible that Rhodes began to realize that Kruger would never voluntarily surrender Transvaal independence and that his own health was such that, if he wished to achieve his ambitions during his lifetime, he would have to force the pace. From 1894 he was gradually lured by conditions on the Witwatersrand into making what was in effect an attempt to force the Transvaal Republic under the British flag. It was a decision that was fatal to his own plans and to the peace of South Africa.

We saw what the effects of the discovery of gold were in the Transvaal: a cosmopolitan, restless, vigorous, and urban population of Uitlanders thrusting into the middle of a slow-moving rural Boer community whom it soon outnumbered; a highly specialized industry with the intricacies of which the Boer government found it difficult to cope; genuine Uitlander grievances, and genuine fears that if the grievances were to be redressed the Transvaal would be handed over to foreigners. The Uitlanders, controlling all the wealth, clamoured for political control which Kruger and the majority of his Volksraad were determined not to surrender.

In Johannesburg a body called the National Union had been formed in 1892 to agitate for reform, and in June 1895

Rhodes, Beit, and other gold-mining capitalists began to organize for an armed rising which, when it occurred, would be supported by a force of Chartered Company police and volunteers, operating from Bechuanaland under Jameson. Arms and ammunition were smuggled into Johannesburg in oil tanks with false bottoms, and secret depots of stores and fresh horses were established between the border and Johannesburg; as soon as the rising began, the arsenal at Pretoria, from which the main supplies of arms and ammunition would be obtained, was to be seized.

The main features of the plan were that a rising would take place in Johannesburg, that Jameson would go to the assistance of the Uitlanders, and that the High Commissioner and governor of the Cape, Sir Hercules Robinson, would then go to Pretoria and, in the guise of peace maker, dictate terms to the Transvaal. The Secretary of State for Colonies, Joseph Chamberlain, knew about the plot though he was officially ignorant of the exact details.

In November Jameson visited Johannesburg to arrange final details, and he got from the leaders of the National Union a letter with the date left blank asking him to come to the 'rescue of unarmed men, women, and children' who would be at the mercy of 'well-armed Boers'. This fake letter could subsequently be published as proof that Jameson had invaded the Transvaal only at the invitation of the Uitlanders! The date of the rising was fixed for the 28th of December, and Jameson went off to organize his force at Pitsani on the Transvaal border.

As the date for the rising approached the conspirators in Johannesburg began to get cold feet. Hurried messages were sent to Pitsani to implore Jameson not to move; and Rhodes, who was kept fully informed, concluded that the whole thing was off and telegraphed Jameson to wait until further instructions. But the over-confident Jameson had decided, as Rhodes subsequently said, 'to take the bit between his teeth'. He telegraphed Rhodes that he was going into the Transvaal, cut the telegraph wires so that Rhodes could not send contrary instructions, and on the last day of 1895 moved off with his force in the direction of Johannesburg.

The sensational news that Jameson had invaded the Transvaal caused excitement and dismay in Johannesburg, in Cape Town, and in London. For a few days it was touch-and-go whether there would be war or peace. In Johannesburg the Reform Committee hastily began to improvise a belated revolution, and feverish drilling took place. In Cape Town, Hofmeyr insisted that the High Commissioner and Rhodes, as Prime Minister, should stop Jameson and repudiate the Raid. And in London the British Government, most of whose members had had no previous knowledge of Rhodes's plans, dissociated itself from the Raid; to have done otherwise would have meant war with the Transvaal. The Transvaal Government itself acted with great discretion. Leaving the Reform Committee alone for the time being, it concentrated on Jameson's invading force. Boer commandos under General Cronje surrounded the invaders at Doornkop, and after a skirmish compelled them to surrender, and with that surrender the 'revolution' virtually collapsed, as ingloriously as it had begun. Jameson and his men were imprisoned in Pretoria, and the Reform Committee surrendered unconditionally. The Jameson Raid was over, but its effects were to be felt for many years.

The ringleaders of the conspiracy in Johannesburg were tried by the Transvaal courts and most escaped with heavy fines while a few were sentenced to death, the sentence being immediately commuted to one of imprisonment and a fine. As for Jameson and his immediate staff, Kruger wisely persuaded his executive to hand them over to the British government for trial. They were duly tried in London, found guilty, and sentenced to comparatively light terms of imprisonment; Jameson actually served four months only when he was released on grounds of ill health.

But the trial and sentencing of the conspirators was relatively unimportant. What mattered was the determination of responsibility for the Raid. In Cape Town, Rhodes resigned and the Cape Parliament set up a committee of inquiry which did little more than establish the sequence of events. In London, the government was compelled to hold an inquiry into the origins of the Raid, and it was to this inquiry that the eyes of the world, and particularly of South Africa, were turned. Was the British government, through the Colonial Secretary, Joseph Chamberlain, involved in what had been the invasion of a friendly state? If so, what would the British parliament do about it?

The committee of inquiry, set up by the House of Commons, carried out its work against a background of popular approval of the Jameson Raid. The British government had, for reasons of state, repudiated the whole affair; but many ordinary Englishmen regarded 'Dr. Jim' as a gallant empire builder who had struck bad luck. He and his volunteers were gamblers who had risked their lives in a dramatic effort to protect the women and children of Johannesburg and add the Transvaal to the Empire. So many similar efforts had succeeded in the past that the failure of the Raid was galling to British pride; and to the imperially-minded Briton of 1896 Jameson was a hero.

Popular opinion had been further inflamed by an indiscreet telegram sent by the German Kaiser, grandson of Queen Victoria, congratulating Kruger on having squashed the Raid. Britain regarded that telegram as a slap in the face from a serious rival, and reacted accordingly. Though the Liberal Party, then in opposition, had always opposed Rhodes and Chamberlain, it now yielded to public pressure to 'close the ranks' in what appeared to be a foreign threat. And 'closing the ranks' meant seeing to it that Chamberlain, and therefore the British government, was exonerated from any responsibility for the Raid.

The Committee condemned Rhodes and Jameson, in a rather lukewarm fashion, and exonerated Chamberlain. Though proof of Chamberlain's complicity had to wait for many years,[1] most South Africans were convinced of it at

[1] See Jean van der Poel, *The Jameson Raid*, 1951.

the time, and the failure of the British Parliament to repudiate the actions of one of its ministers had most unfortunate results for South Africa. Afrikaners, from the Cape to the Transvaal, had been prepared to believe that the Jameson Raid was organized by Rhodes and the 'Rand lords', with the knowledge of the Colonial Secretary, but that the rest of the British cabinet had been ignorant of the plot. But in that case, they felt, Chamberlain ought to have been forced to resign. When the British parliament, in effect, whitewashed Chamberlain, Afrikaners came to the conclusion that it was Britain, and not just a group of capitalists, that was intent on extinguishing the independence of the Boer Republics. Moderate Afrikaner leaders, such as Steyn in the Free State and Schreiner in the Cape, who had tried to act as intermediaries between the two extremes, now rallied to the support of the Transvaal; and the Free State Volksraad, overcoming its previous reluctance, entered into a defensive and offensive alliance with the Transvaal.

From 1897 both sides began to prepare for war. Britain sent as High Commissioner to South Africa Alfred Milner, one of the ablest administrators she has produced, but at the same time one who was convinced that the only solution of the South African question was to break what he called 'the dominion of Afrikanderdom'—in other words, to conquer the Transvaal. Uitlander grievances on the Rand had not been removed, and continued to be a potential cause of war. There were, indeed, efforts to prevent an appeal to arms which most people wanted to avoid.[1] Hofmeyr and some of the Free State statesmen tried to reconcile the conflicting interests, and a conference between the Transvaal and Britain was held at Bloemfontein in 1899. But neither Milner nor Kruger would give way, and in October 1899 the Transvaal sent an ultimatum to Britain demanding that troops on the

[1] Barney Barnato, in his own individual way, tried to restore harmony in the Transvaal. The general tension of the times may have been partly responsible for his suicide in 1897 when, on his way to the Jubilee celebrations, he jumped overboard and was drowned.

Transvaal border should be withdrawn. The ultimatum was rejected and war was declared. The Free State, honouring its treaty, joined with the Transvaal, and the Boer War began.

Chapter Fourteen

THE BOER WAR

During the first months of the war the Boers had advantages over the British but failed to make the best use of them. Britain had only 25,000 troops in the country, and the commando system enabled the Boers to mobilize superior forces rapidly and invade Natal and the Cape Colony, annexing whole districts. Instead of exploiting the initial success which their mobility gave them, by pressing on to the Natal coast and the central Cape districts, they laid siege to Ladysmith, Kimberley, and Mafeking, and so gave Britain time to rush more troops over from England and India. The reinforcements advanced on the Republics along the main railway lines from Durban and Cape Town, but in the second week of December Buller was defeated at Colenso, Gatacre at Stormberg, and, most serious of all, Lord Methuen's forces were wiped out at Magersfontein.

This week of defeats, known as Black Week, made Britain realize that the war would not be, as many thought, a picnic, nor 'over by Christmas'. Lord Roberts was sent to replace Buller as commander-in-chief, with Kitchener as his chief-of-staff and subsequent successor; recruiting was intensified in Britain, and the offer of Canada and Australia to raise contingents was accepted. By February of 1900 Roberts was ready to invade the Free State in earnest. Ladysmith and Kimberley[1] were relieved, General Cronje

[1] Rhodes was in the siege of Kimberley and greatly embarrassed the military authorities by his restless energy and inability to take orders. After the relief of Kimberley he returned to Cape Town where he died, two months before the end of the war, leaving his immense wealth in trust to establish Rhodes Scholarships.

and 4,000 men were captured at Paardeberg, and the capital of the Free State, Bloemfontein, was occupied. Mafeking, where Baden-Powell was hanging on with great courage and cheerfulness, was relieved in May.

The Boer commandos were scattered by this invasion of the Free State and burghers began to return to their farms; General de Wet actually gave many of them leave to do so because he calculated correctly that Roberts would not be able to advance rapidly beyond Bloemfontein and that a spell of leave would restore shattered morale. The British forces were held up by enteric fever, and when, in May, Roberts was ready to advance, the Boers had reorganized themselves and were able to harass his lines of communication. Nevertheless, he marched on and took Pretoria in June. In August Paul Kruger, old and broken in health, left for Europe in a Dutch warship to die in exile;[1] and in September Lord Roberts formally annexed the Transvaal.

For eighteen months more the Boers fought for their independence against increasingly unfavourable odds. They had lost their capital cities, Bloemfontein and Pretoria, and many of their towns and villages were in British hands; their governments functioned from wherever they happened to find themselves; their treasuries were exhausted; their women and children were taken into refugee (concentration) camps where many of them died. The Boers had hoped, from the beginning, that one or more European powers would intervene on their behalf and that there would be a general rising of Afrikaners in the Cape Colony. Month by month these hopes dwindled: European powers were anti-British but were not prepared to risk war with Britain; and though many Afrikaners from the Cape and Natal became rebels and joined the Boer forces, there was no general rising.

By September 1900 the big battles of the war had been fought and for the next eighteen months it was a matter of raids and counter-raids, of fighting from koppie to koppie,

[1] President Kruger died in Switzerland in 1904.

of guerrilla warfare. Kitchener erected blockhouses to defend the railway bridges and his long lines of communication, and the Boers became expert at blowing up railway lines and raiding supply columns. Since every farm-house was a potential Boer base, the British decided to burn the houses and to destroy the farms which were supplying the Boers with provisions. Boer commandos under General Botha raided into Natal, and under Hertzog, Smuts, de Wet, and Maritz, into the Cape Colony; at one time Smuts was within sixty miles of Cape Town, and Maritz within thirty. The past-master at this game of guerrilla warfare was General Christiaan de Wet. Using lightly equipped small mobile commandos, he attacked and escaped, to attack again from a different quarter. Time and time again the net was drawn tightly around him, and a British general would be sure that at long last de Wet could not escape. But he was never caught, and he always reappeared where and when he was least expected. It is little wonder that his name became legendary among both Boers and British.

The story of Commandant Gideon Scheepers illustrates a number of interesting aspects of the Boer War. A Transvaler by birth, he joined the Transvaal State Artillery as a telegraphist and was seconded to the Free State to organize their field telegraphic service. At the outbreak of war he was under de Wet's command where his abilities and daring were soon recognized. In November 1900 de Wet put him in command of twenty burghers and sent him to the Cape Colony to do as much damage as possible and to encourage Cape Afrikaners to rebel. For almost a year he carried out instructions with skill and courage and then became so ill that his men left him at a farm-house and sent a message to the British to fetch him and give him proper medical treatment. The British captured him, and after treating him in hospital tried him by court martial on a number of charges, including the shooting of natives found carrying arms and the burning of farm-houses in the Cape Colony. On the latter charge he pleaded that, as a soldier, he was carrying out instructions and that the Republican governments had warned Kitchener of reprisals if the British continued to destroy farms, and, in any case, he maintained that he should be treated as a captured prisoner of war and that a British court martial had no jurisdiction over him. His plea failed, and he was condemned to death and shot, at the age of twenty-two.

There were sharp contrasts between the British and the Boer forces. The British Army consisted of regulars and volunteers and had all the familiar features of an army—drill, uniform, discipline, distinctions of rank, and army organization. Many of the men were city-bred and in any case had little idea of the country in which they were called upon to fight or of its inhabitants, whom they imagined to be like hairy apes. Many a captured Tommy was surprised to find his captors humane and clean-shaven, and able to speak and understand English. The Boer commandos were, by contrast, highly irregular. They were unpaid, wore no uniform, knew no drill, elected their officers and, as de Wet and others complained, took leave when it suited them. They were all mounted and were at home on the veld on which Tommies were lost; and they were, to a man, excellent marksmen. Many of them were youngsters of sixteen or seventeen, and even younger, who had left school to join a commando, and they soon became seasoned warriors.

As the war dragged on Boer discipline became sterner under the younger generation of officers, but in the early months of the war the laager of Cronje or Joubert was like an early Voortrekker laager with its women and children, its wagons, and its lack of discipline. When Cronje was surrounded at Paardeberg, de Wet found a way out for mounted burghers; but Cronje refused to relinquish his wagons and was compelled to surrender.

Accustomed as we are to the inhumanity of total war, many incidents in the Boer War make strange and refreshing reading. When General de la Rey took prisoner the wounded Lord Methuen, he sent him back to the British lines so that he should have proper medical attention; and Boer and British generals frequently allowed truces so that the wounded could be cared for. Friendliness between occupying troops and Boer inhabitants was common, and Boer women took pity on hungry and thirsty British soldiers; and concealed Boer marksmen were known to refrain from firing on unsuspecting Tommies because it would have been 'sheer murder'. The present writer's father, a minister of the Dutch Reformed Church, was captured on commando; he sent the British Tommy who was escorting him to the deportation train back to the parsonage with a note: 'Give this man a New Testament. He is a good Methodist.'[1]

But war is war, and no number of individual acts of kindness and humanity can take away its essential inhumanity. The destruction of farms and the establishment of concentration camps may have been a strategic necessity but they involved hardship and suffering for women and children. The camps were hastily improvised and badly run, and Boer families were forced, sometimes at bayonet point, to go to them; medical supplies, doctors, and hospitals were in short supply, and neither British officers nor Boers had any but rudimentary notions of hygiene; when enteric fever and measles broke out, women and children died by the thousand. When a horrified public opinion at the Cape and in Britain insisted on improvements, these were made; but by the end of the war more than 150,000 Boer women and children were in camps and the death roll was 26,000.

These things happened two generations ago and there are many Afrikaners who recall the Boer War from personal experience, or whose fathers and mothers have told them all about it. They recall the cruelty; but they also remember the efforts of Emily Hobhouse, Miss Fry, and many others

[1] Anyone interested in the personal side of the Boer War will find the following books attractive reading: Denys Reitz, *Commando*; Lionel Curtis, *With Milner in South Africa*; and Victor Pohl, *Adventures of a Boer Family*.

to alleviate conditions in the refugee camps; and they remember the gifts and comforts sent by British, German, and Dutch sympathizers. In 1943 a South African officer in Italy told the writer that his own experiences in the British-occupied Transvaal made him more sympathetic to the Italians whose country he was then helping to occupy.

The Boer War was peculiar, too, because of the absence of unity on either side. In Britain, the Liberal Party, which had officially helped to whitewash Chamberlain in 1897, was strongly opposed to the war. Feelings between the Conservatives and pro-Boer Liberals ran so high that foreign observers thought it might end in civil war. Lloyd George, making an anti-war speech in the Chamberlain stronghold at Birmingham, was mobbed and had to escape from the hall disguised as a policeman; and in the so-called khaki election of 1900, the Conservatives received only 53 per cent of the votes cast. The Irish Members of Parliament were completely pro-Boer, and when Methuen's capture was announced in the House of Commons, stood up and cheered.

In South Africa, too, opinions were divided. There were men with English names who had become Free State or Transvaal burghers and fought with the commandos, and there were Afrikaners in the Republics who joined the British forces or who too easily became 'handsuppers', as the Boers called them. In the Cape Colony there were many rebels, and many more who, while behaving correctly, sympathized with the Boers. Most of the Cape statesmen, though loyal to Britain, heartily disapproved of the war; and among their friends in the Republics were men like Hertzog and Smuts who, born in the Cape, now held high positions in the Transvaal or Free State. The Boer War, thus, had many of the aspects of a civil war. It was by no means a clear-cut issue between British and Afrikaner, and it imposed great strain on men's loyalties.

By March 1901 things were going badly for the Boers and Kitchener offered good terms if they would surrender.

He met Botha in conference at Middelburg, but since surrender meant giving up their independence, the Boers would not agree. So the war dragged on for another year while Milner prepared for peace by instituting civil government wherever possible. At last, in April 1902, negotiations that were to lead to peace were opened. Representatives of the two Boer governments met Kitchener and offered to make a treaty of friendship and peace which would remedy Uitlander grievances and provide for a customs and railway union, but the British government insisted that Boer independence should be given up. When the Boer leaders pointed out that they had no power to surrender the independence of the Republics without consulting their people, it was arranged that they should go back to the commandos to discuss the question and that representatives of the burghers should be elected to meet at Vereeniging.

On May 15th thirty representatives from each Republic met and, one by one, rose to describe the miserable plight of the burghers of his commando and the destruction of farms in his district. The majority declared that their burghers had voted for carrying on the fight for independence. It was then decided to elect a committee to negotiate with the British, and Botha, Smuts, de Wet, Hertzog, and de la Rey, all honoured names, were chosen to go to Pretoria to meet Milner[1] and Kitchener. For nine days they pleaded and argued for the retention of their independence, and when it was certain that this would not be granted, for the best possible terms. On May 29th they reported back to the waiting delegates at Vereeniging with the British terms and, after a two-day debate, these were accepted by a majority of 54 to 6. And so, as the Vice-President of the Transvaal said, they stood 'at the grave of the two Republics'. The committee of five generals returned to Pretoria where the Peace Treaty was signed on 31st May 1902.

The Treaty of Vereeniging was a generous document.

[1] Smuts and Milner were distinguished graduates of Cambridge and Oxford respectively.

The British Government agreed to pay £3,000,000 to help repair war damage and to honour the notes issued by Boer generals; the Dutch and English languages were to have equal status; and full responsible government was to be instituted as soon as the country was settled. Reconstruction was no easy task: the army had to be sent back to Britain and women and children evacuated from the camps; 32,000 Boer prisoners of war had to be repatriated from Ceylon, Bermuda, St. Helena and the camp at Green Point; farms had to be rebuilt and compensation for damage fairly arranged; the mines had to be brought back into production and railways restored to normal working order.

A few Boers were unable to reconcile themselves to the loss of independence and left the country, some for South America and others for Tanganyika where their descendants still live. But most people accepted the situation and set about rebuilding the country. Botha, de la Rey, and de Wet went to England and the Continent to raise money for widows and orphans; and relief organizations, particularly that of the Quakers, helped to tide over the worst distress. Milner was Governor of the two new Crown Colonies and had appointed a group of exceptionally able young men as his assistants, mostly graduates from the University of Oxford, who were collectively known as the Milner Kindergarten. Among them were John Buchan, Lionel Curtis, Philip Kerr (later Lord Lothian) and Patrick Duncan, and they were imbued with Milner's love of efficient administration; they made mistakes, but their able and upright administration contributed greatly towards setting the new governments along sound lines.[1] A £35,000,000 loan, guaranteed by Britain, and interest free for two years, was used to promote development. New schools were established, public works undertaken, agricultural shows held,

[1] The other members of the Kindergarten were: Lionel Hitchens, Geoffrey Robinson (Geoffrey Dawson), Russell Williams, Robert Brand (later Lord Brand), and Richard Feetham (later Justice Feetham). The names of the Kindergarten have only to be written down to realize what they were able to contribute to the establishment of upright and sound administration.

irrigation works begun, and new roads and railways planned. Further, local government was instituted.

Economic reconstruction was easier to accomplish than political reconciliation which, after sixty years, is not yet an accomplished fact; and there are South Africans who think that complete reconciliation between British and Afrikaners will never come about. By bringing the two Republics under the British flag, the Boer War had made unification possible; but it had canalized and consolidated Afrikaner sentiment from Cape Town to the Limpopo. Immediately after the war there was much division: those who had fought to the end and were known as 'bitter-enders' would have nothing to do with 'handsuppers'; Free Staters and Transvalers kept alive jealousies that dated to the nineteenth century and were strengthened during the war; and neither Free Staters nor Transvalers easily forgot those Cape Afrikaners who had failed to join them in the fight for independence. But in due course these differences disappeared, and a strong Afrikaner nationalism grew out of the defeat of the Republics.

Milner realized that something like that might happen and he tried to anglicize the new colonies. It was a mistaken policy that defeated its own ends, for it merely hastened the process of consolidation. It was because of his fear of Afrikaner nationalism, too, that Milner wanted to go slow in the matter of granting full responsible government to the two ex-Republics. In the Cape Hofmeyr was reorganizing the Afrikander Bond under a new name, the South African Party; in the Free State Steyn and Fischer were organizing the *Oranje Unie*, and in the Transvaal Botha and Smuts formed *Het Volk*. Milner feared that under responsible government these Afrikaner parties would dominate the political scene, and he therefore proposed constitutions that fell short of full responsible government.

Milner left in 1905 and was succeeded by Lord Selborne, and in 1906 the Liberal Party in Britain was returned to power with a large majority. Campbell-Bannerman, the new

Prime Minister, had always favoured immediate responsible government for the Transvaal and Free State, and in 1906 and 1907 this was granted. Constitutionally the way was now open for closer union between the four self-governing colonies in South Africa; economically, a closer union that would abolish customs barriers and have a common railway policy had become highly desirable; and though there were still many differences, the four colonies had long had much in common in law, religion, social customs, and pastimes.[1] Lord Selborne, in a famous Memorandum, set forth the advantages of closer union, and the political leaders in the four colonies agreed to meet in a National Convention to consider the question.

The Convention met on 12th October 1908, the ninth anniversary of the day on which the opening shots of the Boer War had been fired, and the men who now came together had all been concerned with the actual fighting or with the politics of the war. Among others, there were Merriman, Sauer, F. S. Malan, and Dr. Jameson from the Cape; Hertzog, Steyn, and de Wet from the Free State; Morcom and Smythe from Natal; and Botha, Smuts, Fitzpatrick, Hull, and de la Rey from the Transvaal. Rhodesia was represented by three observers without power to vote; and Sir Henry (later Lord) de Villiers, Chief Justice of the Cape, was chairman. The National Convention met at Durban, but adjourned to Cape Town in November. Early in 1909 the draft constitution was published and was considered by each of the four parliaments, after which the Convention met for a final session at Bloemfontein. The

[1] In 1906, four years before Union, the first Springbok rugby football team to leave South Africa toured Britain and won golden opinions on and off the field. They were selected from the four colonies, and the team established a reputation for brilliant and open back play which South Africa has, alas! not always maintained. Probably the greatest centre three-quarter that South Africa has produced was a member of the team, Japie Krige; and it was about him that someone remarked that 'when Japie Krige runs down the field he does more to foster good relations between English- and Afrikaans-speaking South Africans than a hundred political speeches'.

draft was then taken to London where it was passed by the British parliament as the South Africa Act, 1909. Union came into being on 31st May 1910, exactly eight years after the signing of the Peace of Vereeniging.

The Natal delegates to the Convention favoured a loose federation rather than a close union, but they had only slight support from the other colonies. To safeguard the interests of the two smaller colonies, provincial councils were instituted with powers to control, among other matters, elementary and secondary education; and a provision was inserted that these powers might not be altered by the central parliament until ten years had elapsed. Unlike Canada and Australia, South Africa therefore achieved a unitary constitution by which sovereign legislative powers rested with the Union Parliament. This consisted of an elected house of assembly and a senate that was partly nominated by the Cabinet and partly elected by electoral colleges consisting of the members of parliament and of the provincial councils for each of the four provinces. The Executive consisted of a governor-general and ministers on whose advice he acted, and who were responsible to parliament. There was a Supreme Court of the Union which had an appellate and provisional divisions.

There were two points on which the Convention nearly came to grief. The first was the question of the capital of the Union; the strongest claimants were Cape Town and Pretoria, the south and the north, and, historically, the old and the new. At one stage this question threatened to wreck the Convention, until eventually a compromise was reached by which Cape Town became the legislative capital and Pretoria the administrative, while Bloemfontein was the seat of the Appeal Court.

The second question was the franchise. When the Cape Colony was granted responsible government in the nineteenth century it was on the basis of a non-racial franchise, that is European and non-European citizens had the vote on equal terms. The Republics set up by the Voortrekkers had specifically stated that there would be no equality between black and white, and at the conference at Vereeniging Britain had agreed that the question of the non-European franchise would be left over until the ex-Republics had responsible government. In Natal, for all practical purposes, non-Europeans were voteless.

At the National Convention the Cape delegates, Afrikaans-speaking and English-speaking, strongly favoured the common franchise for all races, which they had found to work well. The Transvaal and Free State delegates—Botha, Smuts, Hertzog, Steyn, and others—would in no circumstances agree to giving the African the vote. Even had they agreed they would not have been able to persuade their electors in the two northern colonies to approve of a constitution that enfranchised Africans. The Cape delegates stuck to their guns, and the compromise that was reached left the voting qualifications as they were before Union but limited membership of parliament to Europeans; and to safeguard the Cape franchise it was entrenched in the constitution by a clause providing that it could be altered only by a two-thirds majority of both Houses of Parliament in joint session. It was a compromise between the old Cape tradition of a common franchise and the republican tradition of no equality between black and white, and each side hoped that, as time went on, its policy would become acceptable to the other. Until the present time it is the ex-Republican view that has prevailed.

The South Africa Act was hailed, in 1909 and afterwards, as a great act of statesmanship on the part of Britain and South Africa. Britain, the victor, magnanimously entrusting her former enemies with full political power; the ex-Republics, the defeated, generously accepting this gesture of friendship; Briton and Boer shaking hands, and the divisions of the past being healed: such was the general interpretation of the Act of Union. Nevertheless, there were and still are other opinions—opinions of those who argue that closer union was too hastily entered upon, that the pace was forced as Rhodes had tried to force it, that the differences between the ex-Republics and the older British colonies were still too great, and that a loose federation might have made possible a more slowly maturing and lasting friendship.

There is another and more serious criticism of closer union. While it may be conceded that Union did, to a large extent, make for friendship between the two white groups, British and Afrikaans, it failed to protect the voting rights of non-Europeans. In 1908 the Cape Colony showed all the signs of developing into a state in which Europeans and non-Europeans co-operated on a common, non-racial franchise; and the existence in southern Africa of such a community would, by its example, have had a great influence on present-day relations between Europe and Africa. The compromise on the franchise failed, in the event, to safeguard the non-racial franchise, because, by entering into closer union, the Cape Colony lost its autonomy. A loose federation would have enabled the Cape to maintain and develop its traditional policies, to the benefit of Africa.

By concentrating on restoring good relations between Boer and Briton, the National Convention did not give sufficient thought to that 80 per cent of the population that is neither Boer nor Briton. If a compromise on the common franchise was the price of Union, the Cape statesmen may well have paid too dearly for it. In the British House of Commons, Keir Hardie said that to leave Africans in the northern colonies unrepresented in the Union Parliament was like writing above the portals of the British Empire: 'Abandon hope all ye who enter here.' Looking back on 1908 it is possible to say that the member of the National Convention whose interests were most affected was the one that was not there—the African.

Chapter Fifteen

UNION AND DIVISION

The Union of South Africa came into existence on 31st May 1910, and during the fifty years that followed, the people of South Africa were called upon to cope with all the nineteenth-century problems that had flowed over in to the twentieth as well as with those peculiar to the latter century. The first of the two great unresolved questions of the nineteenth century was that of relations between Europeans and non-Europeans which had begun as a problem of frontiers. When all attempts to maintain peaceful frontiers broke down, successive governments had annexed African territories and brought the tribesmen under European political control; and in doing so, Europeans in South Africa had created something unique in Africa at that time: colonies within colonies. Britain and other colonial powers had acquired colonies overseas, thousands of miles from the mother country. When South Africa became a Union, and for all practical purposes an independent state, she automatically became an empire whose colonial subjects lived within her borders. The problem of South Africa in 1910 was, as it still is: how to deal with her colonial subjects.

The second question that flowed from the nineteenth century was that of relations between Briton and Boer. After thirty years of British government at the Cape, frontier Boers had trekked away to establish an independent republic free from British control. After several attempts, and in spite of British interference, they succeeded in establishing two republics and in maintaining their independence for fifty years. But British finance-imperialism, exemplified by Rhodes and Jameson, the Uitlanders, and the Boer War, destroyed the independence of the Free State and Transvaal, and in doing so roused Afrikaner sentiment throughout South Africa. The enmity and bitterness evoked by these events were not laid to rest by generous post-war treatment and the grant of responsible government; and the question of relations between Boer and Briton, like that of relations between black and white, was in 1910, and still is, unresolved. It is against the background of these two overriding questions that the history of the Union of South Africa must be viewed.

The twentieth century added problems of its own. These were not peculiar to South Africa but they pressed more hardly on her because they came upon a country that had not had time to develop its administrative services and was politically divided. Union removed the territorial barriers to economic expansion and this resulted in the world-wide phenomenon of urbanization—the trek to the towns. African and Afrikaner moved into the towns to become part of the industrial machinery that was developing; and the process was accelerated by two world wars, by post-war depressions, and by the collapse of agricultural prices and the gold standard in the 'thirties.

For no less than ten out of the first fifty years of her existence, South Africa was deeply involved in two world wars, and in neither did she present a united front to her enemies. Only four years after Union the South African Government entered the First World War as an ally of Great Britain, and as a result of this had to suppress an Afrikaner rebellion. In common with the rest of the world she experienced post-war periods of boom, inflation, and depression; and she was faced with a revolution on the Rand. In the Second World War there was no open rebellion, but the Smuts Government had to fight the war knowing that a strong Afrikaner minority was totally opposed to it and that some, at least, hoped for a German victory.

All these hindrances to unity, whether their origin is in this century or that, interacted upon one another and complicated the tasks that faced the people of the Union of South Africa. The unresolved relations between Boer and Briton, and between both and their non-European colonial subjects, made immeasurably more difficult the tasks with which all states have to deal. Industrial development, urbanization, housing, health, education, unemployment, war and defence, foreign affairs, communications, social and cultural amenities, sport, church organization—in the approach to none of these was the Union of South Africa, in 1910 or since then, able to put forth a united effort backed by all its citizens.

The first task in 1910 was to elect a Union Parliament and organize the public services, and to set matters in motion, Lord Gladstone, the first Governor-General, invited General Louis Botha to become Prime Minister, to form a Cabinet, and to hold a General Election. Botha led the South African Party which comprised the various Afrikaner parties and received support from many English-speaking South Africans who were anxious to co-operate; and he gained a big majority over the two predominantly British parties, the Unionists led by Jameson and the Labour Party led by Col. Creswell.

Botha's pre-election Cabinet had been constructed on a provincial rather than a party basis, and it soon became clear that the more conservative Afrikaners from the ex-Republics were not at home in a party that contained both British and Afrikaners. Botha and Smuts went out of their way to conciliate English-speaking South Africans who, as Milner had been, were nervous of Afrikaner domination; and in doing this they laid great stress on the Empire and on the value of Imperial connexions, and made complimentary references to Milner and Rhodes in their public speeches. By 1912 Afrikaner nationalism had begun to revive after its defeat in the Boer War, and the revival was linked to a powerful and successful movement to establish the Afrikaans language in place of Dutch and to promote its use in schools, in the church, and in business; and Afrikaner nationalism would have nothing to do with a policy of conciliation that praised Milner and Rhodes and was, it was felt, likely to be carried out at the expense of Afrikaner interests.

General J. B. M. Hertzog was the leader of the Afrikaner nationalist movement and his position in the Botha Cabinet soon became untenable. Hertzog, like Smuts in the Transvaal, was a Cape man who had received his legal training overseas, he in Holland as Smuts at Cambridge, and had then gone to the Free State. At the outbreak of the Boer War he was a judge in the Free State while Smuts was Attorney-General in the Transvaal, and each became a general in the service of his adopted state. Both fought till the bitter end and took part in the peace negotiations and in the National Convention. But from 1910 their paths began to diverge: Smuts followed Botha in the belief that the important thing was to bridge the gulf between Boer and Briton as soon as possible by allaying British fears and by active political co-operation; Hertzog was convinced that partnership between Boer and Briton would never be happy until the Afrikaners had been rehabilitated after their defeat and their language and nationhood unequivocally recognized.

Hertzog argued that the restoration of Afrikaner morale could be accomplished only by a strong nationalist movement in which the Afrikaner could feel entirely at home. He was, he protested, not anti-British; but neither was he pro-British, and he saw no reason to place the interests of the British Empire above those of South Africa. The nationalist movement was, in reality, a continuation in the political field of the Boer fight against Britain for independence; and as it was in the Cape in 1806 and 1836, in Natal in 1843, the Free State in 1852, the Transvaal in 1877, and South Africa in 1899: Afrikaner opinion was divided on the question of relations with Britain. There was no room in the cabinet for both opinions, and after two particularly strongly-worded speeches by Hertzog, Botha dropped him from the cabinet in 1912. Soon after, Hertzog formed the Nationalist Party.

In 1913 the Botha government tried to deal with the most fundamental and ancient aspect of relations between Africans and Europeans, namely, land. During the nineteenth century many Africans had been deprived of their land by conquest; and though tribes were usually allowed to remain in occupation of tribal areas, or reserves, as they came to be called, those areas were always smaller than they had been before conquest. As population increased pressure on the diminished reserves became greater and hundreds of thousands of Africans became landless. Many of them were permanently absorbed as unskilled labourers in industry, while others became labourers on European farms and the rest squatted on vacant land paying rent to absentee landlords. But, with a few negligible exceptions, they could not acquire land in freehold because it had become traditional that Africans and Europeans should be territorially segregated. The Land Act of 1913 gave legal force to this tradition by demarcating areas where Europeans might not own land and prohibiting the sale of land to Africans elsewhere. Government realized that existing tribal lands were inadequate and set up commissions to buy additional land for African use; but the opposition of European public opinion was so strong that the commissions failed to carry out their task. And the position of Africans worsened because, by controlling squatting, the Land Act made it more difficult for them to rent land from Europeans.

In 1913 another race problem, which had been maturing since 1860, came to the surface. In 1911 the government of India put a stop to the thoroughly evil system of recruiting indentured coolie labour in the villages of India for the sugar and tea plantations of Natal, and in the same year Indians in South Africa began to agitate against laws that discriminated against them and prevented them from entering the Free State or acquiring land in the Transvaal. In this they were led by Gandhi who had come to Natal in 1888, as a barrister on professional business, and remained for more than twenty years during which, among other things, he organized an Indian ambulance during the Boer War and —this time with the rank of Sergeant Major—during the Zulu Rebellion of 1906, and began to forge the mighty political weapon of passive resistance which he subsequently wielded with such remarkable effect in India.

The Union Government, alarmed at the agitation for Indian rights, first negotiated with Gandhi and then passed an Immigration Act restricting further immigration of Indians. Gandhi replied with a programme of Five Points, demanding the repeal of discriminatory laws, and led a passive resistance march across the Drakensberg into the Transvaal. His arrest was followed by strikes on the sugar plantations, and Smuts, as Minister of Justice, once more opened direct negotiations with Gandhi. Agreement was reached and was embodied in the Relief Act which did not remove discriminatory legislation but was accepted by Gandhi as a basis for further reform. Shortly after this Gandhi sailed for India and the questions of Indian rights and of the conflict between Indian and European economic interests remained unsolved.

The three-year-old Union government had its fair share of troubles: African land and labour, Indian rights, and next, strikes by European workers. Trade unionism in South Africa was modelled on the movement in Britain and had the same objects: the protection or improvement of the standard of living of the workers; but in South Africa 'the worker' was the semi-skilled and skilled European worker, and the term excluded non-Europeans except in the Cape, where Coloured workers were admitted to the unions. Moreover, for most European workers 'protecting standards of living' meant preventing Africans from doing skilled work at rates of pay lower than would be acceptable to Europeans; and the small Labour Party, backed by the growing trade unions, was largely responsible for persuading Parliament to pass a law empowering government to regulate the issue of certificates of competency in skilled mining and engineering jobs. This was the Mines and Works Act of 1911.

Powers under the new Act were not used until 1923 when government made regulations which prevented Africans from obtaining certificates of competency. The regulations were tested in the courts and declared *ultra vires*, and after much European trade union agitation the Nationalist-Labour Government passed the Mines and Works (Amendment) Act in 1926, the Act commonly known as the Colour Bar Act. The original Act of 1911 was, thus, not used until much later; but its existence gave white skilled workers on the mines a powerful bargaining position by creating an artificial scarcity of skilled labour. And the miners used this to enforce their demands for the recognition of trade unions and for better pay and conditions of work. When the employers resisted these demands, the miners struck—first in 1913 and again in 1914.

The 1914 strike was a serious affair. Starting on the coal mines in Natal, it spread to the Transvaal mines and then to the State-owned railways and became, in reality, a general strike that attempted to paralyse the life of the country. The Botha government declared martial law and called out the burgher commandos and the Defence Force, and the strike collapsed in the face of such swift and vigorous action, nine leaders being imprisoned on a charge of treason. Smuts, as Minister of Defence, persuaded the government to deport the nine leaders without a trial in the civil courts, and they were taken, in the greatest secrecy, by special train to Durban where they were put on board a chartered ship, the *Umgeni*, and sent to England, to the embarrassment of the British government. By the time the news of this leaked out it was too late for the courts to interfere, for the *Umgeni* was on the high seas and outside the jurisdiction of the courts. Sir James Rose Innes, later Chief Justice, says in his

Autobiography that this high-handed action on the part of Smuts was a 'fascist exploit'; the strike leaders had been deported without a trial and, therefore, without a chance to defend themselves. And, as Rose Innes says, 'the executive had conspired to hamstring its own judiciary' because the whole plot had but one object: to deport the strike leaders before the courts could 'interfere'.

South Africa was soon faced with difficulties more grave than industrial strikes. In August 1914 the First World War began and South Africa found herself at war with Germany. The war presented little difficulty to English-speaking South Africans. Bound to Britain by ties of kinship, language, and sentiment, they responded readily and with enthusiasm; in the cities and large towns, with their predominantly English-speaking populations, recruiting was begun and flags were waved with a great deal of anti-German fervour. The situation was not so simple for Afrikaners. Only twelve years earlier the Boer Republics had been defeated in a war of independence, and to many Afrikaners the temptation was strong to use Britain's adversity to regain their independence. Indeed, many of them hoped and believed that Botha and Smuts would themselves lead such a movement; but even if independence could not be regained, they failed to see why South Africa should become involved in a British war.

Botha and Smuts, and a strong minority of Afrikaners who followed them, took other factors into consideration: in the first place, they had pledged their word at the Treaty of Vereeniging and regarded the long struggle between Briton and Boer in South Africa as over; to reopen the quarrel would, they knew, be futile, and to reopen it in August 1914 would be dishonourable. Further, the strategic position of Table Bay and the coast was of such vital importance in a world war that Britain could not, and Germany would not, respect South African neutrality. Finally, to have attempted to remain neutral would have meant civil war, for English-speaking South Africans would almost certainly have revolted and would have received help from Britain and Australia. To join whole-heartedly with Britain might mean an Afrikaner rebellion; but it would probably not be widely supported and would receive little help from outside.

Faced with the choice, Botha and Smuts unhesitatingly threw the whole of their influence on the side of Great Britain. The Government undertook responsibility for the defence of South Africa and thus made it possible to withdraw the last remaining Imperial troops; and Botha agreed to the British request to capture the important German wireless stations at Luderitzbucht and Swakopmund in German South-West Africa. The decision to invade German territory was bitterly opposed by the Nationalist Party in Parliament, and protest meetings were held in the rural towns and districts of the two ex-Republics; senior officers of the Defence Force and burgher commandos spoke openly of refusing to obey orders and of resigning their commissions.

As so often in the history of South Africa, Boer leaders were divided. Generals de Wet, Beyers, and de la Rey were the moving spirits in organizing protest meetings, and it was on a journey to such a meeting that de la Rey was accidentally killed. He and Beyers set off by car from Pretoria to Potchefstroom on the very day that the police, who were hunting for a band of criminals known as the Forster Gang, had been given instructions to stop all cars entering or leaving Johannesburg. Beyers, ignorant of the instruction, failed to stop when challenged, and the policeman fired with the intention of stopping the car. The bullet ended de la Rey's life. There is strong circumstantial evidence[1] that de la Rey was opposed to actual rebellion and would have gone no further than political protest; but Beyers and de Wet gradually drifted into open rebellion.

In the Free State, ex-President Steyn and Hertzog were against rebellion and tried to restrain de Wet. But matters had gone too far, and when Maritz, officer commanding

[1] See James Rose Innes, *Autobiography*, chap. XXIV.

troops on the South-West Africa border, accepted vague German promises to restore the Republics and went over to the enemy, rebellion broke out in the Free State and Transvaal in his support.

The Rebellion was not widely supported and there were probably not more than 12,000 rebels in the field; it was badly organized and with a lack of forethought and co-ordination that one would not have expected of such experienced leaders as de Wet and Beyers; it was, in fact, much less an organized revolt than a spontaneous rising whose objects and plans were ill defined. Botha took the field with 40,000 men and defeated Beyers near Rustenburg in the Transvaal, and de Wet at Mushroom Valley in the Free State; de Wet, who had so often escaped the British net during the Boer War, was captured, and Beyers was drowned while crossing the Vaal River. The Rebellion collapsed and the rebels were tried and sentenced to various terms of imprisonment and to deprivation of civil rights for ten years; one only, a Defence Force officer named Jopie Fourie, was shot for treason.

The decision to take the field personally and to use mainly Afrikaans burghers must have been one of the most difficult that Botha and Smuts had ever been called upon to make. It certainly was courageous and wise. The rebellion they were suppressing was led by men who had been their comrades in arms in the Boer War, and some of the burghers who helped to capture de Wet had fought under him, and escaped with him, fourteen years earlier. Relations between these men were close and personal, and none of those who now opposed one another could forget their common experiences during the Boer War. These points are well illustrated by two stories. It is said that when Botha, using every ounce of his personal influence over his Boer War followers, telegraphed to General Coen Britz to ask whether he would join him, that redoubtable warrior wired back: 'Yes. On which side are we fighting this time?' And the second story illustrates how little Botha himself could forget the Boer

War. On the morning of the Battle of Mushroom Valley he had made his dispositions and was awaiting the expected attack by de Wet. He anxiously scanned the horizon through his field glasses, and when at last he saw de Wet's commando approaching in the distance, he said to one of his officers: '*Hier kom hulle. Hier kom die Engelse.*' (Here they come. Here come the English.)

The rebellion was over by the end of 1914 and the government was able to turn its attention to German South-West and East Africa. The former was taken without serious difficulty by the middle of 1915, and volunteers were called for to fight in East Africa and overseas. Troops were sent to East Africa to join the composite force operating against von Lettow, and Smuts was in command of the campaign for a time until he went to Britain in 1917 to become Minister of Air in the War Cabinet and to be used on many special missions, thus earning the Nationalist nickname of 'Handy-man of the Empire'. A brigade was sent to France and covered itself with glory at Delville Wood, in the Somme offensive; and thousands of South Africans joined Imperial units, particularly the Royal Flying Corps (later R.A.F.); altogether 76,000, out of a total of 685,000 European men of fighting age, went overseas. A Cape Coloured Corps, under British officers, was raised and fought with distinction in East Africa and overseas; and a Labour Corps of Africans[1] went to France.

The World War that had occasioned such division and strain in South Africa came to an end in November 1918, and Botha and Smuts represented the Union at the Versailles Peace Conference. Once more, as sixteen years earlier, Boer generals sat round a peace conference table with British generals and statesmen; but this time they were on the same side. Peace was signed in the Hall of Mirrors at Versailles

[1] A number of these lost their lives when the troopship *Mendi* was sunk. Among them was Jonas, son of Ou Andries, whom the present writer remembers with affection as his earliest playmate and his instructor in the art of milking a cow and modelling clay animals.

on 28th June 1919, and on that day General Botha scribbled on his agenda paper, in his own language: 'To-day I remember the 31st of May 1902.'

South Africa had weathered the first eight years of Union but she was battered by the storms; and it was soon clear that she was not in good shape to meet the social and political storms that lay ahead. Her main problems became increasingly intense and called with greater urgency than ever for wise policies. It is worth repeating what the problems were: relations between Boer and Briton, and between European and non-European, and the problems arising from industrialization which interacted strongly on those relations.

Botha died soon after his return to South Africa in 1919, and Smuts became Prime Minister and Minister of Native Affairs. Within three years he thrice used armed forces to enforce the law. In 1920 an African religious sect, calling themselves Israelites, illegally squatted on commonage ground at Bulhoek near Queenstown; all efforts to remove them having failed, the government sent armed police and soldiers who killed 163 and wounded 129.

In 1922 a Hottentot tribe in South-West Africa, known as the Bondelswarts, refused to pay a recently imposed dog tax which bore hardly on them, and the government sent troops, machine-guns, and two bombers to enforce the law. The Bondelswarts resisted and were shot down, more than 100 being killed. South-West Africa was an ex-German colony that had been placed under South African mandate, so the whole affair came before the Mandates Commission of the League of Nations, without any tangible results for the Bondelswarts.

More serious from the government's point of view than these two events was the so-called Rand Revolution of 1922. Faced by rising costs, the Chamber of Mines reduced wages and proposed to employ Africans on jobs reserved for Europeans, in other words, to lower the colour bar. White miners struck, and during the course of the next two months a small group of Communists, known as the Council of Action, managed to gain control of the movement and to change the strike into a revolt in which the principal slogan was: 'Workers of the world, fight and unite for a White South Africa!' And an appeal was made to the Nationalist and Labour parties to proclaim a republic. The revolution was well organized and had its own intelligence service and headquarters staff; commandos were drilled and recruits were taught the art of dealing with the police. African workers kept out of the strike but they were frequently attacked by irresponsible commandos who, not unnaturally, took the revolutionary slogans seriously. For some days the revolutionaries were in virtual control of Johannesburg, and then Smuts announced in Parliament that he had proclaimed martial law. Having made the announcement he slipped quietly away to a waiting special train which took him to Johannesburg to direct operations. The Rand Revolution was crushed at the cost of 230 lives.

It was in 1923 that South Africa first began to take serious note of an African movement that was to agitate the country for seven or eight years and enjoyed more publicity than any similar movement before or since. An African named Clements Kadalie, a native of Nyasaland, was in Cape Town in 1919 and there founded the Industrial and Commercial Workers' Union of Africa, commonly known as the I.C.U. It was not a trade union as the term is understood to-day, but more like the early all-in unions formed by British workers in the 1830's; all African workers, irrespective of trade, were invited to join, and the avowed objects were to obtain better wages and abolish colour-bar restrictions. The movement found a ready response among Africans, hard hit by rising costs of living, and tens of thousands of them paid their half-crown subscriptions. As early as 1921 the leaders of the Nationalist Party, Hertzog and Malan, thought it worth while to keep on the right side of the I.C.U. in the Cape Province where Africans still had the vote on the common roll: Hertzog sent Kadalie a friendly letter and a donation for his funds, and Malan sent a sympathetic telegram to a meeting of Africans held in Queenstown.[1]

In 1923 the I.C.U. began to spread rapidly to the other provinces. Kadalie was a man of remarkable physical and mental energy and a dramatic political orator. To see him in action was to understand the hold that he came to have over his followers: in an open-air meeting, on a hot day, he would begin his speech calmly; as he warmed to his subject he would take off his coat, and the waistcoat would follow soon after; finally he would pluck off his collar and tie with energetic and dramatic movements, and stand in his shirt sleeves, no longer the well-dressed organizing secretary but a worker among workers. His influence among Africans was immense, and most Europeans regarded him as a menace; but both Smuts and Hertzog handled him and his movement with great care.

Kadalie was at the height of his power in 1927 when he went to visit Europe and was everywhere received by trade unionists as the representative of African workers. Having persuaded trade-union executives in London to send him an adviser, he returned to South Africa to find dissension in the ranks and intrigues against his leadership. The I.C.U. was a mass movement rather than an efficient workers' organization, and sharp division of opinion developed among the leaders: the left wing stressed political action, the right industrial, and Kadalie hesitated between the two; and lack of experience in organization and the handling of funds further weakened the movement. The adviser sent from Britain, Mr. (later Senator) W. G. Ballinger, was an experienced trade-union organizer who tried to reorganize the I.C.U. on strict industrial lines, and its decline as a mass movement was, in a sense, inevitable if reorganization was to have any success.

The decline was rapid and the success small, for the diffi-

[1] For this, and the full story of the I.C.U., see Edward Roux, *Time Longer Than Rope*, Victor Gollancz, 1948.

culties of the successful organization of African workers were, and are, immense. The weakness of inexperience can be cured by time; but by far the greatest difficulty is the law of the land, rooted in the traditional attitudes of white rulers to black subjects. Pass laws, the Native Labour Regulation Act, and Masters and Servants laws impede the free movement of Africans and make the withholding of labour, the most powerful weapon of the workers, virtually impossible for all but day labourers. The initial success of the I.C.U. frightened parliament into passing the Riotous Assemblies Act which, together with certain clauses in the Natives Administration Act, gave the executive extremely wide powers to prohibit meetings and to apply political controls to African industrial organizations and their leaders; since 1948 these ministerial powers have been drastically extended by the Suppression of Communism Act and the Criminal Laws (Amendment) Act which leave all trade unions, European and non-European, at the mercy of ministerial edict.

These controls are fundamentally political. On the industrial side, the Colour Bar Act of 1926 and the use made of the Apprenticeship Act attempted to bar non-Europeans from acquiring and using skill; the legal recognition of African trade unions was withheld, and the Industrial Conciliation Act of 1924, which provided machinery for settling industrial disputes, excluded 'pass-bearing Natives' from its operation. The Wage Act of the following year did, it is true, have no racial bar; but its operation was cumbersome, and workers are not represented on the Wage Board as European workers are on Industrial Councils. The great majority of European workers, particularly in the Transvaal, feared African competition and were hostile to African trade unions, even to the extent of 'scabbing' when they tried to strike. Despite all the difficulties, however, a number of African trade unions were organized, often with the advice and help of European sympathizers, and achieved improvements in their conditions of labour. But the large bulk of African workers remained then, and still do, unorganized.

The events that followed the end of the First World War brought into sharp relief the new shape that South Africa was assuming. The nineteenth-century pattern of a predominantly rural community, with one large mining centre and a few harbours, was changing. Between the two world wars the balance of European population shifted from country to town as heavy and secondary industries developed behind customs tariffs and favourable railway rates; industrial output quadrupled, and imports and exports doubled; the railway network increased by 25 per cent, arterial roads were constructed, and harbour accommodation was enlarged; agriculture, banking, and commerce kept pace with industrialization; and African labour flocked to the new towns and cities.

This rapid industrial and commercial expansion brought to light the inherent weaknesses of the social and economic structure of South Africa. As long as the relations between white and black were seen in terms of boundaries, to be settled by war and annexation, or of unskilled migrant labour on mines and farms, the issues were comparatively simple: the African could be ruled, and his labour used, as something separate from the social and political life of the country. Industrialization hastened the break-up of tribalism; it brought vast numbers of Africans to the towns and cities to live, for the most part, in overcrowded and insanitary slums; it destroyed the customary social bonds of tribalism faster than they could be replaced by European standards. In short, industrialization uprooted the African from the land and created a landless proletariat.

The Industrial Revolution in Britain had produced similar results; but in Britain the new working class was British, and the ruling class was able, albeit reluctantly, to absorb the workers into the economic, political, and even the social structure of Britain. In South Africa the proletariat was non-European, and the European ruling class found it difficult to admit the African into the changing economic system and wellnigh impossible to absorb him politically and socially. That was, and remains, the dilemma of South Africa. Economic integration is a prerequisite of industrial expansion, but it leads to political and social demands; and the refusal to accede to those demands leads to economic disequilibrium.

This overwhelming problem has had the greatest influence in determining the shape of party politics since Union; even the second great influence, the rise of Afrikaner nationalism, was conditioned by the first though it frequently obscured the real issue. In 1924 the Afrikaans-speaking Nationalist Party made an electoral pact with the Labour Party, which was still predominantly English-speaking, and defeated the South African Party (by then united with the old Unionist Party) under Smuts. The new Pact Government, as it was called, remained in power with Hertzog as Prime Minister until 1933 when a new shift in party politics took place, largely as a result of the economic depression of the early 'thirties. Britain went off the gold standard in 1931 in an effort to stave off disaster, and Ramsay MacDonald headed the new National Government; Hertzog's Government, taking its stand on republican sentiment rather than economic fact, refused to follow Britain's example, with the result that capital fled from the Union and the depression deepened. Public demand for a national government arose and soon became overwhelming, and Hertzog and Smuts, after twenty years of opposition, formed a coalition which became the United Party under Hertzog as Prime Minister.

Hertzog had started the Nationalist Party to rehabilitate the Afrikaner and promote republicanism; but when the Imperial Conferences of 1926 and 1930, largely at his instigation, established Dominion Status and placed South Africa's independence beyond doubt, he came to the conclusion that his object had been achieved and that republicanism was no longer an important issue. That was why he was able to join hands with Smuts who was a firm believer in association with Britain and the Commonwealth. But many of Hertzog's followers, under the leadership of Malan, disagreed with him and formed the so-called Purified Nationalist Party which remained the parliamentary Opposition until 1948. In 1934, therefore, the Afrikaner front was split as it had been in 1912 and on so many previous occasions.

The establishment of the United Party was, implicitly, the result of a bargain: Hertzog accepted, for the most part, Smuts's views on relations between Boer and Britain and with the Commonwealth; and Smuts accepted Hertzog's view on relations between black and white. That view was that African and European affairs should be separated as far as possible and that control should remain with the Europeans as guardians of their African wards. Legislative effect had been given to this policy by such Acts as the Natives Administration Act, the Colour Bar Act, and the Riotous Assemblies Act; but Hertzog's aim was to remove Africans from the common electoral roll in the Cape Province and give them separate, or communal, representation. In 1926 he had introduced bills to effect this but had failed to obtain the two-thirds majority constitutionally required before African voters could be removed from the common roll. In 1936 he had the support of Smuts and the majority of his followers, and despite vehement opposition from Africans and from European liberals, the bills were passed. Africans in the Cape were taken off the common roll and given three (European) representatives in the House of Assembly, while Africans throughout the Union elected four (European) Senators. A Natives Representative Council was set up, with advisory powers only, and consisting of elected and nominated Africans and a number of European officials. Such a Council might have been useful in the nineteenth century in a tribal reserve, as a first step towards self-government; but it was unlikely to satisfy Africans in the industrialized twentieth century. By 1946 the Council had ceased to function and it was abolished in 1949.

The outbreak of war in 1939 found South Africa, as in 1914, divided. The Nationalist Party was solidly opposed to war and clearly hoped for a German victory, calculating that the defeat of Britain would offer a chance for South Africa to become a republic. Hertzog and a small Afrikaner following were, perhaps, not so optimistic, but they could not bring themselves to fight what they regarded as a 'British' war and favoured a vague policy of benevolent neutrality. Smuts and the majority of the European population saw that a policy of neutrality, benevolent or not, could not be successfully sustained by a divided country sitting astride the sea route between West and East; that South Africa's economic and political future was linked to Britain and the Commonwealth; that Hitler's Germany represented a real threat to national freedom and independence; and that ties of kinship and sentiment between South Africa and Britain were far too strong to be disregarded. Smuts gained the day by a majority of thirteen in Parliament and South Africa entered the war as an ally of Great Britain.

South Africa played a bigger and more independent role in the Second World War than in the First. She maintained two full-strength active service divisions and an air force, and her 'little ships' served on coastal defence and on the deadly Alex–Matruh–Tobruk run; she took part in the conquest of Abyssinia, North Africa, Italy and Madagascar, and thousands of South Africans fought in British units wherever those were to be found, even to the Battle of Britain in which 'Sailor' Malan distinguished himself. As in Britain, women played an important part in the services and in releasing men for active service. Cape Coloured and Africans served with the forces, chiefly in a non-combatant capacity as stretcher-bearers, transport drivers, orderlies and batmen, but also as gunners and sailors. And South African industries and agriculture were geared to the Allied war effort.

The dynamic personality of Smuts was everywhere in evidence, dealing tactfully with Boer War comrades who might waver in their allegiance, imparting courage and energy to civilians and soldiers, and keeping a firm grasp on military and strategic matters. Sir Winston Churchill kept in constant touch with him and his advice and consent were sought on all major questions; and his speech to British Members of Parliament in London, during the darkest days of the war, is still recalled with gratitude by those who heard it for the encouragement it gave to a sorely stricken people. Mrs. Smuts, too, played a great role in her own, highly individual way. Born in 1871, she and Smuts were fellow students and companions at the Victoria College (later Stellenbosch University) and were married shortly after his return from Cambridge. After the Boer War they bought a wood-and-iron structure that had been a British Officers' Mess and erected it on their farm, Irene, near Pretoria. This was their home for fifty years. Until the Second World War Mrs. Smuts had little share in public life, and seldom, if ever, accompanied her husband on his numerous political occasions. Then, at the age of 68, she began to play a notable part. At Irene she welcomed high and low with simple and unpretentious hospitality. Judged by the inmates, the famous visitors, and the fateful political discussions that took place in the ex-British Officers' Mess at Irene, it must surely rank among the most famous houses in South Africa. Affectionately known to all as *Ouma* (Granny)—her husband was the *Oubaas* (the old Master)—she delighted everyone, and especially the troops, by her simplicity and directness, her unconventional dress, her complete disregard of formalities, and her unawareness of the 'importance' of military rank.[1] She regarded the men and women in the forces as her children and called them her 'boys and girls'; and she was tireless in organizing comforts for them. Altogether, she did much to maintain morale in a divided

[1] The story is told that a particularly high-up V.I.P. was making the presentation speech to Mrs. Smuts after she had performed the opening ceremony of a servicewomen's club in Cairo. He had been speaking for ten minutes and gave every sign of going on indefinitely, when *Ouma* plucked his sleeve and said: 'You must stop now. I want to see what's in my parcel.'

country. Her death in 1954 deprived South Africa of one of her most intelligent, lively, and generous citizens.

The Nationalist Party had rejoiced at Hertzog's refusal to vote for war and confidently anticipated a reunion of Afrikaner forces. But neither side was able to forget the bitterness with which they had attacked each other since the Party had split in 1934, and Hertzog and his lieutenant, Havenga, formed the Afrikaner Party as a home for the Hertzogites. The Nationalist Party under Malan maintained a sympathetic attitude to Germany throughout the war. This was shown by public speeches foretelling the doom of the British Empire and urging the election of a government with whom, once the inevitable defeat of Britain had been accomplished, it would please Hitler to negotiate; it was also shown in private rejoicings at German victories and in continuous efforts to undermine the morale of Afrikaners in the armed forces by openly regarding them as traitors. There was no open rebellion, but a good proportion of the government's energies was required to prevent sabotage of essential services and maintain security.

The Second World War quickened the pace of industrialization while disguising some of its results; it intensified the problems arising from relations between European and non-European, increasing the fears of the former and the dissatisfaction of the latter; and it promoted the growth of nationalism on the one hand, and liberalism on the other. After the war, the United Party failed to adapt itself to these changed conditions and appeared to be addicted to the belief that, under Smuts, things would somehow or other right themselves. The Nationalist Party played skilfully on all the post-war irritations and discontents of housing shortage and rising costs, and on the uncertainties and fears inherent in relations between black and white. Malan made an election agreement with Havenga, who had become leader of the Afrikaner Party when Hertzog died in 1942; the republican issue was put into cold storage, and the policy of *apartheid* was proclaimed as the 'solution' to the problem of relations between European and non-European. The Malan-Havenga coalition gained a small majority of seats at the General Election of 1948, though a majority of votes was cast against them.

Most of the political and social history of South Africa between 1948 and 1963 revolves round the relations between white and non-white South Africans. It could hardly

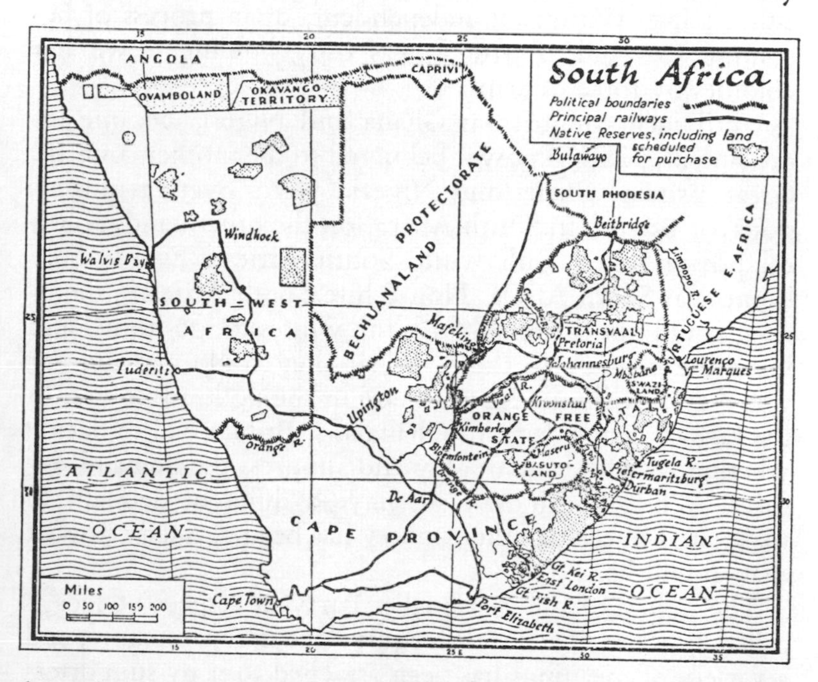

have been otherwise, for during those years revolutionary changes were taking place on the continent of Africa. Most of Africa that had not been conquered by European powers in earlier centuries was partitioned among them during the nineteenth and early twentieth centuries. In 1948 only Liberia, Ethiopia, Egypt, and South Africa were independent states while the rest of Africa consisted of colonies or protectorates belonging to Britain, France, Belgium, Portugal, and Spain.

The Second World War, however, profoundly influenced world opinion on colonialism. Africans themselves began to demand freedom and independence, and most of the European mother countries, strongly influenced by Russia and the United States of America which emerged from the war as the two greatest powers, saw the wisdom of yielding to these demands. By 1963 the great majority of the former colonies of Britain, France, and Belgium were either self-governing or independent, or in process of becoming so, while Portugal was only holding down her colonies by force of arms.

Until such countries as Ghana and Nigeria became independent, political power belonged to the mother country, Great Britain. Ghana and Nigeria were 'overseas possessions' of Britain. In South Africa, on the other hand, political power rested with white South Africans whose only home was South Africa. Non-white South Africans, therefore, could not reasonably ask the whites to 'go home' and leave the country to them. What they could and did ask was that they should have a share in the political power. In the face of demands from Ghanaians, Britain had to decide whether to withdraw or stay and suppress the demands by force. White South Africans have a different decision to make, and since 1948 the country has been divided on what that should be.

The policy of the Nationalist Party in respect of race is called *apartheid*. The English equivalent is 'separateness', and a variety of meanings has been attached to it by supporters and opponents. The theory of *apartheid* is that white and non-white are so dissimilar in culture that they can never live together as a community. If they were to try, the numerically stronger non-whites would swamp the whites, politically, culturally, and economically. The only solution, therefore, is to partition the country into areas where whites alone will have full rights and privileges of citizenship and those where only non-whites will have these rights and privileges. The natural areas for Africans are the reserves (see p. 224), the original tribal homes that were reduced by conquest. The policy for the white man should therefore be to develop these reserves and hand them over to the tribe or tribes living there, who will then, in effect, be given their independence as Britain gave its independence to Ghana.

Opponents of *apartheid* maintain that though it may seem good in theory the facts are against its being carried out satisfactorily. Here are the most important facts: (1) The reserves constitute about 14 per cent of the area of South Africa and it cannot be expected that close on 11,000,000 Africans will be content to leave 86 per cent of the country to just over 3,000,000 whites. Nor is there any prospect that the whites will voluntarily surrender more land. (2) While the climate of most of the reserves is good, their soil has been denuded by bad farming methods, overstocking, and inadequate provision for the periodic droughts and floods. It has been conservatively estimated that it would take at least a generation and cost more than £100,000,000 to restore the fertility of the soil, and even then the reserves would not be able to carry the anticipated African population. (3) With the exception of the Transkei and Zululand the reserves are scattered and none of them, not even the Transkei and Zululand, are likely to be self-supporting countries. They have no harbours and few railways, and it is not proposed to give them any of South Africa's harbours. (4) Estimates of population growth show that when the reserves are fully occupied there will still be 6,000,000 Africans living in white areas. According to the theory of *apartheid* they would be regarded as migrant labour and would have none of the rights or privileges of citizens. It is unlikely that they will be content with such a position. (5) South Africa has been developed with non-white labour and more than half her industrial and mining labour to-day comes from outside her borders. Any policy that tends to drive Africans back to the reserves must seriously slow up the economy of the country. Moreover, if Africans continue to constitute the main labour force in white areas it is unlikely that they will go on doing so without having the rights of citizens. (6) Even if it were possible to solve the question of black-and-white relationship by *apartheid*, there would still remain almost 1½ million Coloured people and ½ million Asians. The culture and languages of the Coloured are European, and the Asians have lost all contact with India, so *apartheid* cannot be morally justified in their case. (7) Finally, opponents of *apartheid* maintain that if civilization rather than colour were made the test, there is no reason why Europeans and Africans, who are absorbing Western culture, should not live under the same political and economic system. There will be stresses and strains, but these are found, and have to be overcome, in most modern societies.

The majority of white South Africans, whether they are members of the Nationalist Party or not, would prefer to have social and political separation of the various population groups, but they realize that strict economic segregation is no longer possible. They accept the traditional view that Europeans and non-Europeans should live in separate residential areas, and that their education, religious exercises, amusements, sport, and social amenities generally should be separate. They differ on the extent of the separation and on whether it should be left to common sense or made the subject of legislation. Most whites want to maintain political domination and fear that if non-whites vote on equal terms with them, and on a common electoral roll, that domination will be lost.

It is possible to speak of non-white opinion only in general terms since it is either not represented at all, or is inadequately represented, in parliament and other elected bodies. Moreover, Africans, Coloured, and Asian are not homogeneous groups. They range from the mass of illiterates to a small number of well-educated men and women, and their standard of living from grinding poverty to comparative comfort. The masses live so much below the bread-line, and in such insecurity, that they are less concerned with social and political rights than with finding work and food; they are subject to a great many restrictions, and both fear and resent the police who must enforce the law. The better off and better educated bitterly resent these restrictions and their lack of political rights and economic opportunities. The African National Congress, the Pan African Congress, and the Indian Congress were outspoken opponents of *apartheid*, but in 1960 they were declared illegal. Coloured peoples' organizations, teachers' associations, and non-white trade unions are all struggling, in one or other form, for greater political and economic freedom, and most of them regard *apartheid* as a bar to their aspirations.

Since 1948, when the Nationalist Party government came into power and began to implement its *apartheid* policy, it is possible to trace several trends in legislation; and though these have been concurrent it is convenient to describe them separately. The first was the attempt to enforce *apartheid* in social and economic life. Notices announcing *Blankes* and *Nie-Blankes* (white and non-white) appeared in post offices, railway stations and airports, and other public places, making separate ticket offices, separate entrances and other services compulsory; and a Separate Amenities Act regulated admission of white and non-white to public places. The Mixed Marriages Act and the Immorality Amendment Act of 1950 made sexual intercourse across the colour line illegal. The Extension of University Education Act of 1959 provided for three university colleges for Africans, one for Coloured, and one for Asians; after that date non-whites might no longer be admitted to the 'open' universities of Cape Town and Witwatersrand except by special permission of the Minister. Amendments to existing industrial legislation made it impossible for white and non-white workers to belong to the same trade union and enabled the Minister of Labour to reserve jobs for particular racial groups.

The most comprehensive step taken by the government was the Group Areas Act which was passed in 1950 and has been amended many times since then. It is a complicated and intricate measure that aims, as a long-term policy, at strict residential segregation of the different racial groups and, towards that end, prohibits members of one racial group from acquiring or occupying property in an area designated for a different group. Closely connected with this Act was the Population Registration Act of 1950 which made it compulsory for all persons above a certain age to be in possession of an identity card on which, among other things, his or her race is shown. Many Coloured people were so light in colour that they were able to 'pass' as white and so enjoy the privileges of more select residential areas, better schools for their children, superior travel facilities, and political, economic, and cultural freedom. The Population Registration Act was designed to put an end to 'passing' as well as to facilitate the administration of the Group Areas Act.

The government has from time to time expressed itself opposed to 'mixed sport'—that is, white and non-white taking part in the same games or competition. It has not yet, however, legislated directly against it although it has threatened to do so. It has used the Group Areas Act and its control of passports and of entry into South Africa to limit mixed sport; and the threat of legislation has been enough to inhibit most white sporting bodies from going against the government's wishes. This is increasingly causing difficulties with international sporting bodies that do not recognize a colour bar.

The social and economic legislation necessitated by *apartheid* was strenuously opposed in parliament, in the English-language press, by a number of extra-parliamentary organizations, and by the main non-white political organizations before they were banned. Even more vigorous was the opposition to legislation to enforce political *apartheid*. In 1951 Malan's government introduced a Bill to take Coloured voters in the Cape Province off the common electoral roll, a right they had enjoyed ever since the Cape had received representative government a century earlier. (With small exceptions, Coloured people had no vote in the other provinces.) Since the Cape Coloured franchise had been entrenched in the South Africa Act of 1909, a two-thirds majority of both houses of parliament, in joint session, was required in order to remove it. When the government decided to disregard the entrenchment the public reaction was swift. Mass protest meetings were held and more than 100,000 voters signed a petition against the Bill. Ex-servicemen and women organized what was called the Torch Commando, under the leadership of 'Sailor' Malan, the Battle of Britain pilot, and thousands of them converged in convoys on Cape Town to present resolutions to Parliament. A mass meeting of 50,000 people was preceded by a march of 10,000 ex-servicemen and women, carrying torches, through the main street of Cape Town.

Demonstrations on such a scale were not previously known in South Africa and the government was clearly perturbed. Nevertheless it was not to be diverted from its purpose, and the Bill was passed by a simple majority; whereupon four Coloured voters appealed to the courts, and in 1952 the Appeal Court declared the Act to be null and void because it had not been passed according to the procedure required by the South Africa Act. The government then tried to achieve its purpose by a High Court of Parliament Act which would have enabled Parliament, in certain constitutional cases, to by-pass the judiciary. This, too, was declared invalid by the Appeal Court. During 1953 and 1954 the government tried to get a two-thirds majority by persuading the Opposition to co-operate and so solve what had become a potentially dangerous constitutional crisis. When the Opposition refused, Strydom, who had succeeded Malan as Prime Minister, decided to 'pack' the Senate as Asquith had threatened to pack the House of Lords in 1911. The Senate Act of 1955 enabled the government to appoint enough senators to give it the necessary two-thirds majority and so to remove the Coloured voters from the common roll and to give them four representatives (who must be white) in the House of Assembly, and one nominated senator. In 1960 the 'enlarged' Senate, having served its purpose, was reduced to its normal size.

It is basic to the policy of *apartheid* that Africans should not be represented in the South African Parliament but should be given a greater or lesser degree of self-government in their own reserves. The Nationalist Party has always held that Western parliamentary democracy is not suited to African traditions and that they should develop their own tribal institutions. The Bantu Authorities Act of 1951 enabled the government to establish district, tribal, regional, and territorial Bantu authorities for the purposes of local government. Chieftainship and tribalism were revived where, under the impact of Western economy and culture, they had died out; and where they still existed they were vigorously encouraged. Realizing the importance of education to this policy the government established a separate Department of Bantu Education and laid great stress on the use of Bantu languages and the revival of tribal traditions.

The policy of Bantu authorities met with strong opposition from tribesmen and from urban Africans who felt that they were being denied citizenship in white areas on the plea that they might, at some future date, achieve it in the reserves. Many chiefs welcomed the restoration of the powers of chieftainship though, in reality, they held office at the pleasure of the government and not, as in former times, by the wishes of their tribesmen. Chiefs who refused to co-operate with the government were indeed denied official recognition and, in a few cases, were deposed and banished. In some areas, notably in the Transkei, the government could maintain order and ensure that its appointees were obeyed only by proclaiming a state of emergency and the use of force. Despite such opposition, the government persisted in its policy and by 1963 six territorial and a large number of regional and tribal authorities had been instituted. In 1959 the government announced that Bantu authorities were approaching the stage where self-government might be introduced and that, accordingly, representation of Africans in Parliament would be abolished. This was done by the Promotion of Bantu Self-Government Act of 1959, and in 1963 the Transkei Constitution Bill was introduced to give limited self-government to the largest African reserve. In this Act the government modified its view that Western democratic institutions were not suited to African conditions and made a concession to the elective principle: the legislative assembly of the Transkei is to consist of 64 nominated chiefs and 45 elected members.

When the Bantu Authorities Act was passed in 1951 the government set up a commission (generally known as the Tomlinson Commission from the name of its chairman, Prof. F. R. Tomlinson) to study the social and economic conditions of the reserves. This important commission reported in 1954 and made recommendations on how best the policy of establishing the reserves as homelands for Africans could be carried out. The report estimated that it would require the expenditure of more than £100,000,000 over a period of ten years to rehabilitate the soil of the reserves and to establish the industries necessary to give them a diversified economy. It maintained that tribalism and rule by chiefs were not compatible with a modern economy and recommended that private, rather than tribal, ownership of land should be instituted and that 'white' capital and enterprise should be encouraged to enter the reserves. These recommendations were not acceptable to the government and only a fraction of the money recommended has been spent.

Long before 1948 South African governments had passed laws designed to ensure that power remained with the whites and to control African political organizations and their leaders, who were usually called 'agitators'. A few of these laws were mentioned on p. 234. The practical application of *apartheid* involved a number of additional restrictions on the freedom of Africans to move from place to place, to seek work where they wished, to build homes for themselves and have their wives and families living with them in urban areas, and to organize in protest against such restrictions. Sometimes, when the courts found a particular section of a restrictive law invalid, the government rectified the matter by amending the law and placing ever-increasing powers in the hands of ministers and officials to avoid the delays of going to court. Each new law provoked further opposition which, in turn, had to be curbed if *apartheid* was to be successfully applied, and so a vicious circle was created of more restrictive legislation to enforce existing restrictive laws. The police were given wide powers of search and arrest without warrants, often on evidence that did not stand up when the case came to the courts. Thus, in December 1956, 156 men and women from all racial groups and from different parts of the country were arrested on charges of high treason. The accused included doctors, lawyers, journalists, clergymen, and teachers, and after a trial that dragged on with many adjournments and during which charges under the Suppression of Communism Act were added to the charge of high treason, they were all found not guilty. The trial had lasted for over four years, till March 1961.

From 1959 onwards African opposition to the restrictive laws required by *apartheid* hardened. In March 1960 the Pan African Congress organized a demonstration against the pass laws which took the form of going to the nearest police station and asking to be arrested for refusing to carry a reference book, the new name by which a pass was officially known. They believed that if enough Africans did this the law would become unworkable; and when the police arrested a few of the leaders only, their followers became angry and demanded that they be released. In the demonstrations that followed the demonstrators were fired on by the police, who were inexperienced in handling crowds, and at Sharpeville in the Transvaal 69 Africans were killed. Similar demonstrations took place in Cape Town when

Parliament was sitting; and the government reacted by declaring a state of emergency and calling out the troops.

After Sharpeville the government banned both the Pan African Congress and the African National Congress, whose president is chief Albert Luthuli, and tightened up its control measures. African political opposition was driven underground and no more large-scale demonstrations were possible; but isolated acts of sabotage, such as blowing up electric pylons, took place with increasing frequency. To meet this new threat Parliament passed the so-called Sabotage Act in 1962 which gave the government the power to place anyone it suspected of subversive activities under house arrest without going to court to have the suspicion proved or disproved.

We saw earlier that the Malan-Havenga coalition of the Nationalist and Afrikaner parties won the General Election of 1948. In 1951 the two parties merged, with Malan as leader, and for the first time since Union a party was in power whose members were almost entirely Afrikaans-speaking South Africans. The parliamentary opposition consisted of the official Opposition, the United Party under the leadership of Smuts, a Labour Party of six members, and three members representing Africans in the Cape Province. Smuts, who had played a leading part in South African politics since shortly before the Boer War, died in 1950 and was succeeded by Mr. J. G. N. Strauss. At the General Election of 1953 the United Party, the Labour Party, and the non-party Torch Commando came to an electoral agreement in a determined bid to unseat the Nationalist Party. Despite all their efforts, however, the Nationalists increased their parliamentary majority though they did not yet have a majority of votes in the country.

After the election a number of people who were dissatisfied with the policies of the existing opposition parties and believed that the only hope for racial harmony lay in the abolition of economic colour bars and in a non-racial franchise, formed the Liberal Party whose membership was open to all races. The new party was led by Mrs. Margaret Ballinger, an experienced parliamentarian who, at that time, represented Africans in the House of Assembly; though it was small and did not win any seats in European constituencies, it remained an active extra-parliamentary force.

The Torch Commando was disbanded in 1954, but in 1955 another extra-parliamentary organization came into being. This was the Women's Defence of the Constitution League which soon became known as the Black Sash from the fact that when their members demonstrated in public they wore black sashes. This organization of white women voters (no non-white women have at any time had the vote) began as a protest against the government's proposals to circumvent the constitution by enlarging the Senate; but it remained in being after the Senate Act was passed and directed its energies to protesting against legislation that discriminated against people on grounds of colour or otherwise deprived citizens of individual liberty, to educating public opinion on political matters, to canvassing the need for a more adequate constitution, and to assisting non-whites who are the victims of restrictive laws.

Malan retired from active politics in 1954 and was succeeded by Mr. J. G. Strydom, leader of the Nationalist Party in the Transvaal; and in 1956 the United Party, dissatisfied with the leadership of Mr. Strauss, elected Sir de Villiers Graaff in his stead. When Strydom died in 1958 the Nationalist Party chose Dr. H. F. Verwoerd to succeed him, and the two main parties under their new leaders faced each other in the General Election of 1958. Once more, the Nationalist Party increased its majority. In this election the Labour Party failed to return any members; and in 1959 the United Party split when twelve members, led by Dr. Jan Steytler, formed the Progressive Party. This party included in its programme a qualified franchise open to all races, the substitution of a federal constitution for the existing union, and the inclusion in the constitution of a bill of rights to safeguard individual and group freedom.

On 5 October 1960 a referendum was held in which white voters in the Union and South West Africa were asked whether or not they wanted a republic, and there was a majority of about 74,000, or 4 per cent of the electorate, in favour of a republic. In April 1961, therefore, the South Africa Act of 1909 was amended to substitute a president for the crown as head of the state. Earlier, in March, Dr. Verwoerd attended a conference of Commonwealth prime ministers in London and formally applied, as Ghana and India had done in similar circumstances, for continued membership of the Commonwealth if South Africa became a republic. There are differing accounts of what actually took place, since Commonwealth conferences are not held in public; but the upshot was that after a long discussion of South Africa's racial policies, Dr. Verwoerd withdrew his application. And so, on 31 May 1961, South Africa became a republic and ceased to be a member of the Commonwealth; and the constitutional ties that existed between Great Britain and South Africa since 1806 were broken.

Although a General Election was not constitutionally necessary until 1963, Dr. Verwoerd decided to appeal to the electorate in October 1961. It was generally supposed that he took this step, partly to strengthen his own position in the Nationalist Party, and partly in the hope of attracting English-speaking voters dissatisfied with the United Party and alarmed at the increasingly strong attacks on South Africa from outside. He achieved his first objective and had sufficient success in the second for him to appoint two English-speaking politicians, who had at one time been United Party M.P.s, to his cabinet. Only one Progressive Party candidate was elected. The parliamentary strength, therefore, of the first Republican Parliament was as follows: Nationalist Party, 105; United Party, 50;[1] Progressive Party, 1; representatives of Coloured voters, 4.

[1] For a short time there was one member representing the National Union Party, but he joined the United Party to give a total of 50.

The first reaction to the election of a Nationalist Party government in 1948 had been a loss of confidence by investors which resulted in a flight of capital. Another result was virtually to put an end to immigration, though more immigrants were sorely needed. As time went on, however, confidence in South Africa's economic stability returned. By 1951 the newly-discovered Orange Free State gold fields began to come into production, and in 1952 the first plant for producing uranium was opened on the West Rand Consolidated Mines; both these events gave a much-needed boost to the country's economy by attracting new capital from abroad. From 1961 onwards the government undertook an active campaign to attract more immigrants, though it was by then too late to tap the main stream of emigration from post-war Europe that had flowed so liberally to the other dominions, particularly to Australia.

In secondary industries, too, South Africa's economy continued to attract the capital necessary for expansion. The government's vigorous policy of housing for Africans in urban areas, sometimes involving the compulsory sacrifice by Africans of long-established rights of ownership of fixed property, ensured a reasonably stable labour supply near the large industrial complexes of the Witwatersrand, Pretoria, and Durban. Only in the Cape Province (chiefly in the Western Province urban areas) has the theory of *apartheid* interfered with a recognition of the need for a plentiful supply of African labour, for that area, the government maintains, must be reserved for Coloured labour. Thousands of Africans have, accordingly, been endorsed out; that means that they are forbidden to seek work there or to remain there unless they can prove that they were born in the Cape or that they have worked for one employer for ten years or have been in continuous employment for fifteen years. The application of this policy has caused great hardship by breaking up families and by compelling Africans to return to the reserves where there is no employment for them; it has also produced a great deal of illegal entry and, as court records show, bribery and corruption to avoid prosecution.

One further step of considerable economic importance was the introduction, in 1961, of a decimal system of coinage. The rand, equivalent to ten shillings, became the unit instead of the pound, and there are 100 cents to the rand. The 20 cent and 10 cent coins are equivalent to two shillings and one shilling, the 5 cent piece to sixpence, and the 2½ cents replaces the 'tickey', as the threepenny bit is usually called. The cent has a slightly higher value than the penny, and decimal coinage, therefore, increased the cost of articles of food and small articles that were formerly priced in pennies. Sugar at 6 cents a pound is more expensive than at 6 pennies a pound.

South Africa's policy of *apartheid* has attracted a great deal of world attention and has often embittered her relations with other countries. This is particularly the case in connection with her control over the territory of South West Africa. Before the Nationalists came to power South Africa had become involved in a dispute with the United Nations over this. In 1920 the Union was appointed Mandatory Power over this sparsely-populated area, and at the end of the Second World War Smuts held that it had become an integral part of the Union and he applied to the Trusteeship Council for permission to incorporate it. This application was rejected, and when South Africa, in turn, refused to enter into a trusteeship agreement with U.N., the question was kept on the agenda and became the annual occasion for an attack on South Africa's racial policies.

The Nationalist government maintained that South Africa was no longer bound by the Mandate system since the League of Nations was defunct, but Malan agreed to U.N.'s proposal to submit the matter to the International Court of Justice for an advisory opinion. This opinion, given in 1950, was to the effect that U.N. was entitled to exercise the supervisory functions formerly exercised by the League of Nations and that the international status of South West

Africa could not be altered without the consent of U.N. Before the opinion was handed down, Malan had decided to give the territory representation in the Union Parliament, a decision supported by Smuts and the United Party. This was done by the South West Africa Affairs Amendment Act of 1949 which, though technically it did not constitute outright incorporation, did so for all practical purposes.

Year after year the Trusteeship Council or the General Assembly, or both, tried to bring South West Africa within the cognizance of U.N.; but, despite the opinion of the International Court, South Africa was able to persuade enough supporters that this was a 'domestic matter'. As more and more African and Asian states were admitted to U.N., however, the attacks against South Africa became more unrestrained and the majorities against her larger. What was really on trial was the doctrine of *apartheid* which all non-white nations had particular reasons to detest; and in the cold war between East and West the United States and the countries of Western Europe did not want to alienate the new African and Asian states. They therefore found themselves compelled to oppose South Africa, and by 1961 only Portugal, whose own colonial policies were under fire at U.N., voted for her, though a few nations abstained from voting.

In 1960 the governments of Liberia and Ethiopia, both members of the original League of Nations, instituted proceedings against South Africa in the International Court asking it to adjudge and declare that, in the administration of South West Africa, she had violated the terms of the Mandates because she had altered the status of the territory without the consent of U.N. and had failed to promote the interests of the inhabitants of the territory. The case is unlikely to come before the Court until 1965. If, as seems probable, it goes against South Africa, the way would be open for direct intervention in South West Africa by the United Nations.

The establishment of the Republic of South Africa was a triumph for Afrikaner nationalism. Fifty years after they had gained their independence, the Free State and Transvaal republics lost it in the Boer War. But what the Afrikaners lost on the field of battle they more than regained at the polling booths, for they achieved political control over the Cape and Natal as well as over the Free State and Transvaal. But whether Afrikaners or people of British descent, or both together, rule, they cannot evade South Africa's oldest and most crucial problem: the reconciliation of her colonial subjects.[1]

The history of South Africa has been, and will be, dominated by the fact that its population consists of people of different cultures and languages who have to adapt themselves to the difficult situations created by the contact and clashes of those cultures. Such adaptation is never easy, but, as most South Africans of whatever colour realize, on that adaptation depends the future of their country. The Republic is a multi-racial state of close on 16 million people of whom just over 3 million are in effective political and economic control. The remaining 12¾ million are colonial subjects with very little say in the councils of the nation; and to a large extent they are debarred by law and custom from playing that part in the building of a nation to which their ambitions and abilities urge and entitle them. Whether South Africa will sink into oblivion, a classic example of a multi-racial society that failed, or become a force for the maintenance of civilized standards and culture on the continent of Africa, depends primarily on whether her white rulers can associate their non-white subjects in a national state that is representative of all its inhabitants.

[1] See p. 220.

INDEX